ian regimes, with fewer pretensions to morality, moral questions tend to be submerged in favor of the common goal.

The political moralist then might profit from a search for the *more* moral politics, rather than absolute virtue. In accepting the mean, the "diseases" might be kept within their constructive limits and might aid in achieving the transformations of the system necessary to guarantee that the other, more noble, human endeavors continue.

Carl J. Friedrich is Eaton Professor of the Science of Government, Emeritus, at Harvard University. He is well known as the author of a number of important works in this field, including *Constitutional Reason of State,* the *Survival of the Constitutional Order; Man and His Government; Totalitarian Dictatorship and Autocracy* (with Zbigniew Brzezinski); *Constitutional Government and Democracy;* and, most recently, *Europe: An Emergent Nation?*

THE PATHOLOGY OF POLITICS

Books by Carl J. Friedrich

Europe: An Emergent Nation?
Trends of Federalism in Theory and Practice
Constitutional Government and Democracy
Impact of American Constitutionalism Abroad
Introduction to Political Theory
Totalitarian Dictatorship and Autocracy (*with Zbigniew K. Brzezinski*)
Transcendent Justice: The Religious Dimension of Constitutionalism
Philosophy of Law in Historical Perspective
Man and His Government
Constitutional Reason of State: The Survival of the Constitutional Order
Age of Power (*with Charles Blitzer*)
Age of the Baroque: 1610–1660
War: The Causes, Effects and Control of International Violence

Edited

Nomos: Yearbook of the American Society for Political and Legal Philosophy (Vols. 1–8)
Public Policy: Yearbook of the Graduate School of Public Administration, Harvard University
Politische Dimensionen der Europäischen Gemeinschaftsbildung
From the Declaration of Independence to the Constitution (*with Robert G. McCloskey*)
Studies in Federalism (*with Robert Bowie*)
Totalitarianism

CARL J. FRIEDRICH

THE PATHOLOGY OF POLITICS

VIOLENCE, BETRAYAL, CORRUPTION, SECRECY, AND PROPAGANDA

HARPER & ROW, PUBLISHERS

New York, Evanston, San Francisco, London

1817

 For information address Harper & Row, Publishers, Inc., 49 East 33rd Street, New York, N.Y. 10016. Published simultaneously in Canada by Fitzhenry & Whiteside Limited, Toronto.

FIRST EDITION

STANDARD BOOK NUMBER: 06-011367-7

LIBRARY OF CONGRESS CATALOG CARD NUMBER: 79-138723

To the memory
of the resistance
fighters against tyranny—
more particularly my friends
Theodor Haubach and Adolf Reichwein,
executed after July 20, 1944

Dum desint vires, tamen est laudanda voluntas.

CONTENTS

PREFACE

This volume, on which work was begun many years ago, was originally intended as part of *Man and His Government*, 1963, in which an early form of the discussion of resistance and revolution is included. Since then, several of the topics, notably violence, have come into the foreground of public attention. As a result much material has come to hand, but the basic issues have not been significantly advanced. Historians, jurists, sociologists, and political scientists have made valiant efforts to cope with these and I have sought to do justice to these efforts though I may have failed to take account of some of them. If so, I owe apologies to the authors and their readers. In any case, I hope to have acknowledged the work of friends and colleagues adequately.

It remains to express my thanks not to any office or foundation none of which was in fact asked to support this research and writing, but to my friend William A. Robson, who encouraged me by including in 1966 a programmatic article on "Political Pathology" in the *Political Quarterly* of London, which he has so successfully edited these many years. A succession of seminars have been devoted, both at Harvard and at Heidelberg University, to the exploration of various aspects of these pathological phenomena; I have in the notes given credit to some of the outstanding contributions made by members, though by no means to all of them. I have benefited greatly from these discussions, and appreciate the work done by my students more than I can say. My secretary, Miss Rosalind Cummings, has been unfailingly cheerful in her help, and so has Miss Edith Kaiser, my research assistant in 1968–1969. All the manuscript was read and its literary style improved by my wife Lenore, who taught me to write English and never has failed. How many books would ever get written without such a power behind a throne?

CARL J. FRIEDRICH

THE PATHOLOGY OF POLITICS

CHAPTER 1

INTRODUCTION: POLITICS AND MORALS

Ich bin ein Teil von jener Kraft
die stets das Boese will und stets
das Gute schafft.

—Mephistopheles in Goethe's *Faust*

CORRUPTION, violence, betrayal and treason, secrecy, and propaganda all are political phenomena that are ubiquitous, though universally condemned. In relations between persons, the kind of behavior they refer to is surely wrong, and hence they are important elements in the general public dislike of and revulsion from politics, especially in democratic societies. Adversaries of democracy have usually stressed these aspects of political life, often under the general term *corruption;* they have usually promised their "abolition" in the new order in which the wise, the brave, or the scientifically instructed were to rule. Actually, these practices have not at all disappeared in such more authoritarian systems; they have increased in volume and virulence, though hidden from public view, when there is no longer any effective opposition. The political scientist may well ask: Can these practices be eliminated? Is politics possible without such behavior? Or do corruption and violence as well as the others have a distinct and important function in the body politic? Is their ubiquity an indication of such functionality? If so, what is this function? What are the several roles they are meant to play in the game that is politics?

But while corruption and the other phenomena here discussed are ubiquitous, it is equally patent that when they become too widespread they become destructive of the political community. Their function seems to depend upon their being limited, and only within these strictly circumscribed limits can they function without creating a serious threat to the survival of the political order. Hence the moral disapproval to which these practices are subject has itself the important function of helping to keep them within bounds! The moral consciousness which looks askance at violence or corruption does of course condemn all of it. From this fact has arisen the doctrine of "reason of state," usually attributed to Machiavelli.[1]*

The doctrine of reason of state constitutes a special application of purposive rationality, as contrasted with valuational rationality—a contrast familiarized by Max Weber as *Zweckrationalitaet* and *Wertrationalitaet*. Purposive rationality is characteristic of behavior in which *all* is done that is considered likely to accomplish the desired purpose, irrespective of any scruples springing from ethical and/or religious beliefs and values. Thus reason of state commands conduct which serves the interests of the state and is one form of political rationality, others being concerned with other political entities: "reason of party," "reason of church," and so forth. Obviously the well-being of any organization can become the concern of a particular rationality; business is familar with the problem, particularly in times of crisis, when personal ethics is sacrificed to the good of the firm. A specific instance is the kind of sacrifice of personal convictions which the Communist party expects its members to make and which has produced such bitter reactions as are set forth in *The God That Failed*.[2]

The problem is a very ancient one. We find Thucydides struggling with it. He tells of a discussion between the imperialist

* A section of Notes follows page 233.

Athenians and one of their victims, the inhabitants of the small island of Melos. According to the tale, the Athenian ambassadors who wish to persuade the Melians to abandon their allies and join Athens suggest that might makes right and that "by the necessity of their nature, men always rule, when they have the power." Justice prevails only among men equal in power, and "the powerful exact what they can, while the weak yield what they must."[3] The matter is often left at this point, as if Thucydides approved of this bald doctrine. But there are some indications that he thought the arrogant candor of the Athenians to have been a cause of their later troubles. By arguing thus, he does not abandon the basic doctrine, of course. He merely suggests that a certain amount of pretense of recognizing the beliefs and values which most members of a community cherish is part of a skillful purposive rationality. Indeed, even a moral justification of such hypocrisy may well be offered in terms of its value in ensuring the survival of the community in its particularity. The problem of reason of state involved the question of the importance of a political order as an essential condition of a moral, of an ethical existence. Hence the argument of a political rationality in its more specific form can arise only when a creed, a belief system of ethical convictions, exists. For only then do we face the question of how to justify its violation by the necessities of a political entity, a state, a church, a party.

It is important to appreciate that in the absence of such a belief system, the problem of political rationality reduces itself to one of pure technicality. This is often the case with revolutionaries. The Communists, for example, are quite openly believers in a radical rationality of means, and the same holds true for many of the youthful rebels who call themselves anarchists and clamor for a revolution.[4] In Mao's opinion, the revolutionary goal of the liberation of colonial peoples hallows any means calculated to achieve that end. This opinion is in turn an echo of Lenin's notions. Obstructing this calculation by moral objections merely shows bourgeois prejudice, and hence Marx's well-known exclamation that "justice is a bourgeois prejudice." In a sense this had also been the situation of Machiavelli; as a disbeliever, he glorified the state as man's greatest work of art and anything serving this purpose needed no justification. To be sure, as for Marx, a well-constructed political order would seem to Machiavelli the precondition of a moral life of man. The source of its ethical inspiration would appear to be the heroic founder of such an order, whereas for Marx it appears to be a collection of "liberal" sentimental notions derived from Rousseauistic romanticism. Morals and politics are thus brought into harmony, their requirements coincide, and there is no further need for any such conflict resolution as the doctrine of reason of state was meant to provide.

But for most men the problem persists, and it does so particularly in the sphere of the phenomena with which we are here concerned: violence, corruption, betrayal, and so forth. That a certain amount of violence is required for the maintenance of political order many men agree. That corruption is helpful in many tight situations practical politicians acknowledge by their actions, if not their words. That betrayal is recurrent in politics the study of any party history will show. All of these kinds of behavior, condemned as immoral by most men in the Western belief system, and indeed many others, are by many political philosophers as well as ordinary folks considered pathological, a part, that is, of the "sickness" of contemporary politics; they are also at times spoken of as "cancer" of the body politic. Organic analogies are justly suspect, considering to what use they were put in earlier times, with the king as the "head." But how persuasive they are can be seen from the fact that the expression "head of state" persists to this day. Hence, if we keep in mind the dangers lurking in such analogic reasoning, it might yet be admitted that a political order as a system exhibits greater similarity to an organic than to a mechanical system. At present, mechanical analogies have become very popular in political analysis, especially in systems analysis, and "mechanisms" are seen on every hand, as are "equilibrium" and similar mechanical phenomena. Actually, a political order and a political community appear to be ill described by these terms, possessing, as order and community do, a life cycle characterized by growth and decay. These life cycles assuredly should not be equated with organic life cycles; they have their own rhythms, and the disturbances (pathologies) are of a particular kind. A good many of these disturbances appear to be linked to the processes here under consideration. When they get out of bounds, when they exceed certain rather narrow limits, the political order breaks down and is eventually threatened with extinction.[5]

What is implied here is that these phenomena, these kinds of morally objectionable behavior, have a *function* in the political order. They are not only system-maintaining and like conflict may even be needed for the functioning of a system, but they are, as we shall hope to show, system-developing, that is to say they are particularly important for the organic process of growth and decay. There has been a good deal of argument and discussion over the question of function. I should like to associate myself with those who would define a political function as the correspondence between a political process or institution and the needs and requirements of a political order (Durkheim). I include in these needs and requirements its development, and hence political change, and not merely the maintenance of the *status quo*, as is so often done, especially by Parsons and his followers.[6] And while I recognize the significance of Merton's distinction between manifest and latent functions,[7] I do not believe that the distinction is particularly useful for the phenomena here considered; for in one sense their political function is always a latent one, in another sense the actors who engage in them usually are very conscious of their utility and functionality, so that for them they are indeed manifest or at least not latent. It has been observed that this distinction leaves undetermined whether or not their consequences are shaped in some naturally determined way or whether they are the result of a choice by the actors which governs the conditions in some way; for both of these possibilities occur in the sphere of potentially pathological political behavior.[8] In a number of situations, violence is the result of such a choice, as will be shown, yet that choice is made on the assumption that the situation naturally requires the particular alternative adopted. The arguments of policemen and rebels amply illustrate this conclusion. Typically, valuational and purposive rationality are intimately intertwined.

In the foregoing paragraphs reference has been made several times to systems and systemic relations. It seems therefore desirable to make some prefatory remarks and clarify some points concerning these terms. For systems analysis has become an object of intense theoretical discussion, and indeed controversy, not only in political science, but in many other fields, notably biology. It is obviously not possible to enter into this topic at length here, but a few general remarks may be in order.[9] We are confronted with a system of some sort when several parts that are related and yet distinct and different from each other compose a whole in which they bear a functional relation to each other which establishes a mutual dependence of these parts upon each other. There are systems of thought and there are those of mechanical parts (machines), as well as physical and organic biological systems, besides social, economic, and political systems. Such systems are real—that is to say, *in* the things systematically related to each other—and not merely imputed to the data by the observer as is sometimes held. This is readily seen where the interdependence is so strong that the destruction of a particular part entails the destruction of the entire system. Such parts may be called constitutive (or vital)—primary—as compared with supplementary or assistant—secondary—parts. Even though merely secondary, certain parts may have a very significant role to play. The well-being of the system may depend upon them, even though its survival does not. Thus the queen bee is a constitutive part of the hive, whereas the drones are not (fertilization may be provided by a drone from another hive). Indeed, if there are too many of them, they may become destructive and then the working bees will destroy them before winter comes. What is particularly interesting in organic systems is the potentiality of growth and decay. In these processes both vital and assistant parts play a role, and certain parts may become lethal, if they become too large or too numerous. The cancer phenomenon in biological entities is paralleled in systems formed by human beings. This aspect is of particular importance in the case of the phenomena studied here. They are dangerous when they exceed certain limits.

Let me recall now what has just been said with regard to political function (and function in general), namely that it refers to a correspondence between a political process or institution and the needs and requirements of a political order. It is clear, then, that each part, whether primary or secondary, has, in a system, a function by which its relation to the system is defined. If this function declines to the point where the particular part hurts and maybe destroys the system, we speak of a disfunction; we say it has become disfunctional.[10] In the passage from one to the other of these states, the part may for a time be nonfunctional, as is the hair on the human body, as well as a noninflamed appendix. The drones in a hive with a live and active queen that has been fertilized constitute likewise a nonfunctional part. Certain writings in this field have failed to draw this distinction and this leads to serious errors; for a nonfunctional part is in a sense no part at all, and the history of politics is rich in illustrations.

Parts that have become nonfunctional may be put to another use and thereby acquire a new functionality, for example, the duchy of Lancaster; more frequently they remain a potential threat of becoming disfunctional, as the electoral college in the U.S. In any case, the phenomena here considered, namely violence, corruption, betrayal, secrecy, and propaganda, are secondary parts of all known political systems (secondary because it is quite possible to imagine a political system without one or another of them). It may be said of them that they have a propensity to multiply, and when they exceed a certain narrow limit, they become noxious and eventually lethal to the system.

In this connection, some general points need further developing. The most important of these is one which relates such disfunctional transformation to the growth and decline of political regimes. Both types of political change are rooted in the transformation of the values, interests, and beliefs associated with a political regime. If a particular regime rests upon a given set of values, interests, and beliefs, i.e., that $R=f(v, i, b)$, then a change in these givens, transforming them into v', i', and b', will produce behavior which threatens and may eventually destroy R. Thus a regime resting upon the prime value of freedom, the interests of the bourgeoisie, and a belief in Christianity or at least its ethics, will be jeopardized if a growing number of its participants come to give priority to the value of social justice, while their predominant interest is that of the workingman and their belief a secular humanism. This much is obvious enough. But what is at times overlooked is that such a change may express itself in behavior which to the exponents of the established system appears to be corruption, betrayal, secrecy, propaganda, and violence. This subjective reaction of the "establishment" is itself a sign of the developing pathology. Even so, if these several forms of deviant conduct remain within limits, they may serve to transform the regime, and do so gradually in such a way that continuity and a certain degree of stability are maintained. Thus a political system may undergo in the course of time very radical changes, as happened in Britain between 1740 and 1890,[11] which in the longer perspective appear not to constitute a change of system, except in an adjectival sense. The British parliamentary system became in this period of time democratic and legitimate, whereas it was oligarchic and of rather doubtful legitimacy at the start.

The difficulties of such an analysis spring in part from the very concepts in terms of which it is cast. For it would be arguable that Britain was governed under several systems during this period of 150 years: oligarchic parliamentary, democratic parliamentary, democratic plebiscitary (cabinet). Such subdivisions could be increased and the analyst would be confronted with the task of describing and explaining the transformation of one system into another. It has been customary not to proceed in this fashion, but rather to consider the system as one, with changing characteristics, as is done in biological systems, where we don't speak of several men in describing A in his youth, his middle age, and his senility, but seek to understand the process in such terms as maturing, aging, and decaying. Thus, in the longer perspective, a regime exhibiting certain common characteristics (a measure of separation of powers, including an independent judiciary, the protection of some basic rights even if they change, and a monarchical "head of state" even if wholly symbolic) is seen as *one* system undergoing cycles of growth rather than as several. Even the values, interests, and beliefs of the earlier stage R may be not so much superseded by R′ as transcended and preserved in it—to use a famous Hegelian terminology—even the workingman in Britain aspires to being a "gentleman" and is so addressed by his political rivals. Generally speaking, it may be said that these particular processes serve the function of orderly political change. They may, however, also help to preserve a regime under these conditions. By corruption challengers of the establishment may be offered positions of power and influence, by betrayal they may employ their following for the purpose of securing for themselves material advantages in exchange for abandoning the challenge, or the establishment may by propaganda succeed in reinterpreting the activities of its members in terms acceptable to the values, interests, and beliefs of the challengers. If these things happen on a considerable scale, but not to such an extent as to destroy the regime's intrinsic rationale, they may actually help to preserve the regime intact.

What has just been pointed out shows that violence and so on, when not reaching pathological proportions, may be important factors in the process of system maintenance rather than its development. They offer the chance of mediating conflicts and tensions; they operate like internally generated tranquillizers. We hope to demonstrate these propositions in much greater detail in the chapters which follow. By toning down the tensions which certain changes bring into being they make it possible for the system to operate successfully. They implement the formally institutionalized procedures for conflict resolution, more especially the entire range of arbitral and judicial methods employed in dispute settling.[12] But such formalized and institutionalized methods fail, in the very nature of things, in many crucial situations of challenge. The reason is that notions of justice on which judicial procedures are based are linked to the established values, interests, and beliefs, and hence fail in the very situations where such tensions are most apt to arise. Here the effort to maintain the system and/or develop it leads to the several morally dubious ways of manipulating such situations or "getting around them."[13]

Corruption may become so all-pervasive, however, that an effort at institutional reform will have to be made, if the political order is not to become so static as to generate explosive revolutionary ferment, with the consequent violence and betrayal of its underlying belief system and institutional core. It can be seen at such a juncture that corruption is closely linked with the other pathologies, especially violence and betrayal.

Any attempt to elucidate these phenomena further and to develop theoretical propositions about them may concern itself primarily with their genesis, their operating, or their distinctive patterning. For in all political analyses genetic, operational, and morphological theories are imaginable and should be distinguished. They will all turn up at various points in the analyses which follow. The forms of corruption, monetary and other, may even prove themselves to have a distinct causation as they operate in different ways. They are no doubt similar to a certain extent and therefore may be substituted for each other. The same holds true for the other forms of political pathology. A study of the patterns seems a prerequisite for a study of genesis, and this in turn is presupposed when one seeks to understand how a particular practice or behavior operates. In the actual exploration of these phenomena it has not proved practical to maintain such a sequence; for genetic inquiry has led to further differentiation of pattern, and the study of the actual functioning of such behavior patterns, however they came into being, has suggested further and perhaps more penetrating ways of analyzing the genesis of such practices. So while we shall not rigidly adhere to the distinction of the three kinds of theory, it is well to keep the distinction in mind in drawing conclusions from the analysis.

Genesis, operation, and pattern are all linked to the problem of morals and politics. To put it very broadly, a general decline in morals generates a number of these practices, or rather aids their spread. This has given rise to the widespread belief, expounded by a number of political philosophers in the past, that *the* cause of corruption and so on is moral decline. In response to such notions, men like Savonarola have appeared on the scene to preach a moral rebirth as the one and only way of combating the spread of these evil ways at a point at which they have come to exceed the limits which are allowable for their remaining functional. Such endeavors have usually provided a noble and inspiring spectacle rather than generated a radical reduction of the pathological practices. This kind of change has only rarely succeeded and then as a concomitant of political institutions and processes, as happened in England during the great reforms.[14] Moralizing on politics has rarely produced significant results, but that does not mean that morals do not have a considerable impact on politics. For one, the moral objections to the phenomena here under consideration have helped to keep them under control and within limits. From this fact arises a serious misgiving about publishing the present work, since undiscriminating readers might from the argument that under certain conditions and within narrow limits the phenomena here considered are functional derive the wholly mistaken conclusion that they are so under all circumstances and without any limits. The moral condemnation of treason (betrayal), for example, stands, since it is derived from transcendent beliefs which make betrayal unjust and contrary to the categorical imperative.[15]

This is not the place to explore the other ways in which morals impinge on politics; for our primary concern is with how politics impinges on morals, or rather how political rationality may tend to shape human behavior regardless of moral injunctions. In pursuing this problem, we do not pretend that the phenomena here presented, violence, betrayal, corruption, secrecy, and propaganda, are the only kinds of such behavior, that is to say that they exhaust the problem of political pathology. There are undoubtedly others[16] such for example as lying, the functionality of which has long been recognized, as in the saying that an ambassador is an honorable man sent abroad to lie for the good of his country. And while most men would maintain that social life and more particularly political life could not be carried on without a certain amount of lying, rigorists like Kant have argued that lying is never justified and any notion that it is reveals itself upon closer analysis to be merely apparent *(vermeintlich)*.[17]

Lying is, to be sure, for most practical purposes involved in propaganda, and there is a popular notion that propaganda consists of lies—a notion which we shall analyze and criticize below (Chapter 12). In any case, the phenomena here studied have always been in the foreground of attention of those who were concerned with the decline and disintegration of political orders and communities; they have in recent years been also in the focus of public concern.

Another self-imposed limit should be mentioned here. It is not proposed to describe these phenomena in comprehensive detail; each one of them would require more space than this entire study occupies. Attention is focused upon the problem of the limit at which they become disfunctional, that is to say pathological. And while historical parallels are brought in for the sake of comparative evaluation, primary attention is upon recent modern times and upon Western democratic systems. For while totalitarian and other kinds of dictatorship offer interesting parallels, the information concerning them in this twilight zone of politics is rather unreliable and can only be used with great caution. All sorts of indications suggest that corruption is rife in these regimes, but the only ones we can be sure about are the Mussolini and Hitler regimes, for which the documentation is now ample and confirms what was previously surmised.[18]

As noted before, the problem of system maintenance while

naturally in the foreground of any notion of functionality must not be allowed to become a static norm of unchangeability. More particularly democratic systems are organized in such a way that change is not only possible but treated as intrinsically desirable. Whether an abstract and general belief in progress sparks this attitude, or whether change is not so optimistically assumed to be for the good, it is seen as inherent in a political order; the institutionalized amending clauses in all modern constitutions testify to this outlook. Hence functionality and disfunctionality cannot be simply related to a *status quo* which it is the task of politically active men to maintain; indeed the functionality of certain processes and institutions consists exactly in the fact that they facilitate change. The assumption is rather that the change needs to be orderly and gradual and should ultimately redound to the benefit of the community at large. In mathematical terms the change remains a function of the preceding state of the whole. Hence at the present time, violence is often argued to be a good thing, because it forces an antiquated institutional mold out of its rut and into new and better ways; notably it is said that the student rebels were justified in employing a measure of violence in bringing about university reform. Leaving aside whether the argument is factually correct, that is to say, leaving aside whether violence was needed to bring about these reforms as well as the question whether the reforms are actually an improvement, it is clear that such a way of arguing means to assert that violence in this situation was functional not because it ensured system maintenance, but because it caused system alteration—and maybe even system substitution. The traditional "reason of state" argument has typically been cast in terms of survival, that is to say of system maintenance.[19] The broader argument of political rationality needs to free itself of this conservative bias; for the political community like all living entities needs to adapt itself to changing conditions, and the dynamism of modern technology for one thing produces continually highly significant changes, for example, modern mass communications, which significantly alter the political environment and hence call for adaptation. Functionality is here understood in this dynamic sense.

Politics and morals are therefore closely intertwined and Aristotle was right in treating them in close conjunction. But they are not for that reason one and the same, as religious and moral fanatics have at times been inclined to maintain. Nor are morals merely handmaidens of politics, as Machiavellians are prone to say. Nor do morals dominate politics, nor again does politics dominate morals. All these positions are arguable, but the consequences are undesirable. For morals and politics have each their own and inherent rationale, and the decision of their rival claims will always remain an open one. For the different schools of morals and divinity the resolution of the conflict will differ, and so it will for the political regimes and their ideologies. What the political scientist can attempt to undertake is a more modest task, namely to determine within what limits a violation of ethical norms may contribute to the good of the political community. It would be fortunate if I could pretend that the answers and suggestions which follow are precise and capable of measurable quantification. Unfortunately this is not the case; vague terms such as more or less suggest at various points what a more thorough statistical knowledge may eventually enable us to do in quantifying the results of these studies. At the present time, I must be content with having to some extent clarified the issues and stated the problems in more definite terms than was hitherto the case. Maybe all that can be said is *Dum desint vires, tamen est laudanda voluntas.*

PART I

Violence

CHAPTER 2

THE PROBLEM OF POLITICAL VIOLENCE

THE problem of the functionality of violence is implicit in traditional political and legal parlance. For on the one hand we learn that the state has a "legitimate monopoly of force or violence" or the monopoly of sanctions for the allocation of values, and such statements imply that violence is functional to the political system or order when employed by its legitimate rulers or power wielders, but not when employed by others.[1] On the other hand, those thinkers who approve revolution imply the functionality of violence in conjunction with political change, radical political change, and the same may be said of those who favor resistance to the lawless abuse of political power.[2] The same may be said concerning the field of international relations.[3] War has in the past been considered a rightful employment of violence for the settlement of disputes between states, and hence functional to the international system; yet there has been a long controversy over the question of what kinds of wars, and here the argument of aggression has been one source of disagreement, while the broader argument over just and unjust wars has been the other. Both these arguments have become more embittered in this century, and the advent of nuclear warfare has highlighted the suggestion that all wars are disfunctional because of the destruction they entail for victors and vanquished alike.[4] These assertions have lent new vigor to the moral condemnation of war—from Erasmus to Kant—and to their religious antecedents.[5] In a sense these judgments are a special application of the general condemnation of violence as immoral, especially the killing of other human beings. It is common to all the world religions, Christianity, Buddhism, Confucianism, and others. Therefore, violence is clearly one of the instances of the clash of moral and political (pragmatic) beliefs and values we are here considering. It is perhaps the most important field in which political pathology occurs.

In this chapter I shall address myself to that violence which is considered legitimate and of which the "state" claims or is said to claim a monopoly. It is essentially the armed forces and the police which are to be considered. Both are intimately linked to the development of the modern state as it emerged from the anarchy into which the Protestant revolt had plunged the medieval order or what remained of it. There is at present so much indignant revulsion at what is termed "police brutality" by those who are coming into conflict with the police in America[6] and a number of European states that one tends to forget how central the organization of the police was to the establishment of the centralized bureaucratic order which successful rulers built in those centuries. Liberalism and constitutionalism fought the police for so many generations that in the course of that struggle the state came to be denounced as a police state—an order which ruthlessly by the deployment of violence sought to maintain the established authoritarian order against the ground swell of democratic forces. This repressive role was by no means the original destination of these agents of legitimate violence. It was "prosperity" which was the primary goal of the "police state" in its early days.[7] The efforts of a Cecil in England or a

Colbert in France promoted economic prosperity and industrial growth because they believed in the doctrine of mercantilism, which has rightly been described as a "system of power."[8] As Colbert put it in a famous letter: "Trade is the source of public finance, and public finance is the vital nerve of war." These mercantilist princes, inspired by the misleading example of Spain, believed that the accumulation of treasure was the basis of success in war. Prosperity was clearly an objective of primary importance in making a country more powerful. Hence much revenue was expended by the government to provide capital for new industries, to develop trading companies, and to build up shipping, mining, roads, and forests. Such a government looked upon the economy as an enterprise to be planned and promoted for steady growth. And where did the violence come in? Force was needed to break down the resistance of those who had been in control under feudalism and the guild "cartels" in the towns. An enactment like Elizabeth I's Statute of Artificers adopted by Parliament in 1561 is an eloquent case in point. It "imposed" a freer trade and production: police violence had to be used to break down the many pockets of resistance before it became the living law of the land. On the European continent such legislation could not be secured from the feudal assemblies, corresponding to Parliament, which had become representatives of entrenched economic interests and hence "reactionary." Perhaps the best known and researched situation is that of the *intendant* in France—a royal emissary seeking to enforce the economic innovations which were being resisted by local estates and other interests. It is evident from even these brief hints that the two forms of violence, the police and the military, were intimately tied to each other, but that the police was an agent of economic progress.

The argument was then cast in terms of "reason of state." "Reason of state" was at the time defined as "a necessary violation of the common law for the end of public utility."[9] Clearly, this traditional doctrine is an early form of argument about functionality. Linked to this idea of a special means-end rationality is the notion of particular "necessities" occasioned by a state's interests. To the modern mind the word *state* has become all-embracing in its connotations; it is thoroughly permeated with the ideas of sovereignty and independence. This concept of the West implies the notion of a political system, and whatever is needed for the functioning of this system must be considered functional. The nameless hundreds and thousands of faithful servants of the crown emerge as the core of modern government. This hierarchy of officials, this bureaucracy, is the state, and they had better ground for saying *l'Etat c'est nous* than had Louis XIV, the *roi soleil.* In their cold-blooded pursuit of functionality, the *intendants* proceeded ruthlessly, autocratically. They showed as little regard for law and custom as did their masters, men like Richelieu. The *intendants de justice, de police, et des finances* did what was necessary from the government's standpoint. In a sense, they personified the practical working of the doctrine of *raison d'Etat.* They employed violence without or even contrary to law; vested rights were set aside. At the point of the sword taxes were collected.[10]

We can see in such a case how continental European police systems came to be so highly centralized and came to be associated with the repressive violence of autocratic monarchical regimes. Their legitimacy was derived from the traditional legitimacy of the sovereign, which Jean Bodin had rationalized and systematized in his famous treatise on the state,[11] as well as from the results achieved by such planners and developers; for economic success, that is to say prosperity, has been a legitimizing ground for centuries and in many kinds of societies.[12] Such performance legitimacy, as I have called it, never suffices, but it greatly contributes to a traditional or charismatic or rational legal basis (to use Max Weber's somewhat inadequate terminology). When the performance declined and was eventually questioned by liberals such as Adam Smith, the violence looked more and more arbitrary and unjustifiable. The old feudal order having been liquidated, there was less and less ground for police activity in the economic field. Yet, to this day in many European countries, democratic and other, such traditions are reflected in institutions like the building police which imposes restraining as well as commanding rules upon the property owner, forcing him to obey sanitary, esthetic, and other regulations. It has been argued that the beauty of European cities is owed to this kind of central control over building and to some extent this is probably true.[13] Yet in the end all this depended upon how good the controllers were.

In any case, it is clear enough that the use of violence for the enforcement of economic progress was functional in relation to the system of the monarchical national state, the development of which it fostered and promoted. The regulation and supervision, reinforced by violence against recalcitrant elements of the population, was, it seems, an indispensable ingredient of the system, mercantilist and industrial, that these national states entailed. In fact, in the countries east of the Rhine, the government never quite released its grip on industry and commerce. Consequently, all these countries tend to look upon governmental restrictions with greater equanimity than do Americans and other "Westerners." The problem of the police has become primarily that of "law and order." But the vast extension of regulatory legislation in recent years, in America as elsewhere, has thrust upon the police many of the activities which occupied the police of the autocratic police state: housing laws, sanitation laws, moral and anti-vice laws. The cop has to serve as slum inspector, he has to watch garbage cans and milk bottles, he has to be critic and censor of theater and publishing, he is involved in sex.[14] The guardian of law and order is no longer merely the protector of the weak and violated against the strong and the attacker, but the agent of the government in all its ramifications.

The American police are by their history ill fitted for this role. Their role was historically derived from the British tradition of a measure of local autonomy. The frontier life of most American communities well into the nineteenth century made the police a highly valued ally in the contention of various factions for local control. In due course, many of the big city police became instruments in the hands of local boss rule, and indeed vital to it. They thus became involved in crime and its exploitation and protection, and indeed highly necessary for the functioning of this "system" of rule. "The worlds of crime, vice and politics in which he [the policeman] lived were not the public's worlds: thus while they turned their backs, the tradition became fixed."[15] To the extent that the development and maintenance of big city machines may be considered functional within the American democracy, as they have been from time to time,[16] this sort of police force must likewise be held to be a necessary part of it. That it became disfunctional as American democracy turned into a welfare state seems highly probable. And the race conflict and student rebellions over Vietnam have further complicated the assessment.

Before pursuing this argument further, let me glance at the comparative picture presented by European police methods and procedures. Bordua has summarized the comparison thus:

> Until World War II, the larger continental European countries had centrally controlled police organizations. . . . These were often supplemented by more heavily armed security police units that were essentially military in nature. The combination of central control, rigid selection of recruits (often through the army), special recruitment and training of command personnel, produced highly efficient police systems whose personnel were generally free of the influence of the local politics and corruption that have plagued many departments in the United States.[17]

The often substantial amount of violence deployed by these police systems is considered a vital part of a functioning political order, and it is at times overlooked that they have served to repress political criticism and especially all challenges to the established order of things. Movements of radical social reform have been thwarted, and such police systems have therefore tended to become disfunctional to the extent that such change is of vital importance to the viability, and even the survival, of the system in question.[18]

The English police system, much admired for its popularity among the majority of the people, is a blend of the American and Continental European arrangements. While the London Metropolitan Police is under the central government, the local departments are not, except for some inspection and grants-in-aid. A Royal Commission on the Police (1962) reported on (1) the constitution and functions of local police authorities, (2) the status and accountability of members of police forces, (3) the relationship of the police with the public and the means of ensuring that complaints by the public against the police are effectively dealt with, and (4) the broad principles which should govern remuneration. The report is a thoughtful one and formulates 111 recommendations. Among these, some stand out. The Royal Commission itself speaks of three objectives their report sought to achieve: (1) a system of control over the police for achieving maximum efficiency and the best use of manpower; (2) adequate means for bringing the police to account; and (3) proper arrangements for dealing with complaints. While recognizing that the police does not adequately secure the first two, yet the Commission thought that these ojectives could "be achieved without any fundamental disturbance of the present police system," except that they pleaded for "more effective central control."[19]

The ombudsman parliamentary commissioner instituted since the report has provided a complaint procedure via the House of

Commons.[20] But, interestingly enough, the Commission could not persuade itself that a national police service was needed, even though "there is a substantial case for creating such a service." Some of the commissioners thought it would "prove a more effective instrument for fighting crime and handling road traffic than the large number of partially autonomous local forces."[21] Without going into the details, especially that concerning the constables[22] whose authority is "original" and not subject to the crown, it is evident that the British system continues to be neither as decentralized, not to say chaotic, as the American, nor as centralized as the Continental European. It is based, as are other police systems, upon the notion that violence (force) is functional to a political order, and indeed is inherent in it.

The greatest part of this violence is, of course, potential rather than actual, and much police work relies upon the rule of anticipated reactions. It has been argued with cogency that many crimes would not be committed if there was a policeman in sight. In a remarkable experiment, known as Operation 25, the crime rate in a very bad district in New York, the 25th, was reduced by 55 percent within a few months as the result of an increase in the number of policemen: the manpower was more than doubled, from 213 to 648.[23] This raises the interesting general question of what ought to be the ratio of uniformed police to the population for effective control of violence? If it is true that safety and civic peace are obtainable if people are willing to pay for them, what needs to be paid? The answer must be different under different conditions, e.g., rural and urban, or a slum and an upper-middle-class residential section. An observer reports: "A one-man police force sufficed to protect the 1500 inhabitants of the upstate New York village" where he was raised. And he adds, "such communities tend to police themselves."[24] The author can confirm this from his own experience in a comparable village in New Hampshire where he is writing. Evidently the probability of violence in a given population determines the degree of "official" violence to be employed. Violence that is disfunctional begets functional violence in an as yet undetermined ratio. Let us here examine the prevailing ratio of police to population in a number of industrially advanced countries.

In Great Britain, the total police establishment seems to run to 90,900 for a population of 51,350,000. This amounts to roughly 1.7 per mille of population. In the United States we find for 1965 a total of 371,000, of which 83 percent were local and 10.8 percent state police. For a total population of approximately 185,000,000 this would give 0.5 per mille, or roughly one-third of the British force. However, for urban areas, the situation in the U.S. is roughly similar to that in Britain (1.3 to 1.5 per mille) and in metropolitan areas it resembles metropolitan London (2.3 per mille).

In Britain (see map) the police establishment seems to run to about 1.5 per mile, except for metropolitan London, where it runs to 2.6 per mille. At the same time, the Royal Commission reported that "relations between the police and the public are good. . . . Most people have great respect for the police. . . ." The same could certainly not be said in the United States. Here we find, on comparably competent authority, deep concern over the lack of confidence and respect. For while such confidence is probably there for large parts of the population, and in certain areas, it is decidedly not there for the slum dwellers and racial minorities. One wonders, however, how deeply the Royal Commission probed into these kinds of marginal and deviant groups. There is some newspaper and literary evidence, reinforced by recent troubles, which suggests that a good deal of disaffection is found in these groups in Britain as well. In the Federal Republic, where the police has had to live down the deep disaffection generated during the Nazi regime, recent student rebellions have revealed the lack of confidence and respect which the police are suffering from. Although the figures show the percentage to be rather similar, and although the federal decentralization and the breakup of Prussia have given greater control to local authorities than formerly, the police have been able to exercise their function of violence with a reasonable degree of effectiveness. The same may be said of France, where the authoritarian regime of the Fifth Republic reinforced the strongly centralist tradition of the country. France, at the same time, illustrates the dangers inherent in such a centralized system, and has done so through the ages. The police as the pathfinder of autocracy testifies to the potential disfunctionality of such "legitimate" force or violence. For, as the police is expanded, its disposition to overreact is increased. Such incidents as the Kent State killing of demonstrators, whatever the inherent merits of the case, serve to demonstrate the point at which institutionalized violence turns into a destructive and disfunctional force. It does not maintain the system, but weakens it. One swallow, of course, does not make a summer; but if such incidents multiply they can and often have undermined the legitimacy of the regime the violence is supposed to serve. The old saying that you can sit on bayonets, but not for a long time, represents traditional wisdom on this subject.[25]

All this discussion readily leads to a brief comment on the totalitarian regimes of the twentieth century. For these autocracies depend very heavily on the police and greatly expand its function of repression and also that of protection. The police, especially its secret part (see below, Chapter 13), become vital instrumentalities in the maintenance of terror, varying in intensity but always present to some extent.[26] Such terror occurs, of course, also in nonautocratic regimes where it may be present in "zones of terror," such as racial minorities[27] and areas of industrial strife. The most pragmatic indication of the absence of a low degree of terror is the presence of organized groups and publications that criticize the "establishment" publicly and continually. Isolated acts of such criticism may, on the contrary, be evidence of the presence of terror.

The history of the totalitarian regimes is reflected in the evolution and perfection of the instruments of terror and more especially the police. There is no need to elaborate upon this sorry tale here. Suffice it to point out that even under such regimes there is a point at which the deployment of violence becomes disfunctional; it occurred, for example, at the height of the great purges in the Soviet Union, when Stalin called a halt in his famous speech "Dizzy with success. . . ." Commenting upon this limit to the functionality of violence in the purges, it has been said that "in the atmosphere of fear and indecision which the purge engendered, it was becoming increasingly difficult to restock the party and the administrative apparatus with replacements, made necessary by the many removals."[28] From the time of the assassination of Kirov in 1934 to the liquidation of Yezhov in 1938, some one million party members were purged and many of them executed. A similar bloodbath occurred in Maoist China during the "Cultural Revolution" and the number of victims though unknown is likely to have been considerably higher. That these cases represent instances of official violence becoming disfunctional is clear from the reaction of the leaders; but there are no precise quantitative data which would enable us to suggest a formula for this limit. There are numerous indications, however, that this limit is rather flexible, and that violence may be carried much further. This fact suggests that there exists a rough ratio between the degree of autocracy and the amount of violence which is functional to the system. This ratio carries the implication that as violence becomes more widespread, a system may be transformed into an increasingly autocratic pattern in order to legitimize the official violence. Indeed the need for violence may be a main factor in transforming a free and constitutional order into an autocratic one.

Any general discussion of the police would at this point in the analysis take up corruption and the related issue of secrecy (see below, Chapters 8-11). But we are here concentrating on violence and asking the question: At which point does it become disfunctional? The answer cannot be an abstract and general one, because much will depend upon the tolerance for violence in a given society. For the police is part of the society and will reflect in its own behavior the society's values and beliefs. The equation must therefore be a rather complex one. *Lv* (limit of functionality of violence) will equal the number of coercive acts (*ca*) required to keep sporadic non-official violence (*av*) below the level considered tolerable in terms of a given society's values and beliefs. It is obvious that such *ca*'s must remain below the *av*'s; for at a point above this police activity turns into civil war. It has been a striking confirmation of this proposition that public indignation in the U.S., France, and Germany has become extreme and turned against the police in those situations (Shah visit at Berlin, Kent State, etc.) where the victims of violence exceeded in number the police fatalities. It is further confirmed by the continuous and instinctive comparisons made between what the "protestors" did and what the police did. If substantial damage can be shown to have been caused by *av*'s, the public will accept even a high measure of illegal police violence.[29]

The mention of civil war, to be dealt with in the next chapter, raises the problem of the other side of official violence and that is war. For war has been an accepted form of state action in the defense of the population, whereunder defense has been very broadly defined at times to include even obvious cases of aggression, such as Hitler's war against Poland. But since hypocrisy renders homage to virtue by pretending it, such efforts to disguise aggression as defense indicate the priority of the latter. The argument has, through the ages, been further complicated by the issue of justice, which we intend to bracket out here to a large extent.[30] What may be said at the outset is that wars of defense have been more generally accepted as functional to a political order than wars of aggression. This general inclination has been modified by the further inclination to consider wars which end in victory as functional and to doubt war's functionality when it ends in defeat. And indeed so many regimes have been destroyed by unsuccessful wars that, in light of the uncertainty of the outcome, considerable doubt must be said to persist concerning the functionality of all war. These doubts have been greatly increased in the twentieth century as the result of advancing technology, more especially of nuclear weapons. It is banal now even to repeat that a war which results in the physical annihilation of victor and vanquished alike cannot serve any useful purpose, unless destruction becomes an end in itself.[31]

With these preliminary remarks made, we turn to some more specific problems of the functionality of war as it has existed in the past and prior to our century. The elimination of war being a problem of government,[32] the evolution of modern government can be seen in terms of reducing the prospect of its occurring sporadically and between small local units. At any rate, the functionality of war in terms of political systems or of political order can hardly be doubted. At the same time, the moral condemnation of killing has made war a typical instance of the type of phenomena here considered. But the fairly widespread condemnation of war as immoral has made it particularly difficult to acknowledge its functionality. For such an acknowledgment can easily be misrepresented as a "glorification" or at least a "justification" of war,[33] when, as a matter of fact, such an acknowledgment is nothing but a recognition of demonstrable human experience.[34] For defense has always been recognized as a prime objective of any political order.

One may also speak of certain "drives" which lead to war, such as the search for food, procreation, conquest of territory, adventure, and lust of domination.[35] War, seen as organized sanguinary fighting and killing, has resulted from these other "drives" only because one political community was prepared to defend its food, its women, its territory, or its independence against an aggressor who undertook to deprive it of these possessions by violent means. The long drawn-out controversy over whether armed, violent combat was expressive of "human nature," that is to say was "natural," has been inclined to concentrate on surface phenomena, namely the psychological accompaniments of this tendency to defend one's own.[36] The argument has been carried on by highly selective biological and psychological "evidence" from which by uncritical analogy tenuous "conclusions" are drawn. The established historical experience is that human beings have attacked, defended, and hence fought throughout human history, and that a good many among them have morally condemned this fighting and that such condemnation has resulted in widening the territorial basis and the boundaries for such fighting. Sanguinary fighting between towns and cities, between barons and dukes, has ceased, but such fighting between tribes, nations, and states has continued and has been intensified. Had the British and their allies not been prepared to fight Hitler, he would presumably be dominating Europe and perhaps the world at large; had the Israelis not been prepared to fight the Arabs who proclaimed it their avowed aim to destroy Israel, this small state would presumably have ceased to exist; had Biafra not been willing to fight, no civil war would have devastated Nigeria; and had the South Vietnamese not been willing to engage in sanguinary fighting, Ho Chi Minh would presumably have united Vietnam under the Communist banner, and many Americans would still be alive today.

All this is very obvious, but we need to remind ourselves of these and many analogous situations in order to realize the patent functionality of international violence (war) in the field of politics. At what point does such violence become disfunctional? The common-sense answer would seem to be that it does so at the point of defeat. Such a reply misses the key point that the defeat of one is the victory of the other side, and that for the victor the functionality of the war is therefore arguable. It may however be questioned whether victory always constitutes functionality. The classic example is the victory of Pyrrhus, which is proverbial for a victory that is so costly as to be self-defeating. It presumably was not functional for the victor. General reasoning would lead to the hypothesis that war to be functional needs to have results which substantially outweigh its cost for the victor. The question of functionality poses the problem of cost/benefit analysis. It is therefore afflicted with all the difficulties that have beset this analysis in less complicated fields, such as public-works expenditures.[37] When William James set forth his notions about a "moral equivalent of war," he stressed the psychological benefits of warmaking such as have been repeatedly set forth since Plato glorified the warrior class in his ideal state; James sought to find other means for securing these benefits. Since both pacific and warlike tribes and states have not only survived but flourished throughout human history, it may be arguable that war may be functional or not, depending upon the value and belief system prevailing in a particular society. But it is a demonstrable fact that many political orders have perished after defeat in war. A speculative philosopher like Hegel could make this observation the basis of a philosophy of history in which success in war was claimed to be the indication of spiritual superiority, or at least timeliness—a kind of secular version of the Chinese tradition wherein such success was a proof of divine favor that made the ruler a legitimate claimant by dint of his being a "son of heaven." This pattern of thinking was transformed by Karl Marx and his followers into a rationalization of class war which predestined the emergent class as the victor and the executioner of historical necessity.[38] In this doctrine, too, war of a certain kind becomes functional, but the doctrine is so intertwined with the problems of revolution that we shall comment further on it in the next chapter.

A functional theory of war sees it as the extreme form of social conflict, that is, large politically organized groups of men engaged in organized killing for the real or imagined attainment of believed-in group ends. This functionality of war has been rapidly declining, at least in the advanced industrial societies. There can be little argument about the enormous and mounting cost of modern wars. Pitirim Sorokin has given some interesting statistics showing this steady increase in the cost of war:[39]

SUMMARY FIGURES BY CENTURY PERIODS FOR FRANCE, ENGLAND, AUSTRO-HUNGARY, AND RUSSIA, 1101-1925

		Casualties	
Century	Size of Army	Number	Percent of Army
XII	1,161,000	29,940	2.5
XIII	2,372,000	68,440	2.9
XIV	3,867,000	166,729	4.6
XV	5,000,000	285,000	5.7
XVI	9,785,000	573,000	5.9
XVII	15,865,000	2,497,170	15.7
XVIII	24,849,000	3,622,140	14.6
XIX	17,869,000	2,912,771	16.3
XX (1901-25)	41,465,000	16,147,550	38.9

Source: Pitirim Sorokin, *Social and Cultural Dynamics*, 1937. Vol. III, ch. 2, Tables 15 and 17.

Sorokin makes the further point that in ancient Greece only from 2 to 4 percent of the population of a city was actively engaged in any war. The loss of life in the Battle of Marathon is estimated to have run as high as 25 percent of the men engaged in it, and it was considered terrible; for in other battles of the time it ranged from 1 to 8 percent. The average loss of the French and Italian armies during the Napoleonic Wars was about 20 percent. In England, he adds, the casualties for the first quarter of the twentieth century exceed those of all the preceding centuries from the twelfth onward, taken together. In the light of these figures, it is undeniable that the cost has become very high. Unfortunately, it is not possible to establish anything like a mathematical ratio when the gain consists in the defeat and destruction of Hitler, for example. It is the curse of ideological wars that the benefit cannot be calculated in rational terms, and slogans like "better dead than red" or "give me liberty or give me death" suggest that any cost-benefit analysis breaks down at this point.

In the past, many wars were fought for the purpose of achieving dominion. When that is the goal, can it be said that under modern conditions both victor and vanquished are losers, as is so often done in moral discussions? The end result of the First World War makes such a conclusion seem plausible.[40] That war was waged by the empires of Russia, Austria, and Germany, and the ruling groups who started the war all suffered eclipse. Even those of France and Britain were greatly reduced in their sway; they lost much ground to both their internal and external foes. All the countries of Europe engaged in the war lost in prestige, position, and power and had to surrender a considerable part of their colonial empires. Therefore the war turned out to be disfunctional for the major combatants, and the same may be said of the Second World War, except for the destruction of the Fascist powers. Even here, a skeptic might well ask whether the rise of the Soviet Union as the dominant power in Europe was not worse than the preceding Fascist predominance. Only for the Soviet Union itself can a fairly convincing argument be made in support of the functionality of the Second World War. The cost-benefit argument breaks down where ideological motivations enter; for it is always arguable, as it now is being argued by Maoist China against the Soviet Union, that the revolutionary advance in the service of an ideological goal is worth any sacrifice. The functionality of all forms of violence may always be asserted, and has been asserted, by the totalitarian ideologists of this century. The very fact of their totalist thrust leads to this conclusion.

If and when an effective world government is established, it will be necessary to face the problem of violence. Small wars, in the nature of police actions, will be necessary from time to time to subordinate recalcitrant members of the world community. Such wars would be functional to the world community. This problem leads directly into the subject of our next chapter, namely resistance and revolution involving internal war.[41] To this problem of violence and its functionality we now turn.

CHAPTER 3

RESISTANCE AND REVOLUTION

POLICE action and war are forms of political violence which are employed on behalf of a political order; as such they may or may not be systemically functional, but are presumed to be under ordinary circumstances. There are two other forms of political violence where the presumption is that they are not functional, though under particular circumstances they may well be so: resistance and revolution. The two may be seen as forms of internal war, whenever they are of a certain magnitude.[1] But they are typically condemned as bad and as threatening the political society within which they occur; they are spoken of as an "illness" or "sickness" of the political order, which terms bring out the pathological potential in such occurrences. Among disturbances of the political order, resistance and revolution occupy a distinctive place: they are explicitly or implicitly directed toward changing the political order by force and violence. All revolution starts with resistance, though a good deal of resistance does not lead to revolution. It may also be revolutionizing in effect, without that having been the original intention of the resisters.

When does political resistance occur? It is endemic in political order as such, and the maintenance of order implies a certain amount of disorder.[2] It occurs when the values, interests, and beliefs of the rulers conflict with those of a group of their subjects. Not all such conflicts lead to resistance, but it presupposes them. Resistance may be organized or spontaneous, continuous or sporadic. It is evident that continuous and organized resistance constitutes a more serious threat to a political order than does sporadic and spontaneous resistance. The latter is found in all political orders as disobedience and crime. We know too little about the frequency of such resistance and about the conditions under which it occurs. As in the case of suicide[3] such knowledge would provide significant indices of political disorder. But I shall leave these phenomena aside, much of them not being political anyhow, and concentrate upon the continuous and organized forms of political resistance.

Such resistance occurs as partial and total resistance. Partial resistance often takes the form of nullification of obnoxious laws and orders. Particular groups or regions which constitute subdivisions of the political community—so-called subcultures—cherish values, interests, and/or beliefs which differ from those in the community at large. The nationality conflicts such as those involving the French-speaking Canadians, the Bretons in France, the Welsh and the Irish in Britain, the Austrian Tyroleans in Italy, the French-speaking citizens of the canton of Berne in Switzerland, and many others are typical instances of violent resistance to the decisions of the rulers representing the dominant majority.[4] Such groupings may be cultural, economic, religious, or several of these factors in combination. In all democratic states there is a tendency to anticipate the possible resistance by prior consultation and adaptation to the deviant wishes of the subgroup. Such a procedure may, in fact, be institutionalized, as is the case in Puerto Rico, where a "resident commissioner" is elected by the people to sit in the U.S. Congress in a consultative capacity; he often persuades the Congress not to make applicable to Puerto Rico some legislation which would be unwelcome to Puerto Ricans and might engender resistance.[5]

The arrangements made for Puerto Rico largely correspond to the theory of John Calhoun, though a perfected commonwealth would carry these procedures a step further.[6] According to Calhoun, there is only one way in which the government can be structured so that the abuse of power can be prevented and checked—and the violence which such abuse might entail anticipated and avoided. The "organism" by which this goal can be achieved is "to furnish the ruled with the means of resisting successfully this tendency on the part of the rulers to oppression and abuse." In Calhoun's view, such "resisting" could be nonviolent, if any distinct subcommunity differentiated from the rest by a separate "interest" (which includes values and beliefs) must concur by a distinct vote upon any decision affecting it. As he put it, there must be a "concurrent" majority. "The government of the concurrent majority . . . excludes the possibility of oppression, by giving to each interest, or portion, or order . . . the means of protecting itself, by its negative [veto], against all measures calculated to advance the peculiar interests of others at its expense."[7] Each well-defined political subculture must have a veto power, that is the power to nullify the acts of government affecting it. In light of the conditions prevailing in an advanced industrial society and its pluralism, such a doctrine would appear an open invitation to anarchy; for a great deal of legislation of the welfare state is directed precisely toward advancing the interests of one group at the expense of another (redistribution of income, desegregation, health protection, and so forth). Yet Calhoun himself did not see it that way. He considered anarchy the "greatest of all evils," and it is precisely this evil which he hoped to combat by the recognition of the need of concurrent majorities; for thus violent resistance would be avoided, which has often been considered the most patent form of anarchy. But it may well be asked whether a certain amount of such violence is not functional to a political order, as a corrective and providing the anticipatory incentive for taking divergencies into account.

To resume the argument, then, resistance, organized and continuous, may occur when and if the values, interests, and beliefs of a substantial group or region are jeopardized by the political action of a more inclusive community to which this group or region belongs. Recent experience in the United States with desegregation has shown this as clearly as experience in Algeria and the Congo. Calhoun was therefore at least in part right in claiming that in order to avoid violence it is important to make sure that any potent subgroups who could mount violent resistance are in agreement or accept a genuine compromise. It would be important to know precisely at what point such resistance becomes organized and continuous. Clearly this is the case where the survival of the group as a distinct entity is at stake. The tendency in recent years for such violent resistance to spread appears clearly related to the egalitarian and leveling tendency of popular regimes in which the majority has the final say. Not only constitutional but totalitarian systems are in this sense "popular," or more accurately "populist." In this century the most frequent source of such violent conflicts has been national and, more especially, linguistic diversity. Language is the most patent expression of cultural identity, though it need not be, as the case of Ireland shows.

An inspection of these cases of cultural identity and diversity shows that the attempt of the majority to deprive a cultural minority of its language and other symbols is much more apt to precipitate violent resistance than an effort to superimpose a second language as the *lingua franca* of the entire community.

Even the latter effort may, however, bring on violent resistance, as the development in India shows where the constitutionally sanctioned effort to superimpose Hindi as the common language has been strongly resented by other language groups, and denounced by some as "Hindi imperialism";[8] the constitutional provisions have had to be abandoned after outbreaks of ferocious violence in Madras and elsewhere. In the Soviet Union, cultural diversity has persisted, with the Russian language being imposed by the central authorities; here too, in spite of the difficulties of resistance under an autocratic regime, violent resistance has occurred from time to time in the Ukraine, in Turkestan, and in Kazakstan.

Charles Merriam some years ago described these phenomena in terms of the "poverty of power"; he recognized the difficulties of such analysis "owing to the wide range of situations under which resistance may be made."[9] His analysis was not limited to violent resistance; he included what has come to be known as "passive resistance."[10] All such resistance has a tendency, an inherent propensity, to become violent, however, as recent experience in the United States has once more shown. Thus the Black Panthers are the natural sequel to Martin Luther King's movement. For when the established powers do not yield to passive resistance, as they only rarely do, an opposition element will raise the banner of violence as "the only means" for forcing the issue. How frequently has the claim been made in regard to the student rebellions, and especially their violent manifestations, that "one has to admit they got results"? The results may not have been what the violent demonstrators wanted, whether it be university reform or withdrawal from Vietnam, but actions occurred, steps were taken which moved in the desired direction.[11] Similarly the bomb-throwing Tyroleans forced the Austrian and the Italian governments to agree on a "solution" to the language problem of the Austrian-speaking minority.

The violence in Northern Ireland testifies to the explosiveness of religious divisions, as does the establishment of Pakistan and the resistance occurring in some totalitarian regimes; among the conspirators against Hitler, the religious motivation was paramount.[12] Some elements may seek to maintain the passive posture, as did Gandhi and Count Moltke out of religious conviction,[13] but political expediency will push others toward violence. How far they will go depends to a considerable extent upon the decisiveness with which the established power will "clamp down" on such violence; any yielding, far from appeasing the violent resisters, will encourage them to increase the violence because it gets results, as they would say. This practical problem of how to prevent violent resistance has in the past preoccupied political thought when it has dealt with the phenomenon. From Machiavelli to our time, the argument has been over the degree of severity required to cope with violence. Much evidence has been marshaled in support of both the repressive and the permissive theses. The conclusion which stands out from all this controversy is that "it all depends." It depends in part upon how strongly the violent resisters are motivated and to what extent self-sacrifice and martyrdom are ingrained in the local culture; it depends also upon whether remedial measures designed to eliminate the cause of the resistance accompany the repression or permission. Becuse of this preoccupation with prevention, theorizing about resistance has in the past largely been focused on the "right of resistance." During the Middle Ages and in early modern times, this focus was highlighted by the question of tyrannicide. There is no need to review these writings in the present context,[14] although we should recognize that the elaboration of the notion of the tyrant as a ruler who abuses his power implied a concern with functionality. In our terms, the argument that violent resistance served to rid a political order of a "bad" ruler suggested its functionality. Expressions such as "despotism moderated by the fear of assassination" testify to the general notions that constituted part of conventional wisdom in this area. But the argument remained general, though often quite sophisticated.[15]

These arguments have been revived under totalitarian dictatorship, but again mostly stressing "moral right" or even "moral duty" as contrasted with function. Indeed, the potentially functional argument of German officers that they were trying to remove Hitler because he was wrecking Germany, and similar statements made in France and Italy by resistance groups, were often looked upon by outsiders as some sort of irrelevant "nationalism" or even a kind of "moral depravity." Yet during the McCarthy period, some of the most effective opposition to McCarthy's dubious methods was similarly defended in terms of protecting the functioning of the American constitutional order.[16] Thus the "tyrant" is seen as a disfunctional ruler whom a functional application of violent resistance must remove in the interest of the system's functioning.

The record of totalitarian dictatorship is instructive, though by no means conclusive. It could be said, in the perspective of the past, that "before the advent of modern tyranny, the idea of tyrannicide not only appeared anachronistic to most people in advanced countries but was generally condemned from the viewpoints of both expediency and morality. . . ."[17] The term "expediency" here hides the problem of functionality. Taking full account of such movements as the German resistance under Hitler, we encounter three "expedient" arguments against tyrannicide. First, there is the danger of uncoordinated, spontaneous violence in the form of individual action; second, there is the danger of disturbing public order; and third, there is the danger that the killing of an individual ruler will not attain the desired end, especially the destruction of the tyrannical regime. Had the problem been more realistically formulated with reference to functionality, it might not have been overlooked that counter-balancing these three expedient considerations might be that which stresses the damage to be avoided. Thus it might, *ex post facto*, now be possible to show that had Hitler been killed in the summer or fall of 1939—the attempt was made—World War II would probably not have occurred—not then, anyway.[18] The crucial functional considerations are brought out by focusing on the resistance rather than the killing of an individual ruler.

Dissenters who resist for the purpose of insuring the functioning of at least part of a political system usually belong to groups which predispose them toward a distinctive viewpoint in a modern industrial society: scientists, scholars, artists and writers, clergymen, and technicians of various kinds. These persons usually are gathered into an institutionalized grouping, such as an institution of higher learning (academy, university, etc.), a factory, a church, or a military establishment, and thus form "islands of separateness" in which resistance may take various forms.[19] These groupings find it necessary for purposes of survival, and hence the maintenance of their vital function, to resist the totalist claim. Such resistance by special-skill groups could be called "functional resistance." Most of it is nonviolent, but some, especially the military, are prone to become violent when circumstances appear favorable. The greatest difficulty is to achieve an effective organization; for a totalitarian regime seeks to prevent any organizing outside its own control.[20] Such resistance is in a very specific sense "functional," since it is directed toward maintaining a particular function, such as the military, intact, and thus may be functional by helping to maintain the system as a whole.[21]

In more open societies, even if not fully democratized, resistance often takes the form of "nullification," that is to say the local powers, tied in to the social and cultural region in which they serve, simply disobey orders from the center and fail to enforce laws and other kinds of commands. Such nullification may go so far that the central authorities feel obliged to intervene by armed force, as did one American President (Eisenhower) in an effort to enforce a federal court order. The resistance may then either subside, as it did in this instance, or it may become more violent and lead to a civil-war type of situation, or it may adopt other methods, especially the so-called passive resistance. Since its declared purpose is to avoid violence, such passive resistance does not properly form part of our topic here, even though such resistance may actually destroy an established rule. Nullification is itself a form of passive resistance or noncooperation. Such acts as the burning of draft cards or tax records are not truly "passive," but instead of being violent they are demonstrative and symbolic. But if the establishment adopts violent methods for their suppression (police action), the likelihood is great that such demonstrative resistance will evolve into violent resistance; at first only the individual who is being arrested may strike the arresting policeman. But eventually his friends will be drawn into the fray.

When the objective of resistance groups becomes that of overthrowing the regime, they are likely to become disfunctional. Sedition, rebellion, and revolution are the successive stages of the process.[22] Revolutions are successful rebellions. They are also rebellions on a large scale. Revolutions are the cataclysmic manifestations of a process that is continually occurring on a smaller scale in personal and group relations whenever necessary changes are unduly delayed. Many small revolutions in these relations anticipate, that is to say "prevent," a big one in the overall political order if they are effectively reflected in adaptive steps (legislation being the modern form of such adaptations and "reforms"). For as various factors of the social order are revolutionized by way of such an adaptive process, the tensions which would make the forcible overthrow of the political order, the "establishment," necessary are alleviated by being channeled into participatory operations. The effort that is being made at the present time to interest rebellious youth in seeking to achieve their goals by influencing elections points in that direction. But it may not work if the rebels prove unpersuasive to the electorate and are thereby excited into even more violent resistance against a system that does not yield to their demands. It is an old argument; in the Marxist movement before the First World War it was perhaps the "hottest" topic of controversy.[23] The "evolutionists" insisted that participating in elections and eventually in a parliamentary government was the most promising road toward socialism, while others refused all such participation and insisted upon class war and revolution, claiming, and not without a good deal of ground, that this was the orthodox position and the true view of Marx.[24] It was an argument that repeated itself between the Mensheviks and the Bolsheviks in Russia, and is now in a distorted way the argument that divides Moscow and Peking (in so far as this division is ideological). In a sense, all of this bitterly contested issue can be considered an argument over the functionality of violence. For the revolutionary groups obviously maintain that the violent overthrow of the existing political and social order is functional to the new order to be erected after such an overthrow.

In spite of such expressions as the "industrial revolution" or the "scientific revolution," revolution as a political process needs to be distinguished from such evolutionary transformations no matter how radical. One of its distinctive features, and perhaps the most crucial one, is the employment of physical violence on a large scale and in organized (planned) ways, that is to say as a "strategy."[25] Such an employment presupposes that those engaged in it believe it to be functional to their purpose, and hence disfunctional to the existing political order. Trotsky once said that "revolutions are the mad inspirations of history."[26] Such a statement is a poetical way of saying that revolutions occur when a basic change in values and beliefs which have not been able to mold political decisions and institutions breaks through into the political realm. Revolutions constitute the most serious form of political pathology. In their course, one political order dies. The difficulty for the analysis arises from the fact that a political order is constantly and continually dying as various elements are being transformed or replaced. Violence is the decisive criterion of the political revolution. An understanding of the revolutionary process obliges us to recognize that it is not death which is pathological; it is on the contrary the most natural occurrence. But what is pathological is sudden and violent death.[27]

At this point it is necessary to consider the question of range. There is an obvious difference between the kind of violent overthrow caused by some of the Latin American revolutions, apart from the many *coup d'états*,[28] and the great French Revolution. The former more nearly correspond to the kind of revolution Aristotle had in mind, typical for the Greek cities, in which aristocracy and democracy were the usual contestants. These were limited revolutions, as contrasted with the great revolutions of European history and their limitless aspirations.[29] In these cases, the political change in all its violence is incidental to the cultural, that is to say the valuational and convictional transformation of which the revolutionary overthrow of the political order forms a part. It is understandable enough that the revolutionary violence employed for this purpose appears distinctly functional in relation to the new and emerging order. Through this link, *revolution* has acquired a positive, affirmative, even a laudatory connotation in Western speech. "I am a revolutionary!" is proclaimed proudly by those who, alienated from the existing scheme of things, wish thereby to express their readiness to employ all necessary means, but more especially violence, to change the political order. Some contexts seem especially favorable to revolutionary action.[30]

The well-known pronouncements in favor of revolution by such great American leaders as Jefferson, John Quincy Adams, and Lincoln would seem to express a cultural disposition in favor of and thereby favoring revolutionary action. The cry "Back to the Spirit of 1776" expresses such a disposition.[31] A country in which a revolutionary spirit is part of the national culture, part of the political belief system (what has rather awkwardly been called "political culture"), will be more vulnerable to this kind of violent appeal than a country of a conservative disposition. But, important as such a tradition may be, certain "objective" givens are probably equally or even more important. In Latin America, for example, one count says that there occurred sixty-eight revolutions in Bolivia during the sixty-five years of her existence to the date of the count. Aristotle thought that deep divisions on the subject of "justice," that is to say what would now be called a strong "polarization" of a particular population, create the prospect of revolutionary violence. It is clear from such a surmise that this discussion leads into the ancient topic of the "causes" of revolution. Aristotle's early attempt[32] has been followed by those of Polybius, Machiavelli, and Harrington, which present essentially refinements of the Aristotelian hypotheses. In more recent times, historians, sociologists, and political scientists have contributed toward this discussion.[33] It would seem that no analytic purpose is served by listing particular values of a highly abstract sort, such as freedom, security, equality, or justice as causes or grounds for revolutionary feelings. The development of a great many stresses and strains is the most general antecedent of revolution, and of revolutionary violence. These stresses and strains may be strictly political; they may also be economic, social, or ideological.

It has been argued that only an accumulation of such stresses and strains will add up to a revolutionary situation.[34] Experience in this century, as well as earlier periods, suggests that the presence of a revolutionary power of great resources may be a revolutionizing factor of great potency.[35] The violent implications of such "interference" or "intervention" became so clear in their disfunctionality in the course of the late sixteenth and early seventeenth century (note especially the Thirty Years' War) that the doctrine of nonintervention in the internal affairs of another country became an important principle of international law. Unfortunately it was more often honored in the breach than in the observance.[36] In any case, the disfunctionality involved was related to the international system, rather than to national or parochial political orders. A situation such as that in Vietnam has demonstrated to everyone willing to consider it with detachment how dangerous in its violent potential intervention can be; here (and in Cambodia) it has become almost impossible to say who intervenes with whom or against whom where; because the doctrine of intervention which permits foreign powers to come to the aid of the government when so requested makes it essential to be able to determine who constitutes such a government, that is to say the problem of legitimacy becomes of vital concern.[37]

Many of those who have sought to arrive at an "objective" or scientific view of the process of revolution have mistakenly neglected its objective. It is not merely a matter of considering what brought on the revolution, but also a matter of analyzing its thrust. Only when the makers "think in terms of a new order, of progress, of changing times" can one speak of revolution in the distinctive modern sense.[38] But the objective needs further differentiation. A number of Western revolutions, notably the British, American, and French, were directed toward establishing a *constitutional* political order. Others, notably the Russian and Chinese revolutions, were intended to place *total* power in the hands of men who wished radically to alter the entire society, and more especially the economic system. Many other revolutions are directed toward greater power and authority for the rulers *per se*, such as the Roman and the Gaullist revolutions. In these latter cases, the revolution *may* obviously be functional in both intention and actual result; at times such a revolution is difficult to distinguish from a *coup d'état*. Realistically, a revolution carried forward by a group which wants to establish a constitutional order and hence forms a "constituent group"[39] is a different process from a revolution made by proponents of great power for the government; both may be functional in relation to a given national state.

More often than not constitutional revolutions are limited in in scope. Their focus is on the political order as such. A well-drawn constitution with an adequately flexible amending process can anticipate the occurrence of such a limited revolution; here the developing pressures of change may crystallize in amendments, such as that by which the Senate of the United States was based on popular election, a step in the democratization of the Constitution. The long, drawn-out process of this democratization, by no means completed, is in itself a "revolution," but not in the specific sense of a political revolution as here defined, since it did not result from violence. An amending process may, indeed, provide for the complete revamping of a constitution, as happened in a number of American states and in Switzerland in 1874. The latter process democratized Switzerland, and hence basically altered her constitutional order; it was presumably preferable that this alteration be achieved without a violent revolution, even though violence would have been functional to the new order. This feasibility of achieving basic alterations without violence reduces the functionality of violent revolution; for what can be achieved without morally objectionable means destroys the justification for the employment of such means.

It is in keeping with this general insight when contemporary constitutional orders increasingly provide for the outlawry of those who abuse its protection for the purpose of advocating its violent overthrow. In this connection, American political tradition has evolved slowly toward an increasingly hostile attitude toward violent revolution, in spite of the origin of the country and the pronouncements of its earlier leaders mentioned above. The problem of fully integrating the fairly large minority of blacks into the U.S. community has once more posed this problem. Blacks are a part of the American people. It has rightly been said that America would not be what she is without them. The greatest tragedy of its history, the Civil War—incidentally the bloodiest war of the nineteenth century—could have been the consummation of its revolution.[40] If Lincoln had lived, it might well have been. For Lincoln was keenly aware of the functionality of revolution under certain conditions. In speaking of the Mexican War he said in Congress on January 12, 1848: "Any people anywhere being inclined and having the power, have the right to rise up and shake off the existing government, and form a new one that suits them better. This is a most valuable, most sacred right. . . . More than this, a majority of any portion of such people may revolutionize, putting down a minority. . . ." And to make doubly sure that this meaning be taken in the radical sense of an overthrow of established institutions, he added: "It is the quality of revolutions not to go by old ideas or old laws. . . ."[41] It may be doubted that a majority of latter-day Americans would agree with him, any more than they did in 1848—the year of the revolutions all over Europe that placed in jeopardy the reactionary monarchies of Prussia and Austria, as well as the liberal one of France. If a profound alteration of the American political order, perfecting its democracy, should be consummated in this generation, it would be more nearly a political revolution; for violence on a considerable scale has been occurring all over the land, and the Black Panthers have become the spearhead of this revolutionary enterprise. The revolution of the liberation of former colonial possessions which has swept the globe has been stimulating it, even though the setting is one in which amending processes of the established constitutional order probably will eventually take care of the necessary changes. That this can happen is shown by the case of Puerto Rico—for the establishment of the associated commonwealth is truly an integral part of the democratization process that has been going on in what has been rather rhetorically referred to as the "permanent revolution" that is America. It is such a revolution only in the non-specific sense of a radical change. Yet the accompanying violence which has been endemic to American life lends it a truly revolutionary flavor. There is little doubt that by the end of the century a black may be President of the United States, just as a black sits on the Supreme Court and blacks are members of America's legislative assemblies and run American cities today. But it is difficult to determine at this point to what degree the accompanying violence is truly functional; the partisans are inclined to consider it so, while its opponents decry it in the name of law and order which become questionable within the context of revolutionary thrusts.

However, the American tradition, having been preoccupied with the "right" of revolution,[42] fails to be concerned with and does not face up to the main point of our interest here, namely that revolutionary violence will in fact occur and has a vital relationship to the functioning of the political order. Its importance for the founding or refounding of such orders is obvious and has often been recognized.[43] But if the systemic relationship is not to a formal institutional setup, such as the state, but to the political community, nations, and similar entities, a revolution may indeed be functional in providing the challenge for an effective reordering which makes it possible for the nation to survive. And not only to survive, but actually to achieve a more advanced form of political existence. All those speculative theories which link the revolutions to what is known as "progress" obviously assign to it the crucial function of stimulating growth. This is actually a prevailing belief among Westerners: the English, French, Russian, American, German, and other minor revolutions have been occasions for the achievement of significant progress in a presumably desirable direction—democracy, freedom, and so forth. It is evident that such reasoning about revolution and its functionality depends for its conclusiveness upon the belief in the desirability of the particular direction, whether it be freedom, social justice, or whatever. Such arguments demonstrate at best that the revolutionary and his sympathizers envisage the revolution as functional. At times this outlook is reinforced by the notion that the revolution seeks to "re-establish" an earlier order which has been corrupted or perverted; however, such reactionary perspectives have usually soon yielded to a transformation into progressive preoccupations (notably in the English and French revolutions).

Whether the scope of a particular revolution is limited or unlimited, pro-constitutional or anti-constitutional, a revolution will, in short, invariably have the remaking of the political order as one of its major objectives. In other words, a political revolution with its attendant violence is inherent in every kind of revolution because of the stresses and strains which it engenders in the body politic. But it may be forestalled in a constitutional order by a flexible amending procedure which would prove, or at least suggest, that a political revolution is not the necessary sequel to such a social revolution, though a radical transformation of the political order is bound to be—a non-violent revolution, if you please. The problem of violence presents itself here in that particular form which preoccupied Sorel and with which we shall deal in the next chapter.

Here it remains to draw attention to a curious kind of situation in which what I have elsewhere called "negative" revolutions occur. These revolutions negate or reject a past political order without any belief in or enthusiasm for a new one. In France, Germany, and Italy the inclination to restore, after the Second World War, a former political regime was the result of resignation rather than hope and expectation. Many have spoken of this situation as one of "restoration" in analogy to the restorations which occurred after the great revolutions in England (1660) and France (1815). These restorations, however, really believed that the old regime could be revived. The resignation in Western Europe after the Second World War extended to the restored systems themselves. The new rulers have therefore lacked any legitimacy, that is to say any supporting conviction on the part of the people subject to them that they were entitled to rule. The violence which preceded these was mostly that of foreign conquering armies, aided and abetted by alienated local elements who had mounted a certain resistance, most notably in France. But the truly revolutionary elements were those who hoped for a Communist regime; this was in fact prevented by the restorations, because of a lack of popular support. The revolutionizing violence being that of foreign armed forces, one could even mockingly speak of these peoples as "forced to be free."[44] If I may allude to a famous and generally misquoted passage in Rousseau's *Contrat Social*,[45] the presumed paradox is reduced if the revolutionary goal is not only or primarily freedom, but social justice and related tasks of social change. Thus in Germany the primary concern was the re-establishment of the rule of law (*Rechsstaat*) rather than freedom.[46]

Similarly, the revolutionary upheavals in the course of which colonial regimes were overthrown have not succeeded in establishing viable political orders. But here it was not a resigned restoration of former orders, though this was at times the first step, but rather a half-hearted attempt at instituting orders for which there was no foundation in the belief and value system prevailing in these societies.[47] The result has been a further revolution (or even several of them) leading to the establishment of military dictatorship.[48] All of these experiences point to the conclusion that a revolution, no matter how violent, does not necessarily produce an effective political order. The optimism of the West which inclined toward assuming such a result has proved to be quite unjustified.

In conclusion, let me say that violent resistance and revolution, while endemic in any political order and related to each other, are often effectively controlled. The means of avoiding resistance is to combine enforcement with broad consensus toward governmental activities of every kind, and the same holds true for revolution. It has been rightly said that "it is intrinsically impossible to construct a statistical measure that will predict the occurrence of a revolution."[49] But a potentially revolutionary situation can be ascertained. Hence "the likelihood of revolutions is a function of both positive or conflict-generating factors and negative or conflict-controlling factors."[50] Every political order is subject to change, and unless means are provided for adaptations of the institutions and processes to such changes as occur in the social substructure, such change will lead to violence, either sporadic, as in much resistance, or all-engulfing, as in political revolution. The process of revolution is simply a marginal instance of the range of processes of political change. As such it exhibits certain regularities in its successive phases; breakdown of the established order is the beginning phase. Revolution, when successful, signalizes the death of one political order and the emergence of a new one. It is hence necessarily two-faced in its functionality; it is disfunctional to the dying order and functional to the new order. Resistance, violent resistance, is often the harbinger of such a revolutionary overturn; as such it may be highly functional to the established order, serving as a warning and a stimulator of the necessary changes and adaptations. The violent labor unrest in Great Britain before the great reforms serves as a striking instance of such functionality of violence. There are indications that the same may be true at the present time in the U.S. and elsewhere.

CHAPTER 4

REFLECTIONS ON POLITICAL VIOLENCE IN GENERAL

THE DIVISION of the discussion of political violence into two parts, official and unofficial—the violence or force exercised by the government and that employed outside it or even against it—is somewhat artificial. It relates the discussion to the traditional institutional approach, even though it challenges the antiquated formula about the state "possessing the monopoly of (legitimate) force" which is found in juristic texts on the doctrine of the state and even in Max Weber. The more recent formula about the "authoritative allocation of values" is hardly an improvement and seeks to state the same position. These are normative propositions disguised as existential definitions. In seeming to base our discussion of violence upon the distinction, we might have given the impression that we were inclined to assign a vital importance to "legitimacy" as far as violence is concerned.[1] Such is actually not the case. On the contrary, the concept of functionality is intended to transcend this traditional approach—official violence may be strongly dysfunctional, as we have shown, while unofficial violence may be highly functional.

By speaking of violence in reference to its functionality or disfunctionality, a different set of relations is suggested. The relations are systemic, and what may be functional in the perspective of one system may be disfunctional in the perspective of another. Some may feel that if this is so then the statement that a certain case of violence may be functional is meaningless or so vague in meaning as to be scientifically worthless. The truth is that such a statement is not meaningless, but incomplete; for it fails to specify the system in terms of which such functionality is asserted. It is evident that in any case such statements are valuational and not value free. They assert that a certain case of violence is helpful to a particular system, that is to say it is good for the system. Such an assertion may, of course, hide a condemnation; for if the system is rejected (say by a particular revolutionary projection), then the violence which relates to it in a functional way is intended to be rejected in the bargain.

Georges Sorel, in his famous *Réflexions sur la Violence*, asserted that there was a sharp distinction between the force of the established rulers for maintaining a political order, and the violence of the revolutionaries for challenging such an order. But to me it seems more appropriate to speak of two forms of violence (or, if you please, of force) rather than to use two different words, thereby suggesting that one is dealing with two distinct phenomena.[2] For there is present in both the compulsion of men by those who have the means of coercion at their disposal. The violence may in either case be functional. But there is always present the potential that it may become disfunctional when it exceeds a certain limit. However, to Sorel this kind of approach was highly objectionable. Hostile anyhow to the conventional condemnation of violence, he insisted that he would consider violence only from the points of view of its influence on ideology.[3] Sorel's vision of a great battle, of the *grande bataille*, highlights the apocalyptic core of his thinking. There must be an armageddon, a culmination of violence, before the moral purification of society, which was the ultimate aim of Sorel, can take place.

He adduces the history of the persecutions of Christians and argues that their culmination only brought on the victory. Sorel's argumentation in terms of an "ethics of violence" (*la moralité de la violence*)[4] shows how closely related the question of functionality is to that of moralizing evaluation. But it also discloses the profound difference between them. The *anomie* that a challenge to established moral values creates in the minds of people eventually affects the governing classes from which the rulers are recruited and undermines their capacity to rule. "When the governing classes, no longer daring to govern, are ashamed of their privileged situation, are eager to make advances to their enemies, and proclaim their horror of all cleavage in society, it becomes much more difficult to maintain in the minds of the proletariat this idea of cleavage without which socialism cannot fulfill its historical role."[5] Violence therefore must be escalated. If we abstract from the particular preoccupation of Sorel with the revolutionary proletariat and generalize, we can say that when a ruling class becomes permissive vis-à-vis revolutionary violence, any tendency on the part of those seeking to revolutionize the society to accept compromise and a reduction of the violence will prevent the radical change originally demanded.

In our terminology, such reduction of violence will be dysfunctional in relation to the new order precisely because it is functional in relation to the established old one. Such a view asserts the value of the catastrophe. Hence a contemporary political sociologist has condemned Sorel's view in very sharp terms: "His work discloses a morally and politically pernicious standpoint."[6] Whether it is morally pernicious depends upon one's morality—to an ethic glorifying violence, such as Nietzsche's or Machiavelli's, it would be "good." But politically such a view is not so much pernicious as mistaken. The escalation of violence is not functional in itself, though it may prove so in the end. British and American society, exhibiting only occasional, limited, and sporadic violence, became more thoroughly revolutionized in the course of the nineteenth century than did that of France, because the "reaction," now popularly called "backlash" in America, remained equally limited and sporadic.

On the other side of the equation of violence, it must be said violence may easily become disfunctional also. A regime that depends too largely on the deployment of violence, and more particularly police action, is difficult to maintain. That you can do many things with bayonets but you cannot sit on them is a saying that suggests this elementary truth. It may seem banal, but is too often forgotten not to make it worth mentioning. Sorel welcomed vigorous defense by the ruling classes; for it widened the social cleavage; and he mocked the notion that those among the revolutionaries who sought to attenuate such defensive violence were serving the revolutionary cause. To him the idea of a "social duty" (*devoir social*) which would seek to achieve their goals by non-violence was untenable. Gandhi's Truth Force was a chimera; he preferred the doctrine of massive violence which he discerned in the writings and actions of Lenin. In a remarkable appendix added in 1919 to the *Réflexions*, Sorel replied to the suggestion that Lenin had been influenced by his thoughts on violence: "I have no reason for believing that Lenin made use of some of the ideas in my books; but if that were the case I would be not a little proud for having contributed to the intellectual development of a man who seems to me to be, at once the greatest theoretician that socialism has had since Marx and the head of a state whose genius recalls that of Peter the Great."[7] And he mocks: "Lenin is after all not a candidate for the prize of virtue awarded by the French Academy."

And in suggesting a parallel between the military violence of the Roman legions in establishing the Roman empire and the violence of the Russian revolutionaries in establishing the workers' republic, he exclaims: "How grateful will not the future have to be to the Russian soldiers of socialism!" And he adds, characteristically, "How lightly for the historians will weigh the criticism of the propagandists [*rhéteurs*] whom democracy has charged with denouncing the excesses of the *Bolsheviks.*" What were these "excesses"? They were "excesses of violence" of course. What is here implied is the disfunctionality of some of the violence[8] which is being "justified" by the result. It is so justified by the coming into being of a presumably better society—better in the sense of having been morally reborn. Our concern cannot here be to explore the particular kind of morality which such a rebirth reestablishes and Sorel is notably vague on the point anyhow. But since he is so deeply troubled by the *corruption* of the bourgeois society, its bargaining and propensity to compromise, one may guess that it is a morality not far removed from that of Machiavelli's *virtù.*[9] The outlook is Nietzschean in its dislike of the Christian virtues. At the heart of it is an enthusiasm for heroism such as had also animated Carlyle and others who reacted against the drabness and dreariness of industrial civilization. These sorts of reactions have been recurrent since the mid-nineteenth century; they are just now celebrating a revival with the popularity of writings such as those of Frantz Fanon[10] and a number of Negro writers in the U.S., notably Malcolm X and Rap Brown.[11] Sartre in his preface to Fanon wrote: ". . . he shows clearly that this irrepressible violence is neither sound and fury, nor the resurrection of savage instincts, nor even the effect of resentment: it is man recreating himself. I think we understood this truth at one time, but we have forgotten it—that no gentleness can efface the marks of violence; only violence itself can destroy them. . . . We have sown the wind; he [the new man] is the whirlwind. The child of violence, at every moment he draws from it his humanity. We were men at his expense, he makes himself man at ours: a different man, of higher quality."[12]

It is, however, in this connection very striking that Sorel cites with considerable approval a French writer who had reported on lynch law in the United States.[13] "The decent American," he had written, "has the excellent habit of not allowing himself to be crushed, just because he is decent. A man who stands for order is not necessarily a timid person, as is so often the case with us." And he had sketched lynch law quite in keeping with the American frontier tradition as follows: "A man convicted of murder or theft can find himself arrested, judged, condemned and hanged in less than a quarter of an hour, if a vigilance committee could get hold of him." Sorel, in approving of such "morality," comments further that one would have to concede to the "partisans of softness" that "violence might hinder economic progress and that it could be dangerous to morality, *if it passes a certain limit*" (italics mine). Sorel adds that such an admission would not affect his own doctrine for he "considers violence only from the viewpoint of its ideological consequences." He does not wish to be misunderstood to say that in order to have the workers understand that economic conflicts are weak images of the great battle to come it is necessary to have a big development of brutality and the blood flow in torrents.[14] (This seems now to be the notion of some radicals, especially the Panthers.)

What Sorel is suggesting is far off the mark, just the same. To him scattered outbreaks of violence are not stimulants for effecting social change, but rather the symbolic anticipations of the catastrophic day of violent revolution, the *grande bataille*. And Sorel is furious with those "liberals" who postpone the great day by making timely concessions and thereby obscuring the "cleavage of society" (*la scission des classes*) which is the basis of all socialism for him. For this reason, he could not see or comprehend that the sporadic violence of the vigilante tradition in the United States was merely a transition phase to a more ordered society. Outbreaks of the vigilante type of violence were a persistent feature of American life, at least in the regions near the frontier. In their studies on violence in America, recent writers have been able to show how such periods of violence were related to important transformations of the American system and its regions.[15] Out of the frontier conditions of self-help and amateur warfare the vigilante movements have sprung. A short list of them fills five and a half pages of small print. The vigilante tradition in America, "in the classic sense, refers to organized, extra-legal movements which take the law into their own hands." Three hundred and twenty-six such movements are known to have occurred; the actual number may be as high as five hundred.[16] Although the phenomenon resembles what has happened elsewhere when a regime was breaking down and law and order were in jeopardy, such as the special *Fehme* courts in medieval Germany,[17] vigilantism is by many believed to be something peculiarly American—an indigenous product of frontier conditions, i.e., the absence of effective law and order. In so far as this is true, it suggests that such plural violence operated as a substitute for the centralized violence of the modern state. It is found wherever the political order is loose and ineffective, that is, where a close-knit regime of violence such as that characteristic of the modern state has not yet come into being.

The case of vigilantism is in some respects unique, but it is nonetheless especially interesting, because the new settlers, in the words of one of its students, mainly "desired to recreate the life they left behind them by reconstructing the kind of community from which they came." And he adds: "Basic to the reconstruction of community is the reestablishment of the old community structure and its values. . . . The American community of the 18th and 19th centuries was primarily a property holders community, and property was viewed as the very basis of life itself."[18] It is therefore not surprising to find the upper crust of merchants and landowners assuming the leadership in most of the vigilante movements; many of these leaders later achieved high political office. Vigilantes recalled in later life with pride their participation in such activities, as a number of memoirs attest.[19] Hence vigilantism has had a profound and lasting impact on the American tradition of self-help with which it is closely linked. Vigilantism thereby attests to the functionality of such plural violence in the building and maintenance of the particular political order Americans have cherished, characterized by freedom and the values of an acquisitive capitalist society. In quite a few cases, it was the cheapness of direct action, dispensing with the elaborate procedures of a government by law, which led the wealthy to support vigilante activities. "No better resolution of the conflicting goals of public order and personal wealth could be found than vigilantism which provided a maximum of the former at a minimum cost to the ambitious and well-to-do."[20] Particular individuals saw in this kind of leadership a chance to win a position in the upper crust of a new community.[21] If it was true that "a really large expenditure of funds for the pursuit, capture, jailing, trial and conviction of culprits could easily bankrupt the typical frontier town,"[22] then the vigilante kind of justice was economically preferable to the slower judicial process of more settled communities.

The frame of mind of the vigilantes, perhaps one could even call it their ideology, confirms the potentially functional role of these groups and movements. It was, as mentioned, inspired by the predominant American pattern of values, interests, and beliefs and sought to make it secure in the communities in which vigilantism sprang up. Vigilantes felt obliged "to legitimize," that is to say to justify their violence by fashioning a "philosophy," thereby manifesting their Christian heritage. According to Professor Brown, this philosophy or ideology was compounded of three elements: self-preservation, the right of revolution, and popular sovereignty.[23] All three are, of course, key points in the Declaration of Independence.[24] They were argued in terms of natural law, and provided the basis for the wide acceptance of vigilantism as an expression of American folk culture. What this means is that violence is thus accepted as functional to a particular political order. Phrases such as "red-blooded American" testify further to this aspect of the matter in hand. To put it another way, if the cherished ideas of the community must be violated in the interest of upholding this community, it will and should be done. That such a view constitutes a popularized form of the ancient doctrine of reason of state will readily be recognized.[25] Brown cites a striking manifestation of this outlook, a resolution adopted on January 9, 1857, by the vigilantes of northern Indiana:

> Whereas we are believers in the *doctrine of popular sovereignty* that the people of this country are the real sovereigns, and that whenever the laws made by those to whom they have delegated their authority, are found inadequate to their protection, it is the right of the people to take the protection of their property in their own hands, and deal with these villains according to their just deserts. . . .[26]

Such a doctrine, widespread in America during the nineteenth century, is of course destructive of democratic order; for if, as Brown comments, the people in their several subdivisions are thus superior to all else, even the law, then anarchy reigns and violence erupts.

On the basis of this set of facts, Professor Brown expounds a distinction between "socially constructive" and "socially destructive" vigilantism. Such a distinction closely resembles that between functional and disfunctional violence. Where the problem of order in the community had been solved by the consolidation of the traditional social structure and the solidification of the supporting community values, there we have a socially constructive vigilantism, that is to say functional violence. Where, on the contrary, anarchy was the result of a vigilante movement, there we have the "socially destructive" variety, that is to say violence that is definitely disfunctional. The several instances of vigilantism which are analyzed in some detail by Brown show how easily this type of plural violence becomes disfunctional, by getting out of hand, in other words how great the risk of violence becoming disfunctional actually is. Brown confirms this conclusion in these words: "In short run practical terms, the vigilante movement was a positive facet of the American experience. Many a new frontier community gained order and stability as the result of vigilantism which reconstructed the community structure and values of the old settled areas while dealing effectively with a problem of crime and disorder."[27] That was the functional side. But "perhaps the most important result of vigilantism has not been its social-stabilizing effect but the subtle way in which it persistently undermined our respect for law by its repeated insistence that there are times when we may choose not to obey the law."[28]

The consequence of this lawlessness has been the recurrence of *riots* in America. For those are in a sense the obverse of the vigilantes, and at times the sequel to their activities.[29] Since a riot constitutes a crime, there are of course legal definitions for what constitutes a riot. The standard common-law definition, we are told, unchanged since September 12, 1849, is that a riot is "any tumultuous assemblage of three or more persons brought together for no legal or constitutional object, deporting themselves in such manner as to endanger the public peace and excite terror and alarm in rational and firm-minded persons . . . ," or to put it another way, stressing the legal side, "whenever three or more persons, in a tumultuous manner, use force or violence in the execution of any design wherein the law does not allow the use of force, they are guilty of riot." This definition includes all the elements which make a riot: three or more persons employing violence and endangering the public peace, and the purpose of reinforcing a demand or expressing a protest.[30] Thus while peaceful assembly is constitutionally guaranteed, such a riot is not. There is no recognition in the law as thus defined of the possibility that riots may be functional, that the violence which is flaring up in such a riot could serve the system and help it to function more effectively.

In spite of the law, riots have been common in the United States, and a recent researcher has described thirteen of the major ones in some detail.[31] Surely no one would hesitate to agree that the first of these, the Stamp Act Riots of 1765, which this author labels "the riot road to revolution," were functional in their relation to the emerging American political system, though clearly disfunctional to the colonial regime. America is at present plagued by the question as to when a peaceful assembly is turning into a riot. Legislatures and courts are divided on the subject, and it would lead us too far afield to describe and analyze this legal tangle. But it serves to illustrate the difficulty that at the core of the arguments is always the question as to whether the rioters serve a "useful" function by their riot. The draft riots of the Civil War period were defended on grounds quite similar to those now used in explaining the draft riots of recent years, namely that they served to publicize and hoped to end a "senseless war."[32] They did of course fail in the latter purpose and Lincoln's response to them was similar to that of any governing man or group engaged in a war.[33]

The most extensive riots occurred at New York on July 13–16, 1863. They are believed to have been the largest riots ever until recent years. Seventy thousand are supposed to have participated. Here is a recent brief description of the process: "The riots started as a treasonable insurrection against the United States Government, then became a destructive attack against the well-to-do, and finally a race riot with Negroes as targets. Scores of separate incidents were equal in fury to many full-scale riots."[34] The writer adds, "The New York City Draft Riots offer the best single example of a mob expanding its original objective to anarchy and every sort of crime and violence. . . . The range of mob activities was vast and there were countless individual outbursts of savage fury and appalling destruction. . . ."[35] Even so, it proved completely unsuccessful. The government "never even considered abolishing the draft in New York City, and the clause permitting payment for a substitute remained in effect. . . . The drawing resumed on August 25. . . ."

There is little difficulty in concluding that this particular violence, in contrast to that of the Stamp Act riots, was completely disfunctional. As one reviews the several instances of rioting he finds that riots directed against serious abuses or seeking positive legislative relief for great tensions tend to be effective and hence functional, while riots which get out of hand and which lack such objective fail to achieve functionality. In a democratic system, where the majority is the ultimate decision-maker, according to prevailing belief and some practice, the only way for an alienated minority to get or prevent action is at times to make large demonstrations of protest, but they are subject to counter-demonstrations by elements of the majority who feel sufficiently strongly on the subject. Such confrontations are usually likely to become violent, and thereby the demonstration develops into a riot.

The same holds true for demonstrations which occasion a police supervision which itself becomes the detonator of a violent riot. A difficult dilemma is thereby posed for those who wish to maintain the democratic system. If one restricts the right of peaceful assembly, the dynamics of the democratic process may be seriously impaired; even a creeping trend toward autocratic controls, by the police and the military, may be initiated. If, on the other hand, the right of assembly is fully maintained, riots may become so widespread as to undermine the belief in the viability of the system and it may be so much weakened that a military coup becomes possible because of the widespread indifference that has set in.[36] The tendency of some of the judiciary to sympathize with the demonstrators-rioters and their goals may alarm majority elements in the population to the point where they are even ready to demand such a change of regime. It happened in Germany prior to seizure of power by Hitler, and in France prior to de Gaulle's reassumption of power in 1958. It had happened in France about ninety years earlier in 1850 and led to the establishment of the second empire under Napoleon III. The same process has been observed in a number of underdeveloped countries, notably in Africa. It is almost the order of the day in Latin America and has been for many generations. In all these instances, plural violence has proved to be disfunctional to the existing political order, and that point may be reached even in formally established systems. It often is a matter which turns upon the ratio of official versus unofficial violence. As long as the ratio remains better than one, the chances are good that the violence remains functional or at least does not become disfunctional:

$$\text{If } \frac{V\,(o)}{V\,(u)} > 1, \text{ then } V\,(u) = f\,(s)$$

is a simple formula for that conclusion; it shows how vital to the system is the strength of the police. The term "strength of the police" is not, of course, measurable simply in terms of the number of policemen; for such matters as their equipment, their morale, etc. enter into the equation, and the same holds for the rioters-demonstrators (V (u)). But even though this be admitted, the strength of the police in terms of number is a basic index.

In the United States, as well as Britain and other countries, the recognition of the truth contained in the above formula finds expression in the considerably larger police forces in large urban centers than in smaller towns and in the country. The riot potential is much greater in cities, and such instances as the draft riots in New York and other large centers, as well as recent experience in the United States and elsewhere, bear this out. Large congregations of like-minded people are another source of danger and riot potential. The large factory has been seen as such for a long time. In recent years the university has proved to be equally dangerous. Students have been in the forefront of rioting all over the world. The youthful age of these large groups increases their volatility; for the emotionalism of young people increases their propensity toward violence and the crimes of violence. This is generally true. The statistics of crime in the United States shows it quite clearly.[37] New York has the highest crime rate per hundred thousand in the Northeast U.S., namely 3,544 for 1968 as compared with Vermont, where it was 787, and to the national average of 2,234. The Northeast region as a whole is high compared to North Central (including Chicago) where it was 1,891 and the South where it was 1,870. The crime rate in the U.S. has been rising quite rapidly in recent years, 16.3 percent per year, and 122 percent for the eight-year period 1960–1968.

Fifty percent of the crimes were committed by people under twenty-five years of age. New York City has the highest per capita rate of violent crime, there being 769 per hundred thousand, as contrasted with Pittsfield, Massachusetts, with 40 and Utica, New York, with 31 and Wilkes-Barre, Pennsylvania, with 31—these are small cities. Crimes of violence are strikingly large in the age group 25–29; in that age group 1,680 as compared to 164 in the age group 60–64. For 20–24 it is even higher, namely 2,167; the highest rate for any one year appears to be that for 18-year-olds, namely 501. The story is the same for forcible rape, namely 1,043 for 18-year-olds, over 3,000 for 20–24 (total), and 1,920 for 25–29. Within that general framework of propensity toward violence, it stands to reason that youth is most apt to engage in violent riots. As far as urban conditions are concerned, the figures also confirm the general impression and reveal that large cities are riot-prone. These rough indices all suggest that violence is endemic and therefore must be considered a general feature of human existence.

We have at an earlier point, when discussing war, briefly alluded to the controversy over whether violence is "natural" or not. That it is ubiquitous there can be little doubt. But the psychologists are disagreed on whether it is innate or environmentally conditioned. There appears to be one environmental condition which greatly increases men's propensity toward violence and that is the setting which is provided by a mob. One does not need to go as far as the French sociologist Le Bon,[38] who would assign an individual existence to a crowd, over and above and beyond the persons composing it. It is a questionable illusion that "when a crowd changes into a mob, its individual members lose their identity and merge into a cruel, primitive body which has lost civilized restraints and suddenly has no respect for those law enforcement agencies that resist it." While such a view might provide a welcome alibi for some of the participants, it is more probable that participation in a crowd changes the identity of many of the participants in a way similar to what alcohol and narcotics do to humans. Restraints and inhibitions to primitive behavior are weakened and reduced or even eliminated and the beast in man comes to the fore.

Rage will also do it, and rage is often intensified by being in the company of others who are likewise enraged. Le Bon's notions were much too much built upon the belief in the rationality of man and hence this collectivist explanation of irrational behavior, and more particularly of violent behavior. It is a well-attested fact that women tend to be more violent than men in these kinds of situations leading to riot and the accompanying behavior. It may well be related to their greater emotionality. Is violence then "natural"? It seems to occur quite regularly in situations of emotional strain, anger and sexual passion being familiar illustrations. It is conceivable, and by some psychologists firmly contended, especially Freud and his school, that long-time suppression of this propensity to violence, especially lack of sex, will eventually make a man burst forth into a veritable binge of senseless violence. Writers with a psychological bent have given some memorable descriptions of such outbursts, like Dostoevsky in *The Brothers Karamazov*. Such occurrences—and many contemporary political riots resemble them—are likely to be completely disfunctional, as far as the political system is concerned.

One is inclined to wonder whether certain kinds of spectacles, notably Western movies, Spanish bull fights, and the wild animal killings of the Roman arena are not institutionalized forms of taking care of these urges in unhappy populations which have no other outlet for their propensity to violence. The student of politics has to accept the fact that as in so many other crucial questions the psychologist leaves him without positive guidance. On the phenomena we are agreed; on how to explain them they are as much in disagreement as are political theorists. Anyhow, the political theorist is not able to accept the heroics of Sorel and Nietzsche, even while recognizing that violence has a definite function in politics. Neither the maintenance of a political order nor its change can be achieved without a limited amount of violence. Where that limit lies will depend upon a variety of political and social factors, including the cultural tradition of any given political order. A greater amount of violence has been acceptable to the American people than to Europeans generally, but it has been declining and the indignation aroused by certain violent occurrences of recent years demonstrates that the limit has become narrower. This question had been raised by Sorel in relation to his particular problem of the general strike as a pacemaker for socialism: "Why is it that in certain countries acts of violence grouping themselves around the idea of the general strike, produce an exalted Socialist ideology while in other countries they do not seem to have such a power?" And he answers in terms of "national traditions," but without elaborating.[39] The exasperating conclusion must be that there obviously are limits, but that it is very difficult to determine where they lie. Some recent studies have made a start. There are studies about disequilibrium[40] which suggest that increased disequilibrium is a measure of the revolutionary potential; obviously if the violent measures taken to deal with acts of violence amount to overreacting, the disequilibrium will be increased and hence the limit within which the deployment of violence will operate functionally has been exceeded. Reversely, and especially for the case interesting Sorel, sporadic violence which leads to effective increase in police control may be disfunctional to the revolutionary enterprise.

At this point, it may be well to discuss, even if briefly, the problem of terrorism. Terror has been well defined as consisting of "symbolic acts designed to influence political behavior by extra-normal means, entailing the use or threat of violence."[41] Such terror may be employed for maintaining a political system or for destroying it. Notable examples of the first are the terror employed in the dictatorial regimes of the twentieth century.[42] The terror of insurgents and anarchists illustrates the other type of terror.[43] In either case, terror has definite limits. These are suggested by the non-achievement of the objective, or even its perversion. In any case, terror is an extreme form of lawless violence, whether used for maintenance or disruption of a political system. It is the opposite extreme of the rule of law. In the totalitarian regimes of our time, those fighting the terror have sought to do so by way of strengthening the legal system. As an exasperated Polish scholar once told a Western questioner who wanted to know what the difference was between Stalinist times and the reform: "They cannot call up!" The point was that no party functionary could interfere in court procedures. There is a difference between being able to foresee the consequences of your acts, even under a very severe system of law, and being exposed to unforeseeable acts of violence, symbolized by the police arriving in the middle of the night for the purpose of arresting a political suspect. The arrival was itself a method designed to terrorize people; every noise would awaken such an opponent. The limits of such terror were at times dramatically demonstrated: Stalin at the height of the violence engendered by the great purges of the thirties called a halt in a famous speech "Dizzy with success . . ." which marked a slowdown;[44] a similar stop had to be put to the Cultural Revolution which Mao had unleashed.[45] The need for such "enforcement terror" is very great in totalitarian regimes, because their totalist ideology requires a total transformation of the preexisting social structure. Thus change becomes the order of the day. It is expected to be the task of generations. The process of building the socialist society is not finished with the physical liquidation of the capitalists and their henchmen. The revolution continues, with the accomplishment of each task precipitating a new one. It is this determination to achieve total change that begets the terror.[46] Change typically entails tension and opposition. In a "free" society total change therefore cannot occur, because it would bring forth too massive an opposition, a total resistance. In a totalitarian regime, opposition is crushed by total terror. It eventually forces everyone to comply by the violence of its terror. Yet total change remains a utopian goal. The spreading vacuum and the rise of indifference—a form of resignation—limits the effectiveness of violence. It prevents total fulfillment, because of the alienation of even the party cadres. Thus the repressive violence of the totalitarian regime which at first aims at eliminating the regime's open enemies is gradually extended to other sections of the society. Totalitarian terror grows until a limit is reached where it becomes self-defeating. The vacuum, the indifference of the populace, and apathy among the workers operate to set this limit. The retrenchment of violence is often misunderstood outside as a "liberalization" of the totalitarian system, whereas it is really a striking illustration of the fact that such violence, too, can become disfunctional. Political violence is here too ambivalent.[47] *When* this point is reached the leadership gauges by "intuition."

What is true of such enforcement violence is equally true of the "agitational violence" of insurrectional forces. The effect of repression may be to stimulate the insurgent movement up to a point. So skillful a revolutionary as Che Guevara was "chary of terrorism." Presumably he feared that the repression it engenders would "cost the insurgents more than they can gain by it."[48] It is essentially the problem of functionality which is involved in such judgments of cost and benefit. It is the opinion of many blacks that this limit had been reached by radical black terror in the U.S. by 1970.

The fierce controversy between Moscow and Peking is essentially such an argument about violence and its functionality. The Chinese may seem to have the better of the argument in insisting upon the analogy between Marx's advocacy of the class struggle and the liberation of colonial peoples. For was it not precisely this violence which Marx urged against the "Utopian" socialists such as Fourrier and Proudhon? Even the bloody experience of the Paris Commune—so apparent a case of a limit—does not seem to have convinced Marx of the fact that the use of violence may itself be "utopian." And was not reversely the Marxian notion of a socialist order without violence, enforcing violence without massive deployment of force, the most utopian of all utopias? Are not the orders established in Russia and China the most violent of all utopias, with little chance of any plural, agitational violence, developing? It would seem that latter-day Marxists in Russia, China, and elsewhere are firmly convinced of the functionality of violence for the maintenance of their socialist systems, not only at home but in adjoining lands. Is not the occupation of Czechoslovakia a striking illustration of it, and its sequel a skillful avoidance of its limit?

What do these reflections add up to? They suggest that the widespread employment of violence in this century has frequently, and under varying circumstances, gone beyond the limit of functionality. Violence has, of course, not lost its function, whether it be official or unofficial, quite the contrary. Unfortunately, it has become all too general an inclination of people in politics to substitute bullets for ballots, and bombs for arguments. At the same time, the technology of weapons has kept pace with these political developments. It has offered new means of destruction to small groups of protesters, and has facilitated their escape from lawful freedom into lawless license, while established authorities, usually with the legitimizing assent of the masses who constitute majorities, have increasingly been inclined to employ discretion without the sanction of law, substituting coercion for responsibility. In many political systems at the present time the functional limits of violence whether official or unofficial have been left so far behind that many despair of ever reestablishing them. Violence on all sides has become the monster which leads to continuous escalation of violence as the opposing sides wage war upon each other. A radical rejection of all violence, as preached and to some extent practiced by Gandhi, appears to many the only answer to this holocaust. It is an anarchic blind alley, politically, but it may be the salvation morally.[49]

PART II

Betrayal and Treason

CHAPTER

5

THE UBIQUITY OF BETRAYAL AND ITS POLITICAL SIGNIFICANCE[1]

WHEN Patrick Henry cried, before the Virginia House of Burgesses: "If this be treason, make the most of it!" he said so after having spoken for resistance. He thereby testified to the readiness of Americans to accept treason; the functionality of treason was implied in this rhetoric. The phenomena discussed in the first part of this book, dealing with violence, almost always involved treason—not necessarily in the technical, legal sense, but in the broader sense of betrayal. In a disturbed, divided community, everyone is in danger of betraying some person or group, because of these divisions. In revolutionary times betrayal becomes so common that it tends to lose its stigma, its morally pejorative connotation. Except where complete unity of commitment and loyalty are possible, conflict between two groups to which a person belongs or between two individuals to whom he is committed will occasionally force upon him conduct which to one or the other will appear as betrayal and will in fact be such a betrayal. The case of the man caught in a fight between his wife and mother is the most familiar instance, and one of the most perplexing. He cannot "choose," though both may insist that he do so. Political treason must be seen in this perspective, not only because it gives an intuition of the psychological perspective, but also because it brings out the trap-like inescapability which forces men to become traitors willy-nilly.

The rather legalistic article in the *Encyclopedia of the Social Sciences* suggests that "treason is essentially the violation of allegiance to the community," meaning by the community presumably the political one, though it could be applied to any other community. The article goes on to suggest that "it is the one natural crime punishable at all times in all types of social organization." But aside from the perplexing question of what constitutes a natural crime, betrayal, in French *trahison,* in German *Verrat,* is a violation of trust rather than allegiance. What such a traitor does is to act differently from the way others had reason to expect on the basis of their relationship. From this we may derive the following working hypothesis: There occurs continually a pattern of behavior in politics which consists in this, that a person acts contrary to how a political organization, a government, a party, or an office etc. expected him to act. A more special case, and a common one, is that of making available to a rival organization information about the organization a man is betraying. It is obvious that such a pattern of conduct will be more frequent in social and political contexts in which conflicts are numerous. In revolutionary periods, as mentioned before, betrayal becomes so widespread that practically everyone has committed some act of betrayal. It has been said of our time: we are all traitors.[2] The traitors are "the others." It has been said that "most men are firmly convinced that they themselves do not deserve the name [of traitor], but equally firmly that there are traitors, and that they must be punished very severely. . . ."[3] The traitor shakes the faith of those who belong, and thereby causes them to feel insecure. They react by demanding official violence.

The most specific kind of betrayal is what the law defines as treason. The Constitution of the United States is both specific and and limiting: levying war against the United States, or adhering to their enemies, giving them aid and comfort (article 3, section 3). To the uninstructed lay mind such a definition makes the critics of the war in Vietnam when they demonstrate and shout "Ho Ho Ho" fall under that definition, for they both adhere to the enemy and give him aid and comfort. Yet such persons would (and do) argue that their action, far from being treasonable, is motivated by a genuine concern for their country, that is to say that their behavior is functional rather than disfunctional. I shall return to this problem later.

If one were to generalize from that legal definition, one could say that betrayal consists in supporting a rival organization, giving aid, whether material or other. Surely the accusation "You are a traitor to our group!" is meant to say something like that. The implication often is that this sort of conduct is the result of a character defect, as indeed it might be; and that it results from low motives which no decent man could approve, and this too may be true. We have, therefore, in treason, a typical phenomenon of the kind we are here investigating: morally objectionable behavior that may yet be functional in a systemic perspective. In moral perspective treason and betrayal appear purely accidental, as deviations from a clear norm. The situation is much more complicated in the political perspective. The moral judgment may quite often be correct, but it is quite inadequate for the purpose of diagnosing a situation in which treason and/or betrayal are frequent. For these two patterns of behavior are quite regularly the result of the social and political order which requires them to insure its effective functioning. When a leader has become old and ineffectual, it may actually determine the survival of the party or the government whether enough men will be willing to betray him and save the group which he led effectively in the past. For how else is he to be gotten rid of?

Some of his followers are more prone to betray such a leader or group than others, to be sure. The literature on brainwashing and related phenomena (torture, loss of job, etc.) demonstrates this beyond the peradventure of a doubt.[4] For the political scientist the political conditions of betrayal and treason present the crucial question. Beyond there is the problem of the "limits" of such functional betrayal; at what point does the frequency of betrayal cause so widespread a mutual suspicion that government or even community life becomes impossible?

Generally speaking, there are, besides the "unpolitical" treason committed for monetary reward (Judas type), four primary causes of betrayal and treason, namely (a) a conflict of loyalties, (b) ideological commitment, (c) homelessness and alienation, (d) persecution and exploitation of minorities (or subject majorities). On the subject of the conflict of loyalties, many striking cases are provided by the War of Independence and the American Civil War.[5] But such other contexts as the Sudeten Germans in Czechoslovakia, the French-speaking Canadians, the Tyrolese in the Italian province of Upper Adige, the Irish Catholics in Ulster, and many other cases provide similarly striking instances of the kind of situation in which the individual is confronted with choosing between one betrayal and another, between the loyalty to his kin group and the loyalty to the larger political community of which it forms a part. This type of situation is at present developing in the United States for the black population, and hence mutual accusation of treason and betrayal are the order of the day. Many of the radical "revolutionaries" among the blacks have made statements concerning the United States which are clearly treasonable if viewed as made by an American citizen.[6] But these groups themselves are quite ready to accuse conciliatory black individuals and organizations of betraying the black community.[7] Voices have now become audible among the Negroes who denounce this tendency and assert that "since the negative aspects of black experience are constantly being overpublicized, justice to the U.S. Negroes, not only as American citizens but also as the fascinating human beings that they so obviously are, is best served by suggesting some of the affirmative implications of their history and culture."[8] The same black author insists that "being black is not enough to make anybody an authority on U.S. Negroes. . . ." "Nothing in the world could be more obvious. And yet a book like Claude Brown's *Manchild in the Promised Land*[9] is recommended all around as if it were a profound, knowledgeable, and even comprehensive account of life in Harlem because its author is a Negro who grew up there and had a rough time doing so. . . . U.S. social critics actually insist that *Manchild* reveals what it is really like to be a Negro. It does no such thing. . . ."[10] What is crucial in this argument is the insistence that black Americans are just as much Americans as are white ones. He rejects what is the basis of the argument of Negro radicals, namely that theirs is a separate and distinct community; indeed many argue for separatism of a radical sort. In all this the American constellation is typical for situations in which betrayal becomes the order of the day, because the divisions have become so sharp that whatever anyone does who is involved in it, he betrays someone. Yet, all this betrayal may eventually turn out to have been highly functional for the American system.

At this point we might well ask whether the causes of treason throw some light on its functionality. On the face of it this would seem to be probable. For, since much betrayal is the result of divisive trends, to the extent to which such betrayals serve to remove these divisions they would seem to be functional. These situations have become so familiar in our time that it seems hardly necessary to labor the point by elaboration. We shall, in Chapter 7, deal at greater length with Rebecca West's studies;

for in them she explored with nice attention to detail, and on the basis of an elaborate trial record, the background of the British traitor Lord Haw Haw.[11] Let me anticipate her conclusion here; it is a rather perplexing one. "All men should have a drop or two of treason in their veins," she wrote, "if the nations are not to go soft . . . yet to be a traitor is most miserable." She found that all the men who were tried in Britain after the war, like Lord Haw Haw, were very unhappy men, and would have been unhappy even if they had never been tried. Why? "Because they had forsaken the familiar medium," and because they realized that "they had thrown away their claim on those who might naturally have felt affection for them." And yet all this personal misery was the consequence of their alienation. They had needed, but had not had, a nation which was "also a hearth." In less poetical language, her analysis shows that treason and treasonable activity may well be generated by a failure of community.[12] Both social conflict and breakdown of community generate betrayal and treason; yet such betrayal may have important functions. In a sense, no political system could hope to adapt itself to changes in its social substructure of values, interests, and beliefs if some men were not willing to betray the old order to the emergent one. Betrayal, that is to say treason, provides a dynamic factor by which a static order is transformed. But it does so satisfactorily only as long as the betraying stays within very narrow limits, and presumably also is confined to particular elements, groups, or organizations. If it transcends these limits, it becomes lethal and puts the survival of the political order into jeopardy.

There are, to repeat four other causes of treasonable behavior, besides alienation and homelessness: the conflict of loyalities, ideological commitment, often closely related to such conflict, persecution and exploitation, and finally monetary and similar rewards. The first of these is illustrated by the problems of a member of one nationality, who is a citizen of another nation, the second is that of the Communist party member in a Western state, the third is the case of the black men in America, and the fourth one is Judas Iscariot. The last of these is not of genuine political interest; but we shall say something about it at the end. There may be considerable functionality in the first three cases; it is doubtful in the fourth, indeed unlikely. The conflict of loyalties, especially national loyalties, is recurrently the issue in situations involving national minorities. It is most obvious in the cases where the national minority in one state belongs to the majority in an adjoining one.[13] It becomes particularly fierce when the two nations become engaged in war. The suspicion that there might be treasonable activity developing often leads to repressive measures. The case of the Japanese minority after Pearl Harbor and the outbreak of war between Japan and the United States in 1942 is well-known. Certain well-meaning writers[14] have stressed the violation of civil liberties which these repressive measures involved, and their indignation is quite justified if the Japanese insistence upon their loyalty is accepted as a fact. There was no way of knowing afterward whether these assurances were factual or counterfactual; for the repressive measures were such—involving a good many unnecessary hardships and injustices—that such treasonable behavior became impossible. Comparable action was taken in the Soviet Union against the Volga Germans and other minorities, and the same argument holds. That there existed potentialities of treasonable behavior it is hard to deny; whether it is a case of using a sledgehammer to kill a mosquito is equally arguable. In any case, it is hard to imagine a constellation in which such betrayal could become functional for the political system of the particular national community, though it may well be for the international political system.

There exists also the possibility of conflicts of loyalty between religion and politics. This type of treason was very widespread in the period of the religious wars, at the time of the emergence of the modern state (sixteenth century), and it was in part from the wish to combat this conflict that the exclusive loyalty demands of the state, such as the famous oath extracted by Henry VIII and his parliament, were formulated. In this instance, Thomas More, the high-minded Chancellor of the Realm, went to the gallows for his refusal to forswear his loyalty to the church. As so often in conflicts involving betrayal, both sides to this conflict have been and can be defended, the king for exacting the ultimate penalty for "disloyalty," and the chancellor for making the ultimate sacrifice for his convictions. Was this treason functional? The case has often been compared with that of Socrates' refusal to flee from Athens when accused of impiety, which in the Greek *polis* with its non-separation of religion and politics was akin to high treason. It has often been forgotten, in the admiration for Socrates' sacrifice, that he was challenging the very basis of the Athenian political system, hence that he was engaging in treasonable, in subversive behavior, and that only a very un-Greek ethics, the moral outlook of Christianity and Western rationality, could fail to recognize this patent fact. Again, we conclude that this treason was not functional, but disfunctional, and was properly punished, though probably overly harshly. There have been many similar conflicts between religious conviction and political loyalty, and these conflicts would have been more bloody if European nations had not found the way out of them into overseas settlements; in this rather vicarious sense, the potential treason became functional for the new political order of colonial settlement and emancipation. But, apart from that, these "treasons" have proved highly functional to the development of the political system we are accustomed to call constitutionalism. For the institution of a guaranteed freedom of religion has played a major role in the crystallization of the notion of a personal sphere which deserves to be protected from the government and its interference. One need not go so far as to say that the idea of religious freedom is the origin of bills of rights,[15] but it certainly contributed a major share. Thus we have here a striking instance of the functionality of treason in the evolution of a political system. It has its contemporary dramatic manifestation in the issue of conscientious objection to military service and its ramifications.[16] For intrinsically the refusal to bear arms is treason in the specific sense of giving aid and comfort to the enemy; yet here too, and all morals apart, there has been an increasing recognition of the functionality of such conduct, not only in relation to the national community against which such treason works, but also in relation to an emergent world order (see Chapter 2, above).

These and other cases of religiously motivated betrayal lead over into the ideological motivation. The militant totalist ideologies of our time (as indeed of earlier times) have been very often associated with treasonable activities. A Fascist or a Communist who is deeply convinced of the rightness of his cause presumably believes that its victory would greatly improve his own nation's existence. Thus, from his subjective viewpoint, such treason is invariably functional. To those who do not share this conviction it will appear invariably disfunctional. Hence the bitterness on both sides, and the frequent ferocity of the punishment. The betrayal of military secrets is the very core of such treason, but it can take other forms. The same situation may occur in reverse when a subject of a totalitarian regime seeks foreign aid in attempting its alteration, if not its overthrow. The chance of such plots is haunting the mind of the masters of these regimes. It is characteristic for the treason complex that Western writers and moralists are full of admiration for such traitors and seek to give them aid. Organizations are fostered for that specific purpose; governments in exile are established to provide an alternative focus of loyalty and interest.

Such activities are, of course, supported by the conviction of those engaged in them that they will prove functional to the reestablishment of a better political system, they are revolutionary or counter-revolutionary as the case may be, but treason is an inescapable accompaniment of them, since nationals are caught between two conflicting claimants. Such occasions produce many personal tragedies, and the experience has served as a theme for many novels. The split of France after the German conquest in 1940 was typical for such conflicts of loyalty; for both Vichy and de Gaulle had good claims to the loyalty of patriotic Frenchmen. We shall describe this in greater detail in the next chapter.

There is, of course, also betrayal that is neither the result of intergroup conflict nor of alienation and the breakdown of community, but is motivated by exploitation and oppression. Here it might be argued that what formally appears as betrayal actually is not that, because no community existed for the "traitor." This complex of problems is at present vividly seen in the United States, where elements of the black community not only repudiate America, but deny ever having belonged to it. This notion underlies such an early outcry as Richard Wright's *Native Son,* and still is alive in present-day writings, such as Eldridge Cleaver's *Soul on Ice,* to mention only two striking examples. Years earlier, James Baldwin had quite rightly commented that "their concept of a better world was quite hopelessly American"[17] and it has since been persuasively argued that American Negroes are as much American as all other Americans,[18] and that the other Americans would not be what they are without the Negroes. They are, to put it in terms of nationalist ideology, "part of the American destiny." Hence many of the statements of Black Panthers and similar groups are treasonable in the strict sense of the term. To give just one illustration of "comfort to the enemy," let me cite a sentence from *Soul on Ice:*

"The blacks in Watts and all over America could now see the Viet Cong's point: both were on the receiving end of what the armed forces were dishing out."[19] It was a feeling closely akin to that of the Czechs as they watched Soviet and Polish and German armed forces crushing them, and this similarity offers a clue to the possibility that such treason may be highly functional to a desperately needed change in an existing political system.

A final motivation-cause of betrayal is greed. The monetary reward offered to the traitor by the beneficiary of the treason is what most ordinary persons think about when they think of treason. The other motivations are more or less incomprehensible, but this is easy to understand. Hence betrayal for monetary gain has been in the foreground of attention in popular and legal discussions. From the standpoint of political analysis, these cases are the least interesting. For where betrayal is solely for monetary gain, the act is often irrelevant. It is common enough in business, when a man goes over to the competition for higher pay. There are two famous historical instances it may be worthwhile to recall here, that of the traitor at Thermopylae and that of Judas Iscariot (see next chapter). In both cases, the monetary motif may hide other, more political ones. It offers an easy explanation and the party which benefits from a betrayal may actually have an interest in placing the relationship with a traitor upon a monetary basis. For, by so doing, it is relieved of political and moral responsibility. We are here touching the field of espionage and related activities (see below, pages 210–223). Secret services prefer to operate with paid agents.[20]

In light of what has so far been said, we may now distinguish several forms or types of treason. The first would be that in which older values or beliefs are claimed to be superior or higher values than the new ones; this type of treason is frequent in post-revolutionary periods. A second form is the revolutionary one based on a new system of values in conflict with the established ones. It is the treason of the revolutionary. A third type involves an external enemy. If an American of German origin joined the Bund and collaborated with Hitler's agents, he became a traitor; similarly, if a German under Hitler, like Undersecretary of State Weizsaecker, betrayed secrets to the British foreign office, he became a traitor. Betrayal may fourthly take the form of not responding to the orders of the regime: sabotage is a common form of betrayal in oppressive regimes. This form has been called "negative treason," that is to say treason through more or less complete negation of a political system's operation.[21] Perhaps an extreme instance but really a separate category is that of seeking to get rid of the ruler, especially by assassination. There is finally the case of "involuntary" treason which may occur as a result of more or less arbitrary actions of a regime. Cardinal Mindszenty of Hungary comes to mind, but there are many other instances.

It must be added that these forms need to be subdivided in accordance with the regime under which they occur. There emerges from detailed studies a working hypothesis to this effect: the legal definition of treason is broadened as the autocratic features of a political system increase; in a totalitarian state it may be extremely wide and include even operational mistakes of a purely technical sort which the regime holds to be sabotage.[22] It is therefore necessary to analyze treason in the light of the peculiarities of the ogranization. For what holds true of states does also for other types of political organization. A highly autocratic party will be more inclined to define betrayal broadly than a cooperative one, precisely because betrayal is more likely to occur. The cases to be explored in the next chapter will provide some of the material for these propositions. All in all, types of treason and their forms of operation are closely linked and intertwined.

There is one type of treason which has not so far been mentioned; it is often overlooked in discussions of treason, although it has played a considerable role in the history of "the subject." It is the possibility of betrayal of the led by their leader, of a people by their government. We saw that treason is basically a violation of trust. Therefore, the trust placed in a ruler by the ruled may certainly be violated. This was recognized in feudal times in connection with the violation of the *foedus*, the agreement between the lord and vassal, often expressed in elaborate oaths of allegiance and the like. It is similarly quite meaningful to speak of the betrayal of the German people, in whole or in part, by Hitler, or of the French people by de Gaulle—in reference to Algeria. Many Americans feel that they have been betrayed in connection with the conflict in Vietnam, that their governments have not lived up to their promises and so on. Such men having been brought to power in the expectation that they would perform in a generally understood way, their failure to do so appears as a betrayal. It makes a powerful appeal for the opposition. After Wilson had campaigned with the promise of keeping America out of the war (World War I), the slogan in the campaign which defeated him was "Remember, he kept us out of war!" But betrayal to whom? Can one say that such men support a rival organization, giving it aid? Hardly. Hence the pattern of treason must be broadened, recognizing that failure to act as an organization has reason to expect one to act is a vicarious form of betrayal. It is certain that a leader's betrayal may often be rationalized in terms of some such argument as "reason of state."[23] This is a way of saying or claiming that the particular act or series of acts of betrayal was functional; that it vitally related to the survival of the political system. But such an argument may often remain rather inconclusive.

In this connection one final point deserves mention. In the Middle Ages and in many primitive societies the notion was prevalent that a ruler possessed a sacred, divinely derived quality —in ethnology referred to as *manna*—which made it an act of treason not only to harm or kill the ruler, but also to wish him such harm, and more particularly to wish him death. The notion of treasonable thoughts has persisted to this day. To exorcise such evil thoughts, symbolic ritual has always played a considerable role, and some forms of torture among primitives are part of this ritual. The performance of certain symbolic acts, such as "allegiance to the flag" ceremonies and the *Hitlergruss* (raised arm), are expressive of this ritual of exorcising the devil that is at work in the traitor. There is a contemporary tendency to impute *manna* to the nation or the people and to treat any hostile thought or word as treasonable and by implication as disfunctional.

CHAPTER 6

SOME TREASON CASES ANALYZED: JUDAS AND AFTER

HERODOTUS tells of a Greek who betrayed his countrymen to the Persians at Thermopylae, and he surmises that it was done for money. Similarly in the Christian tradition, Judas Iscariot is reported to have betrayed Jesus for thirty silver coins. Such tales are generally believed, but they are likely to be untrue or prove to be at least inaccurate. They avoid the political issues. Modern research tends to surmise that Judas was a Jewish patriot deeply convinced at first that Jesus was the liberating Messiah, but then deeply disillusioned with him, as he refused to be a secular liberator, a Messiah in the tradition of Jewish folk belief. In this view one might say that Judas was a political activist who rejected the strictly religious, transcendental mission of the "son of God." To Judas, Jesus had betrayed the trust placed in him. It is an intriguing hypothesis for which, of course, no evidence exists. One might by analogy speculate that the Greek at Thermopylae "believed" in the ordering mission of the Persian King and strongly objected to the local resistance offered by the Spartans. Or maybe he belonged to one of the small towns that had fared ill at the hands of its Spartan overlords. The Greeks were not a modern nation, and the divisions among them went deep. Who knows? Such possibilities illustrate the complexity of motivation that an act of betrayal may reveal. It is convenient but usually too easy to eliminate these complexities by arguing that the treasonable act was committed for money. There is an interesting parallel of our time in the murder of Gandhi so dramatically portrayed by Stanley Wolpert.[1] The extreme and violent nationalist clique that planned and perpetrated this murder, so shocking and absurd, claimed the sanction of Hindu religion, of the *Bhagavad Gita:* "Our ancestors were conquerors . . . highest duty is to fight . . . Our God given destiny to conquer . . . I believe freedom so pure and glorious that I have no doubt it will purify and justify any means. . . ." Here we find the characteristic features of treason: the end justifies the means, violence against a false leader who has betrayed us. Non-violence is itself such a betrayal, but of the traitor's cause. We shall see how it recurs among the murderers of Rathenau and of those who plotted Hitler's assassination. For to the thorough nationalist, the nation and what he considers its well-being is the only valid system of politics and what is furthering it is functional, what is not is not. Treason on behalf of the nation is therefore by definition right, that is to say functional. It strengthens the one system that matters. The Indians revolting against British rule were inspired by this sentiment and whoever was could not accept the Satyagraha—the truth force—as the sole means of achieving its overthrow. Nor could he believe that after the liberation the sole means of liberating themselves from the yoke of Western culture and Christianity was spiritual. Such an outlook bears a distinct kinship to the constellation of the American Negro, and the assassin of Martin Luther King could have been a black radical who objected to his commitment to non-violence. For it was not only the Southern whites who shocked many by their welcoming of the death of the great Negro, but also certain elements among the blacks who felt that "it was perhaps a good thing." The murder of Malcolm X fits into this pattern, as does the violence displayed by some blacks against the more conciliatory among them, contemptuously referred to as "Uncle Toms." The political analyst of these tragic conflicts may sympathize with one side or another, but his primary task is that of disentangling the rival claims of loyalty and treason which are hurled at each other by partisans in these conflicts.[2]

When Eldridge Cleaver writes: "The necessity upon Afro-America is to move, now, to begin functioning as a nation, to assume its sovereignty, to demand that that sovereignty be recognized by other nations of the world,"[3] it is clear that he is placing himself and those for whom he speaks outside the American political system; he is, in the precise sense of that term "betraying" America. When Julius Lester speaks of the black man as "a nation" to be achieved through violence, he is doing the same. And he therefore quite consistently recites that "Carmichael was received in Havana as a representative of a people, of a nation, and, in principle, the assembled revolutionaries were recognizing the sovereignty of Afro-America." He characteristically calls Malcolm X's Organization of Afro-American Unity a "government in exile for a people in exile." Stokely Carmichael and Rap Brown are, in his opinion, speaking for that sovereignty, they are speaking in the name of a nation. And he cites with full approval the treasonable statement of Rap Brown: "I am not bound by the laws or the morals of America!"[4] The editor, in commenting that "black people have always been viewed by white Americans as un-American, as not really belonging here,"[5] is exaggerating an important point. Had he inserted "some" before "white Americans" he would have been right. And he might have added that these Americans in doing so were "betraying" America, and were thus provoking the betrayal that is now rampant in the country. It is the heart of a treason springing from persecution, from oppression and exploitation of a minority, the fourth of the causes of betrayal as we stated above (Chapter 5).

The position of the Negroes in America has in this perspective been assimilated to that of a colonial people, and the problem of imperialism has been introduced as a theoretical framework—a skillful propaganda move, since imperialism is and has been a cussword in America. At the same time, it makes the Negro problem also one of ideological motivation. As did Wright in the thirties, the black is seen in the perspective of Marxism-Leninism as a proletarian who is called upon to rebel against his exploiter. Since the ideological cause is probably the most widespread and the most potent cause of betrayal in the twentieth century, the black man with that outlook may also be understood as a case of ideological treason. It is presented in the writings of Stokely Carmichael, who says: "The values of the middle class are based on material aggrandizement, not the expansion of humanity."[6] And therefore the blacks must not assimilate themselves into that class, but ought to separate. If they do separate, then the numerous betrayals now committed in the name of a black national community will prove to have been as functional as were the treasonable activities of American revolutionaries before and during the War of Independence. But even if separation does not work out, or remains partial, as one or more states become black within rather than without the American commonwealth, their activities may be proven to have been functional to the evolution of America as a multinational political order. It may of course also happen, as seems to me most likely, that both integration and separation will progress; for they are not mutually exclusive in fact, though they may appear so in theory.

The problem resembles that of French-speaking Canadians, many of whom desire separation (over 25 percent of the voters of Quebec said so in the provincial elections of April 26,

1970) but many more desire, if not integration, then an autonomous status within Canada. Here too betrayal is the order of the day, and will continue to play its role in the loosening of the political and social fabric as established more than a hundred years ago. It is now often forgotten that the men who worked out the compromises that are embodied in the original organic act, the BNA Act of 1867, thought of Canadians as composing two nations and the great Lord Durham had in his famous report insisted upon this fact![7] In Canada, too, the evolution may follow both the path of integration and of separation. The traitors of today may turn out to be the heroes of tomorrow. It all depends upon the degree of functionality that can be achieved by them. If a better, more workable federal order will be the result of their activities, it is going to be so assessed.

It is typical for these situations that they generate a great deal of what we have termed "involuntary treason." For, once such a cleavage has developed, those caught up in it, French-speaking Canadians, blacks, or what have you, must either side with the established order or join those who challenge it.[8] The challenger betrays the established order; his decision to do so is presumably voluntary, as is that of any revolutionary. But others in his group may become traitors to their parochial group involuntarily, although the challengers tend to treat them as if they had chosen to act so. The situation also occurred in France under Nazi occupation. Many Frenchmen and Frenchwomen were executed by the Maquis because in the Maquis' view these people were betraying the France which they were trying to save. If such persons collaborated with the German police, this seemed rather plausible; yet such defenders could plead that they were acting in accordance with instructions received from what appeared to them the legitimate government of France, Marshal Pétain's at Vichy.[9] All such cases of involuntary betrayal through failure to act, also at times referred to as "negative treason," are unlikely to prove functional, except in an indirect sense. The large middle-of-the-road group existing in Canada and the United States can, in an indirect sense, be said to be highly functional; for it is their behavior which in the end shapes the future order and is crucially important for its emergence.

From the nationalist motivation of oppressed minorities it is no very great step to the ideological motivation, especially if nationalism is itself seen as an "ideology"—a view which I question.[10] Genuine ideologies are characteristically programmatic in a more specific sense.[11] They are related to a new order, as depicted in Communist and Fascist thinking. The two cases which shall here be more fully explored are the presumed Communist betrayals as highlighted by the names of Hiss and Chambers, on the one hand, and the Twentieth of July Plot against Hitler in 1944. For in both these dramatic instances, the prime motivation was ideological, relating to Communism and Fascism, though in an inverse way. For the first was a betrayal motivated by totalist ideology, while the other was a betrayal directed against it and caused by its rejection.

In dealing with such cases from a very special viewpoint such as the one we are interested in here in this study, one runs the risk of seeming uninterested in the issue which was primary when the case arose. In the case of Chambers and Hiss, that issue was whether they had betrayed the U.S. to Communist Soviet agents or not. But whether these men were guilty or not —in the case of self-confessed Chambers there is little doubt of it—since the court found Hiss guilty, we are for our purposes justified in proceeding on that assumption without necessarily assuming it to be true on its merits. Whittaker Chambers engaged, according to his own confession,[12] in three kinds of treasonable activities, namely (1) fomenting trouble with strikers in the twenties, (2) slanting the news received by the *Daily Worker*, (3) passing information to the Soviet Government which was classified (secret). The first of these kinds of betrayal raises the question as to whether the fomenting of disloyalty is as such treasonable. In a functional sense it would seem to be; for since the effectiveness of a country's defense depends upon the loyalty of its citizens, to destroy that effectiveness is to "give aid and comfort to the enemy." It would seem, however, that for practical reasons the inclusion of such activities under betrayal—especially in a democratic system which calls for opposition and criticism as an important part of the system itself—would go too far and confuse the problem. The same would seem to hold for the slanting of news, especially in the case of a publication as radically oppositionist as the *Daily Worker*, anyhow. It would seem a betrayal of his employers, who have trusted him not to distort the news, rather than of the country. There remains then the passing of secret information to the government of the Soviet Union. How was it motivated?

Whittaker Chambers has complicated the answer to this question by writing at length about it. From his autobiography, one gains the impression of a highly neurotic person, given to paranoia and other kinds of psychic deviation, partly hereditary and partly environmentally conditioned—a broken home and all that. This sad background had to do with his first conversion to Communism in the twenties, his operations as a Soviet agent (espionage for the Red Army intelligence service), and his eventual denunciation of Communism and of his former collaborators, among them especially Alger Hiss. His unstable character and his exhibitionist and self-pitying personality (or disposition?) were predestined to frequent changes of allegiance and hence toward betrayal and treason. He betrayed both the United States and the Soviet Union, both the American people and Communism as a world-wide movement, and his religious conversion has, judging by his own language, a "phony" quality.

Yet it would seem that subjectively he thought of himself as an ardent patriot and hence of both betrayals as motivated by concern for the well-being of America.[13] Therefore he believed that his treason was functional—was going to serve the American system by helping it to survive; when he came to realize that this notion was wrong, he forthwith proceeded to betray the Communists. He seems very candid in describing how his treasonable activities were carried on.

Mrs. Margret Boveri has, in her interesting analysis of Chambers and its comparison with Koestler and others, stressed this point. When Chambers, through his work for the *Daily Worker*, had become known in Moscow he was reemployed by the Soviets' secret service—as an agent for the secret service of the Red Army. He felt proud that he had thus been chosen to collaborate with the reds. In his own memoirs he has described these activities, including the request to collaborate, even though indirectly, in the liquidation of a "Trotskyist." The accusation of Alger Hiss and others fits into this picture. But the fact is that Hiss has never admitted what Chambers accused him of. And since a certain emotional vindictiveness on the part of Chambers makes his testimony a bit suspect, a word might be in order on Hiss. He was a member of a sizable group of New Deal "success boys"—smooth operators who closely collaborated with each other in fostering a transformation of the American system which to its opponents appeared revolutionary in scope. We have seen earlier (Chapter 3) how difficult it is to define a political revolution satisfactorily, but it would seem doubtful that the term is justified in its application to America in the thirties. It is, however, important to recall the unquestionably very rapid social change and the accompanying transvaluation of values to understand the background of these operators. They often were so caught up in these kaleidoscopic changes that they lost the sense of betrayal which their rapid adaptation to changing fronts and party lines involved. It is hard to recapture the spirit created by the decision of Franklin Delano Roosevelt to collaborate closely with the Soviet Union and to adopt the party line that the U.S.S.R. was after the war to emerge as a socialist democracy. Anyone who questioned this prospect was suspect and apt to be accused of being a Fascist or a potential Nazi. In this atmosphere working for the Soviet Union could easily be seen as "functional" even when the actions fulfilled the legal terms of treason. For was it not working for the better world to come in which the U.S. and the U.S.S.R. would march arm in arm to combat Fascism (capitalism) and imperialism as the enemies of "democracy"? It was yet years before Stalin was to declare a cold war upon the Fascists and Plutocrats that were the U.S. and Britain.[14] In this context, it might well seem to an ambitious operator merely foresightful to cooperate with persons some of whom might actually be Communists. Mrs. Roosevelt was herself not averse to it, and formed the center of a significant circle.[15] Felix Frankfurter was its intellectual mentor, consultant, and adviser. All this which goes back to the beginnings of the New Deal and the recognition of the Soviet Union must be borne in mind to grasp the context of the ideologically motivated treason of a man like Alger Hiss.[16]

Alger Hiss was an upper-middle-class success boy, who "had no character" according to one of his co-workers.[17] He failed to deal with the underlying problem sketched above, and it is probably true that he "like thousands of his generation and background was attracted by communism, in the mainstream of the New Deal went through the motions of Marxism, whether as sympathizer or as member of a communist organization, since such notions were the order of the day, and that he exercised such influence as he had in a sense friendly toward communism."[18] He himself does not speak of this angle in his own book.[19] This is very strange in a case of ideological betrayal, but probably is deliberate, as any discussion of this aspect could not have hoped to find a sympathetic audience in America at the time. It leaves open the question of functionality. But it shows the limits. For when treason becomes so widespread as it did become in these circles, and if in the end everyone betrays everyone, the faith which men need for maintaining a political community is destroyed. It is perhaps the most unfortunate result of the ideological movements of our time, with their totalist ideologies, that they produce this effect of mutual suspicion and distrust. At the culmination point there is nothing left but the setting-up of some kind of autocratic rulership, deliberately indifferent to ideological claims. The tendency toward military dictatorship is the result. It is becoming more widespread.

Very different is the situation where totalitarian rule has become established but has generated such antagonism among the subject population that it becomes ready for treason (and resistance; see above, Chapter 2). The well-known paranoia of these regimes, fearing this kind of reaction, aggravates the evil. I wish that we had the record of the Hungarian or Czech cases; but most of what has been written rests upon guesswork and hearsay. There now exists, however, very full documentation for the plot against Hitler of July 20, 1944 (as well as earlier ones), and for contrast we also have reasonably full information on the 17th of June, 1953, when the population of East Germany rose against their rulers, the government of the German Democratic Republic and the Soviet Occupation Forces. Both of these efforts failed. Both produced a good deal of treason which might be said to have been functional, when seen in the perspective of what was good for the German people. A number of the participants in the plot of July 20, 1944, were deeply convinced of it. Father Alfred Delp, S.J., wrote from prison: "Others should some day be able to live more happily than we died."[20] And one of the key officers, von Treskow, wrote to his wife: "What matters is that the German resistance dares make the decisive effort" (of killing Hitler and overthrowing the regime).[21] But, at the same time, the plot was intended to be just the opposite for the Hitler regime and the revenge, brutally bloody and cruel, fully demonstrated the regime's sense of being betrayed. This plot, which was the last of quite a few,[22] involved all elements of the German people and was by no means, as believed at the time in Western countries and as has been since often repeated, a "generals' plot." While important high-ranking generals were involved in it, they were not the planners. Both churches and labor leaders as well as scholars and officials played a decisive role. The plot was intended to substitute a constitutional regime, and in the plans for the future, the re-establishment of the rule of law, and through it of decency in public life, ranked at the top.[23] It was not so much democracy in the radical populist sense, as in the British-American tradition of a constitutional order, which was hoped and planned for. Here is the ideological focus, openly reinforced by the Christian faith of many of the plotters. They felt the conflict of loyalties; the idea of becoming a traitor was abhorrent to many; the consciousness of these moral perplexities occupied too much of their time for their own good, and many of them remained hostile to the notion of "killing the tyrant" as a good thing. Count Helmuth von Moltke, the leader of one of the resistance circles named after his farming estate of Kreisau, could not persuade himself that murder could produce good; the doubt which he so persuasively argued weakened the resolution of many to commit this final act of betrayal. But from the regime's viewpoint this was not decisive and they arrested him before the plot, but executed him in its sequel. But his thinking about a post-Hitler regime was in itself treasonable; like the primitives and the Middle Ages they adhered to the notion of "treasonable thoughts"—to wish Hitler dead, to hope for the end of his regime was the ultimate crime of treason.

More than two thousand men and women were executed, often

after terrible tortures and public humiliation.[24] This bloodbath, which destroyed many of the potential leaders of a new Germany, must be considered to be an argument against the resisters' belief in their functionality, and it is arguable that Germany would have been much better off with these leaders available. The argument does not seem to me tenable. Germany has produced a remarkable group of political leaders—as well as business and professional talent of every kind, since the overthrow of the Hitler regime by the Allied armies. The revolt of 1944 served the purpose of manifesting the "other Germany" and this has been increasingly so recognized. The day has become a national holiday, and the celebrations, while not as generally observed as one might wish, have offered opportunities for recalling to a younger generation the evils of the regime and the valor of these men and women who dared to defy it. In that sense the treason was a moral act, precisely because it was illegal, and the response of Allied leaders such as Hull demeaned the ideological stand of Roosevelt and Churchill.[25] Such treason on behalf of cherished ideas is the very core of martyrdom. It always has been. To lay down one's life for one's conviction is, if I may say so as an aside, likely to be the betrayal of a prevalent belief system. It means that no outsider has a right to adopt an attitude of righteous indignation at the failure of men living under a repressive regime to overthrow it. It is one of the basic rules of ethics that no one is obliged to undertake actions that are beyond the possible *(ultra posse nemo obligatur)*. But this is precisely what the martyr for a cause will do, and so to do is in the nature of things "beyond the call of duty." Such notions are clearly politically meaningful only within the context of a functional relation to a future state. The martyrs of Christianity became the saints of a triumphant Christian church; their betrayal of the Roman Empire as seen by its officers[26] was what made them the "functionaries" of a future order. The same may be said of the "saints" of Communism and of national liberation; in the political perspective the sainthood is measured by the rightness of the cause they served, as seen by the beneficiaries of that cause.

We can discern here the way in which the two pathologies, that of violence and that of treason, are intertwined. For not only is the killing of a political leader and the forcible removal of his henchmen an important form of domestic violence, but so is the suppression of such attempts by a regime. The old saying about ballots for bullets here goes in reverse, as bullets do what ballots might have done. In that general sense, treason is, like violence, intrinsically disfunctional, and must be presumed to be so until functional aspects can be shown to exist. These usually take in our time the form of moralizing about an ideological dimension.

Interviews with survivors who had been close to the resistance bring out very clearly that "unauthorized contact with foreign powers was . . . too new . . . and on the brink of treason, especially when the nation was at war."[27] Few people have ever faced the terrific struggle of conscience that a man like the German Undersecretary of the Ministry of Foreign Affairs, von Weizsaecker, must have undergone before deciding to betray to the British Hitler's plans for the invasion of Norway;[28] it is like a corresponding official of the State Department informing the Soviet Union of the plan to carry the war into Cambodia. The more violent peace advocates in the U.S. today would seem to be quite capable of just such treason, and if challenged would also assert that it would be done for the good of the country. For once a man has become convinced that the government's course of policy leads the nation into catastrophe, he is tempted to adopt extreme and unmoral measures for opposing it. If the particular ideology which serves as a motivation is pacifist or pacifistically inclined, the conflict becomes even more perplexing. But what I would want to stress here is that all the ideological arguments are ultimately related to the problem of functionality; if the action can be said to have an effective function in relation to a political system, it appears "justifiable" politically; if not then not.[29] On the whole, passive resistance is what Protestant and Catholic moral teaching permit. However, the injunction that men must obey God rather than men may push even the Christian in the direction of treason and violence. Such a trend is, of course, much strengthened by the demonstration of a future state that would be better; hence the preoccupation with "plans" in the German resistance, which has often been criticized as foolish. Similarly, the failure to produce such plans has been a source of weakness in most of the student rebellions of recent years. Anarchists often suffer from this difficulty, because their dreams about a spontaneous and undirected social togetherness, while quite in keeping with their ideology, is by most men considered "utopian."

In summary and conclusion it might be said that the several cases here presented, though not in much detail, illustrate the fact that motivations and causes suggest different forms of treason and betrayal which do not prove sharply separable from each other. Sir John Harington, the Elizabethan poet, says somewhere: "Treason doth never prosper. . . . Why, if it prosper, none dare call it treason." The controversies over treason in our time illustrate both of these possibilities. Among the resisters to tyranny as well as their admirers in after-time, it is not usual to accept the label of "traitor." Nor is it among the leaders and followers of revolutionary movements. The functionality of treason is the rationale of such movements and conspiracies; but it is not the existing state but some future state that is meant. In the next chapter, it remains to examine the writings on treason which have sought to cope with the resulting problems.

CHAPTER

7

THE HEROIC TRAITOR AND HIS FUNCTION

"I AM fully aware of what I am setting out to do in my dedication to the *real* struggle for peace," writes Oleg Penkovskiy in the opening chapter of his *Papers*.[1] And since he was firmly convinced that his superiors in the Soviet Union were plotting war, it meant that he was betraying them. Like Weizsaecker and his friends in the German Foreign Office before 1939, and quite a few others who betrayed secrets of the U.S. and Britain to the Soviet Union, the motivation here is a dedication to a peaceful world order—a system transcending the national ones of former times. They are all traitors who appear in a heroic coloring to those who share their ideal. The same can be said of the student rebels demonstrating against the war in Vietnam (and against nuclear weapons) and committing acts of violence in challenging the establishment, as did a few intellectuals in the Soviet Union to protest against the occupation of Czechoslovakia. This heroic aspect of treason, so important a feature of the great figures of the American Revolution and the fight for independence (Washington, Jefferson, Hamilton, and many others), is closely linked to the problem of functionality which concerns us. For when a traitor appears as a hero, he does so as the pathfinder to a new order for which the destruction of the old one is an essential precondition; the traitor himself has this function of aiding in the destruction of a system which is presumed to be outworn and even noxious. When Patrick Henry declaimed in the Virginia House of Representatives that "Caesar had his Brutus, Charles the First his Cromwell, and George the Third ("Treason!" cried the Speaker) may profit by their example." He added defiantly, "If this be treason, make the most of it." His was the vision of the new order to come, and he felt the function which the traitor has in such a situation.

Not all traitors are, of course, as fortunate, and Rebecca West is undoubtedly correct when she sums up her findings in the sentence "Yet to be a traitor is most miserable." Had she included in her inquiry some of the men of July 20, 1944, she would have had to qualify this by adding, "unless the treason is the consequence of a deep, unshakable conviction of the rightness of the cause for which the treason is committed." What distinguishes Rebecca West's remarkable study[2] is the fact that she was preoccupied with British cases, naturally, and a corresponding disbelief in ideological motivation as primary. Hence her theory is essentially that treason is the result of "alienation." She uses this fashionable term largely in its original Hegelian meaning rather than in the restricted sense which Karl Marx has given it.[3] She does not, of course, restrict treason to it, but she thinks it is perhaps the most important source. The traitors as exemplified by William Joyce (Lord Haw Haw) were sad men, estranged from their people and needing the enveloping warmth of a national home. They needed a hearth, she thinks. And for this reason she also believes that "there is a case for the traitor." She believes him to be sort of a necessary type. Necessary is her word for "functional." She speaks of the necessity of social change.

Stressing liberty, as the good liberal that she is, she asserts it is "our duty to readjust constantly between public and private liberties." This conviction she relates to social change—"Men must be capable of imagining and executing and insisting on social change, if they are to reform or even maintain civilization, and capable of furnishing the rebellion which is sometimes necessary if society is not to perish of immobility. Therefore all men should have a drop or two of treason in their veins, if the nations are not to go soft. . . ."[4] But her firm sense of nationhood gets in her way. She adds at once, "There is a case against the traitor." Not only the traditional claim of allegiance, but "there are other reasons for regarding treachery with disfavor."[5] She then cites the problems of modern weaponry and the espionage which they entail. Much of this appears to her a lot of wasted time, energy, and funds. She observes that the people engaged in these activities are cynics who, having "no ideological interests at all, but having rejected all moral taboos," will "pursue any prohibited activity, provided it brings them sufficient reward in money, power, or security." This, she thinks, alters the whole character of the security field, partly because these "purloiners of secrets have now to satisfy technical demands which make it possible to class the traitors of the past as amateurs and traitors of the present as professionals."[6] These persons belong to an underworld of illegal and immoral employment of the secrets of modern science and "the public therefore suffers a sense of impotence. . . ." Hence the large and able security organizations "can find the infinitesimally small proportion of the population which takes to spying only by subjecting large numbers of persons to restrictions on their freedom against which it is a good citizen's duty to protest, unless he is told the reason for them, and such explanation is often inadvisable. . . ."[7] Hence "treachery is a problem we will have to live with for a long time, and the nearest we can come to a solution" appears to be education. "The man tempted to become a traitor will be helped if public opinion keeps it clear before him that treachery is a sordid and undignified form of crime."[8] "We should abandon all sentimentality in our views of the traitor, and recognize him as a thief and a liar."

Such statements show that her problem is essentially the traditional moral and legal one which relates treason solely to the group or organization betrayed and which does not ask whether there might not be another, possibly related group or organization to whom the traitor is a hero, precisely because he is willing to face the moral disapprobation of many others in the service of a cause he believes in and which may in fact be right in that it is the cause with the future. Looked at in this perspective, even the actions of so unpleasing an individual as William Joyce might be viewed without indignation, though in his case related to a lost cause. But has not fighting for a lost cause always been recognized as a specific form of heroism? Are only those who fight for winning causes heroes? Surely Roland blowing his horn is almost the ideal type of hero, as have been others like him. It is a sad fact that many heroic fighters for lost causes are forgotten and remain unsung; in general, it is only the fighter for the *seemingly* lost cause which eventually triumphs that acquires popular heroic stature, and the same may be said of the traitor as a hero. He may be executed amidst a sneering crowd, but, when his cause triumphs, a monument is erected to him. The Germans who betrayed Hitler and his government were executed under the most humiliating conditions, deliberately so by the revengeful Hitler, and have since come into their own. The same is true on a less monumental scale of the Frenchmen who died at the hands of Pétain and his Vichy regime.

A curious feature of such situations is that two actions which are very similar in the functional perspective may be judged very differently, because of the setting. Thus Lord Haw Haw's broadcasts to Britain probably did relatively little harm to the British cause; many may in fact have been angered into greater efforts to prove him wrong. Yet he was executed as a traitor. By contrast, one might consider Anne Morrow Lindbergh, who wrote an essay, "The Wave of the Future," for a leading American magazine at a point where it greatly damaged the Allied cause; but since it did not violate any law, its publisher, let alone Mrs. Lindbergh herself, was never even accused of treason.[9] The same might be said about such intellectuals as Charles Beard and others.[10] The belief in the freedom of speech, even in emergency conditions, protected these persons against the accusation of treason, just as it has in recent years protected those making treasonable (in a functional sense) speeches and engaging in treasonable activities during the war in Vietnam.

The war in Vietnam has highlighted a problem that has been important in modern states, and that is the problem of conscientious objection to wartime military service. Not only is the objector himself in a position resembling that of the traitor, but what he says and what those who defend him say often contains treasonable elements, such as the assertion that a particular war is not "just" and the like. And yet, to anyone who looks forward to a world without war, who with Kant is prepared to consider "there shall not be war" a corollary to the categorical imperative of all morals, as well as a sound guide to a future world order, such conscientious objectors appear in the garb of heroes. And if such a world should come into being, there is little doubt that some of these persons will be honored by monuments commemorating their struggle for a new order. Rebecca West recognizes that this vision was involved in some of the treasons of recent years, such as that of the British scientists who betrayed atomic secrets to the Soviet Union on the assumption that such knowledge would aid efforts to establish a lasting peace. Klaus Fuchs, Pontecorvo, Burgess, and Maclean all indicated as much. Alan Nunn May, in his own statement, claimed that he had come to the conclusion that his researches were evil. They were contributing to create a situation dangerous to mankind unless steps were taken to ensure that the development of atomic energy was not confined to America. Rebecca West does not consider this argument "honest." Why not? "It omits the important factor that other members of the Communist party had long recognized him as one of themselves, working underground."[11] She argues that because of the well-known party discipline among Communists, his argument is dishonest. But is it excluded that a Communist may believe to be right what he is ordered to do, even if his reasons may perhaps differ from his superiors'? She adds mockingly that "it would be interesting to know if Dr. Alan Nunn May's passion for the universal dissemination of scientific knowledge led him to take steps to break down the barrier which he describes as existing between the Americans and the British in this matter."[12] It seems to me a quite irrelevant argument. A traitor in a cause is not dishonest because he does not serve it in all conceivable directions other than the one open to him.

It seems to me that Rebecca West's argument demonstrates once more her reluctance to acknowledge ideological treason as a valid type—indeed probably the most valid type in our time. That is perhaps why she can conclude the more recent version of her essay with a disquisition on the "decline and fall" of treason. It is not based on the widespread misconception of the decline and fall of ideology (the "end of ideology"[13] argument) but rather on the proposition that the professional has taken the place of the amateur—Colonel Abel, a Soviet spy in New York, as contrasted with William Joyce.[14] To her, such men as Abel are not traitors because they have no loyalty which they could betray. But this of course does not alter their function, and furthermore there always have been professional spies, and there always will be amateur traitors who make it possible for the professional spy to work. There is no decline, let alone a fall, of treason in sight in our societies rent by conflicts of ideology and loyalty more deep and dangerous than have existed in the past. If anyone doubt it, let him read the Black Declaration of Independence published recently.[15]

The work of Margret Boveri on treason is rather differently conceived from that of Rebecca West.[16] She too, of course, is not preoccupied with the problem of functionality, but rather with the moral issues and their psychic ramifications. At the center of her work stand the treasons committed by the German opposition to Hitler, but her discussion is reinforced by a great deal of personal experience, as detailed in a brief autobiography attached to her work.[17] Interestingly enough, she does not see any "decline and fall" of treason—quite the contrary. She asks herself: "To whom belongs my loyalty?" And she answers: "Naturally to the German Federal Republic which has constituted itself as provisional and whose passport I carry. But with each wish for reunification I betray in a sense this Federal Republic the demise of which I hope for; just as before 1870 all those Germans who dreamed of a united Germany betrayed their several fatherlands, be it Bavaria or Prussia, Austria, Wuerttenberg, Saxony. . . ."[18] This feeling of Miss Boveri shows her hypersensitive approach to the morals of treason and betrayal. It resembles the view that even "he who thinks of another woman, has broken the marriage in his heart."[19] I sympathize with this view; but from the viewpoint of such a rigorous morality, America is today full of traitors. Where is one to draw the line? Surely not just anyone who thinks about how the Constitution might be improved or even what an ideal constitution would be like can meaningfully be described as a traitor. It is carrying the demands of loyalty to a perverse extreme to have it exclude any desire for change or improvement. Since the declared purpose of the German Federal Republic is to be the first step toward a reformed and reconstituted Germany, surely to wish for or indeed work for such a Germany is no betrayal, but in fact the expression of a higher loyalty. This thought is readily apparent, and may be rationalized in functional terms. Since such thoughts and actions are clearly functional to a reunited Germany, they are also functional to the Federal Republic whose long-term prospects of survival and well-being depend possibly and certainly arguably upon the coming into being of a united Germany. Let us carry this argument a step further. Miss Boveri would have to maintain that any person dreaming of or working for a united Europe is betraying his fatherland, be it Germany, France, or what have you. Thoughts of this kind do turn up in certain nationalist quarters. I once heard an ardent Gaullist describe Jean Monnet as a "man without a fatherland" a "*sans-patrie.*" This is manifestly absurd. Subjectively, the "European" is today a man who is convinced that only a getting together of the Europeans will insure the survival of their several national states. Numerous elaborate arguments maintaining this position are at hand and they are widely believed.[20] It is certainly quite possible these Europeans may be right, so that in objective functional terms they are not betraying their fatherland, but are in fact loyally serving it—more loyally than their opponents. Yet, how is this case different from the opponent of Hitler's regime who attempted to overthrow it for the sake of Germany's survival? The subjective side apart, the difference lies in the latter's being clearly disfunctional to the regime, whereas the former is not.

These illustrations demonstrate how perplexing is the approach to treason in terms of morals. It can be further illustrated by concrete instances of debatable behavior. Let us assume a French official, a convinced European, leaks information about plans of his government. He does so because he believes them to be intended to hinder the European development, and he is also convinced that, if these plans are made known, they will be thwarted. Is he betraying his government? The answer must be yes: he is an ideological traitor. Is he betraying France? Here doubts enter, for it all depends on what is good for France. In other words, if his actions are functional to the effective development of France he is a loyal Frenchman, but since this is a contingent matter, it remains "anyone's guess" how to answer the question. Enough of these sophistries.

Margret Boveri defines treason as follows: When I create the impression of being something which I am not: a friend, a democrat, a nationalist, a Communist, a loyal citizen, a fighter for an idea, an obedient soldier, a sectarian, and then I act contrary to this impression, I am a traitor. On this very broad basis, which is akin to our stress on the violation of trust, she argues that it is so very difficult to disentangle the situations in which betrayal occurs because "we are never just one thing, but many." She uses Oppenheimer as an illustration and says. "He was a friend of H. Chevalier. He was an American, he was a leftist Democrat. He was a Jew. He was a natural scientist. He was the leader of a group of physicists, mathematicians, technicians who sought to build the mass destructive weapon of history. In this capacity he was a member of the American armed forces, and hence subject to the same oath and the same duties as any other American soldier." She then shows how these various commitments tended to conflict so that he would have to betray one or the other and concludes, "Robert Oppenheimer is a highly gifted, unusually complex person. The more complex a man, the more numerous his commitments, and hence the more numerous the possibilities for these commitments to conflict with each other, and hence that one of them will be betrayed."[21] From this analysis, she proceeds to assert that nowadays these numerous links do not fit into a unified system of values, and hence people must choose, and each such choice involves the possibility of becoming guilty of treason to the alternative which was rejected.

From this general assertion she argues that "men die in relation to society." What she means is that they become indifferent and resigned, that they become tired. She cites in support an article in the *Times Literary Supplement*[22] which discusses loyalties and points out that an increasing number of people seek to avoid all social activity because such activity would identify them with the established powers. Not giving any positive value to the government or the political system, they merely go through the motions, being totally indifferent. They become "non-citizens." There is plenty of evidence for this development in many countries, including the United States. Formerly people critical of their society or government had a notion of what they wanted to see in place of the existing scheme of things, but the non-citizens of today know only what they are against. Here Miss Boveri comes close to Rebecca West's thinking; for she would accuse the rootlessness of the urban masses, of the refugees and the exiles, for the cynical disrespect and disloyalty toward the system of which they are the beneficiaries. She also stresses the chasm that separates the actual performance from the ideals proclaimed in various contemporary political systems, and states that it is this conflict which produces the cynicism. It is, she says, a form of "homelessness." And she notes in this connection the extent to which politicians and others active in political life will say one thing in public and another in private, and she asks whether the "private" remarks are felt to be a betrayal of the public order by those who make them.

It is evident that widespread practice of betrayal exceeds the limits within which treason may be functional. These cases of treason are rapidly undermining all possibility of mutual trust and as such cause the corrosion of all social bonds which threatens the disintegration of the political system. In short, such betrayal is becoming clearly disfunctional. It may be arguable that only a totalist ideology, maintained by a totalitarian autocracy, is capable of dealing with such a process. By draconic penalties, all such betrayals are punished, and they are all merged into the one treason or betrayal of the party, the state, the proletariat, and the people. The organization monopoly at the same time destroys the multiple loyalties of a pluralistic society and replaces them with the one and only loyalty, the loyalty toward the revolutionary new system. Anything that hurts the system is, in this perspective, a case of treason, and the penalties are correspondingly high.[23] Boveri puts it in the form of a question, Are we not entering a period of blind, because ideologically oriented, thinking without one's own insight? At the same time, she concludes her searching survey and analysis with the suggestion that she would like to have its title understood in another, broader sense of the word betray (*verraten*), in which we might say that somebody "betrays" embarrassment by getting red in the face. Traitors and their treasonable activities betray in this sense, she thinks, the enormous changes that are taking place at the present time. They have shown that we are living in a time of transition. Recalling Judas and Peter, both traitors of the new message, she asserts that they betrayed the new world that was in the making. And that she thinks is also the key to today's ubiquity of treason.

A similar view, based exclusively on American material, has been expounded by Adam Yarmolinsky;[24] who holds that the multiplicity of loyalties and the frequency with which they lead to betrayal are the reflection of social and political unrest in which disaffection is common and overt conflicts force choices implying betrayals. This opinion is amply documented in a report on fifty security cases, many of which actually disclosed that no serious breach of loyalty had occurred. The purpose of the study being in fact quite different from our present one, they leave open the very questions which would be of primary interest and concern to anyone studying the genesis of betrayal and treason.[25]

Morton Grodzins[26] has put forward a proposition which bears a relationship to the problem of functionality. He sought to show that treason is the "ultimate confrontation" of a man with the power of the state. Since his study was based upon experience with the relocation of Americans of Japanese descent after Pearl Harbor, he could and did argue in terms of a person's willingness to fight as an index of his loyalty. Grodzins put it this way: "The strength and universality of national loyalty rest upon the ease and the force with which this positive connection between nation and happiness can be established in the mind of the individual."[27] If many individuals lose this sense, the situation can become disastrously disfunctional; for, as Grodzins rightly remarks, "the very essence of democratic government is the running equilibrium of the groups advantaged and disadvantaged so that no large group of citizens . . . becomes permanently estranged."[28] Such estrangement is vividly portrayed in the statements made by some of the demonstrators involved in the Kent State killing of four students. One student, Kathy Lyons, in an outcry entitled "Can't Stand No More," says, ". . . I was a non-violent spectator. I watched and listened and tried to understand both sides. . . . The State has taken young people like myself and turned them against their own kind. . . . I'm ready to fight for what I believe is right and against those things I know are wrong. All people, young and old, who believe as I do that there is something seriously wrong with the way this country is being governed, should band together . . . until they are overthrown. . . . These are not our wars. We must not fight for them. If they will not let those who have something to say say it, and those who want to live in peace, live it, then we must fight against them for they are wrong."[29] These are words that were said and thought all over the country, and not only at Kent State, and they are being said in other countries as well. Betrayal is becoming the order of the day in terms of a variety of beliefs which are often the basic professed beliefs of the community to which such a person belongs. Such bitterness may become functional if it propels a person into meaningful political activity and participation. But there is no certainty that it will, or that an attempt at it will be maintained; for the impatience of such young persons is making them ill-disposed to the slow and grueling process of politics. Moreover, they are apt to resent the need of adapting to its procedures.

A special problem is presented by the mass media, which are often in danger of committing not only betrayal but formal treason. They may not even be aware of it, and in any case they may feel that freedom of the press should protect them against restraints resulting from loyalty to the government. These problems are, of course, aggravated if a country is engaged in war, whether it has formally declared it or not. A state of emergency does in fact exist, but any journalist may with some show of reason claim that a sharply critical evaluation of the government's posture is of vital importance. Surely a good many writings of American reporters and news analysts have conveyed secret information to the enemy or have "given aid and comfort" to the enemy. Indeed, so openly admitted has this aspect of the conflict in Vietnam been that the enemy could quite candidly claim it to be his strategy to defeat America by such divisive methods as the American freedoms allowed him to foster.[30] An interesting case bearing on this issue arose in the Federal Republic of Germany when the government accused a leading journal, the *Spiegel*, of betraying military secrets and arrested its editors. The government was not able to make its case stick; none of the editors involved were sentenced, although they were also not entirely vindicated.[31] The editors argued and so did their partisans that this kind of betrayal was "useful"—or in our terms, it served a useful function which the right of the freedom of the press protects. A democratic government will benefit from such criticism. In the American case, many would hold that the treasonable activities engaged in by so many of the government's critics have been beneficial to the country. They served the crucial function of getting America out of Vietnam and this was vital to America's survival. This reasoning is somewhat circular; for, since it is based upon criticizing or viewing with alarm the division by which America is rent, it might with some logic be said that all the critic has to do is stop criticizing, and the divisions will heal. But it is not an argument which will have much appeal to him who is convinced that the withdrawal from Southeast Asia is necessary for the good of the country.

The preceding discussion and the chapters on treason have, I trust, shown that betrayal is, in spite of the moral condemnation of it, very widely practiced in politics, and that it can have very important functions in the political process. I hope the discussion has also shown that when treason becomes very widespread, its functionality declines, except for a possible successor state arising from a revolutionary overthrow. In a novel about a German corporal, who after having been captured became an espionage agent for the American forces in the last war, the author, George Howe, entitling his story *Call It Treason,* made the most of it, as Patrick Henry would have wanted him to do. Such acceptance of the American ideals of freedom and democracy has become incredible to many young Americans (as well as Germans). Can they function if they are so generally betrayed? Can they function if they are *not* so generally betrayed? These two desperate questions show how equivocal is the inquiry into treason's functionality. Who in such a situation is the hero? Or are they both?

We have more or less excluded from the consideration of treason and betrayal the cases where monetary reward was the primary motivation of the traitor. These cases are, of course, quite numerous, and many of them constitute in fact corruption. Therefore it seemed better to treat them under that heading. Others belong to espionage and intelligence work, and that will be taken up in Part IV when we consider secrecy.

PART III

Corruption

CHAPTER

8

CORRUPTION IN HISTORICAL PERSPECTIVE

"ANY attempt to analyze the concept of corruption must contend with the fact that in English and other languages the word *corruption* has a history of vastly different meanings and connotations."[1] This is very true; but a core meaning readily emerges from an analysis of these different meanings. Corruption is a kind of behavior which deviates from the norm actually prevalent or believed to prevail in a given context, such as the political. It is deviant behavior associated with a particular motivation, namely that of private gain at public expense. But whether this was the motivation or not, it is the fact that private gain was secured at public expense that matters. Such private gain may be a monetary one, and in the minds of the general public it usually is, but it may take other forms. It may be a rapid promotion, an order, decorations, and the like, and the gain may not be personal, but benefit a family or other group. The pattern of corruption may therefore be said to exist whenever a power holder who is charged with doing certain things, that is a responsible functionary or office holder, is by monetary or other rewards, such as the expectation of a job in the future, induced to take actions which favor whoever provides the reward and thereby damage the group or organization to which the functionary belongs, more specifically the government. It is preferable for our purposes to state the concept of corruption thus, rather than as the use of public power for private profit, preferment, or prestige, or for the benefit of a group or class, in a way that constitutes a breach of law or of standards of high moral conduct; for while such breaches constitute some sort of damage, they are not necessarily involved. But there is typically gain for corrupter and corrupted, and loss for others, involved in such a situation.[2]

This kind of corruption is the specific kind related to the notion of administrative service which the modern bureaucracy conceived as meritocracy has fostered.[3] But there is a much broader notion of political corruption which is implied in judgments such as that expressed by Lord Acton in his famous dictum that all power tends to corrupt and absolute power corrupts absolutely.[4] For while the specific kind of corruption may be involved here too, the meaning of Lord Acton is focused on the moral depravity which power is believed to cause in men; they no longer think about what is right action or conduct, but only about what is expedient action or conduct. Such deep suspicion of power has, it would seem, a religious root, and is typically Western and Christian. It harks back to the notion of the two kingdoms and to the contrast between the earthly and the heavenly city.[5] In this broad and imprecise sense, corruption cannot by definition be "functional." For such corruption, being in fact a decomposition of the body politic through moral decay, is a general category to include all kinds of practices which are believed to be disfunctional and hence morally corrupt.

Acton's famous statement touches the paradox of power and morals (see Chapter 1). Systematically, corruption is a form of coercion, namely economic coercion. Not only the buying of votes and actual monetary rewards, but all the more indirect forms, such as gifts, or otherwise influencing the judgment of those who exercise governmental functions, are instrumentalities in this sphere. Here it is a question of the degree of corruption. For that such corruption is endemic in all forms of government is practically certain. But that there are striking differences in the extent of corruption between governments which are formally similar, such as Great Britain, Switzerland, and the United States, all functioning constitutional democracies, is equally patent. It is possible to state a "law" or general regularity by saying that the degree of corruption varies inversely to the degree that power is consensual. Corruption is a corrective of coercive power and its abuse, when it is functional. Many complications arise from the fact that power often appears to be consensual when it actually is not; or it may be consensual for Anglo-Saxon, Protestant whites, whereas it is not for immigrants or blacks. We have discussed some of this when dealing with violence (see Chapter 2). It would appear that in those situations where a semblance of consent hides the coercive reality, corruption is rife. The power which is believed to be consensual, having to a considerable extent become coercive, lends itself to corruption. Tammany Hall is a sort of example of this situation.[6] As Willie Stark puts it in *All the King's Men,* "Graft is what he calls it when the fellows do it who don't know which fork to use."[7] There is and always has been a tendency on the part of critics of democracy to assert that developments of this kind are typical of democracy. Historical studies have shown that such a judgment is untenable. In monarchical England, Prussia, and Russia corruption was ubiquitous.[8] The real difference is that in open societies corruption is often uncovered by the opposition and brought to public notice by a free press, whereas in autocratic regimes it remains largely hidden. The extensive corruption in totalitarian dictatorships is evident in the now available documents of the Fascist and National Socialist regimes. Reports from the Soviet Union suggest similar conditions.[9] To give a couple of illustrations let me cite Hermann Goering, Hitler's field marshal: "I have seen terrible things. Chauffeurs of District leaders have enriched themselves to the extent of half a million. The gentlemen know this? It is true? (Assent) These are things which are impossible. I shall not hesitate to proceed ruthlessly." This happened in a meeting on November 12, 1938, and treated such corruption as widespread and generally known.[10] Trotsky reported such corruption on a great scale as proof of his contention that the Soviet Union was utterly bureaucratized.[11] These bits of evidence could readily be multiplied. If it had not been for such corruption, many more would have perished under the terror whom corrupt officials allowed to escape.

Corruption in totalitarian regimes may also be of the broader unspecific kind. Thus the ideology has been undergoing what critics have described as corruption, namely a disintegration of the belief system upon which a particular political system rests. Such corruption will often take the form of a perversion of legal rules by misinterpretation. Such perversion, like a breach, challenges the intended generality of the rule; when exceptions multiply, they become the rule. It is obvious that they may thus become the basis of a revision of a basic ideological position which to the true believer appears as a corruption. There can be little doubt that this sort of "moral corruption" is what concerned political philosophers in the past. Aristotle, and after him Machiavelli particularly, but basically Plato in his theory of the "corrupted" or "perverted" constitutions—democracy, oligarchy, and tyranny—stressed the point that these regimes instead of being guided by the law (we would say the public interest) were serving the interest of the rulers. They were, we might say, exploitative, and thus corrupt. Aristotle followed Plato's notions, but substituted the happiness of the ruled, that is to say their well-being, for the law; such general happiness is, of course, closely akin to what is customarily in modern times referred to as the public or general interest. These fundamental general notions of corruption all practically define corruption as disfunctional; for it is seen as destructive of a particular political order, be it monarchy, aristocracy, or polity, the latter a constitutionally limited popular rule, and thus by definition devoid of any function within a political order.

This classic conception of corruption as a general disease of the body politic persisted into modern times, and is central to the political thought of Machiavelli, Montesquieu and Rousseau. For Machiavelli corruption was the process by which the *virtù* of the citizen was undermined and eventually destroyed. Since most men are weak and lacking in the *virtù* of the good citizen except when inspired by a great leader, the process of corruption is ever threatening. And when *virtù* has been corrupted, a heroic leader must appear who in rebuilding the political order infuses his *virtù* into the entire citizenry. Thus the miserable creatures that human beings ordinarily are or become when not properly guided are thereby transformed into patriotic citizens, capable of sacrifice, self-exertion, and other patriotic virtues. But such a leader must not be a Caesar. Machiavelli was sharply critical of the great Roman. He described him as one of the worst figures in Roman history; for he had destroyed the venerable Roman constitution instead of regenerating it.[12] He was, we might say, himself corrupted. In our time, a similar misunderstanding aided Hitler in seizing power. Instead of proving the heroic benefactor who would reconstitute Germany, he proved to be a corrupted destroyer of the German values and beliefs. The evidence we have on the thought of the resistance (see Chapter 3) brings this out very clearly; men like Pastor Niemoeller offer instances of this original misunderstanding and eventual reversal.

Francis Bacon was generally believed to be a Machiavellian. He certainly shows Machiavelli's influence. Yet he was a corrupt man, perhaps the most famous instance of a high English dignitary brought down by his corruption. As High Chancellor he accepted bribes in order to favor certain parties before the court. The complexities of the case are considerable[13] and they are of no particular interest for our purpose. But what is of interest is that he and his friends essentially defended his case on the ground that he was not doing anything that was not generally done. It is a defense that has persisted to this day; he was the unlucky one who got caught. In the functional perspective, the matter may be stated differently; Bacon's case indicated that corruption had gone too far, that the limit of what might be allowed for purposes of moderating the regime's injustices was here exceeded and caused a reaction. In this sense, Bacon's case bears a relation to Profumo's discussed below.

The Roman Republic also had its trials of corruption, and men like Cicero who were interested in regenerating the Republic addressed themselves to the task of unearthing and bringing to trial extreme cases of corruption, especially in provincial administration.[14] But these efforts came too late. The Republic's public ethic was already too generally corrupted, and the limits had by that time been greatly transgressed. Corruption had become so general that corrupt practices rather than the strict morals of the forefathers had become the accepted mode of behavior. This Roman case was a primary instance in the theory of Montesquieu.[15] This nobleman and believer in the aristocracy, or a monarchy moderated by a nobility, devoted a major work to *Grandeur des Romains et de leur Décadence,* a work in which he described the process of corruption which he attributed to the imperial enterprise of the Romans. Their *virtù* gave them the victories over the other regimes of the Mediterranean and the extension of their city from *urbs* to *orbs* corrupted their moral fiber and eventually destroyed the constitutional order which had won them the empire. Some may anxiously ask today whether the Americans are not undergoing the same process. Be that as it may, Montesquieu again saw corruption as the disfunctional process *par excellence* by which a good political order or system is perverted into an evil one, a monarchy into a despotism.

This global concept was pushed to its extreme and thereby to its *reductio ad absurdum* by Rousseau, who argued at one point that man had been corrupted by social and political life, and this notion was elaborated by the anarchists of the nineteenth century from Godwin to Bakunin. It is not the corruption of men which destroys the political system but the political system which corrupts and destroys man. Beyond this, Rousseau was deeply concerned with what he believed to be the corruption of his age, and he looked upon himself as the wise man who must raise a warning voice; for he believed that the right kind of guidance could shape public opinion to avoid such corruption. He believed in the manipulation of opinion as it was practiced in Sparta as a proper defense against corruption.[16] Artists, scientists, and literary men are "both the victims and the promoters of social conditions which necessarily caused them to corrupt their fellow men. . . . The *corps littéraire* only cheers on princes when they oppress their peoples."[17] In short, Rousseau's concern with corruption is primarily with moral corruption, and only indirectly with political corruption, as providing the setting for moral corruption. Political corruption is seen by Rousseau as a necessary consequence of the struggle for power, and he could have agreed with Acton that all power tends to corrupt. According to Rousseau, equality is natural and good laws are directed toward maintaining this equality against the corrupting influence of power-hungry individuals.[18]

Although this preoccupation with equality may be reduced

and refined to an equality before the law, Rousseau's outlook provides the setting for the modern and specific sense of corruption. The abuse of power, which constitutionalism is primarily concerned with preventing through the application of the rule of law to public officers (*Rechsstaat*), is at the heart of corruption. Corruption was widespread, as mentioned before, under monarchies, absolute and other, and more particularly in England. In fact, the system which Walpole built is perhaps the most striking instance of corruption functioning effectively to transform a political system and establish a new one; for it is well known that the parliamentary system of government in which the ruling party rests upon majority support in the House of Commons was first organized by Walpole. In a celebrated, if somewhat controversial study, Professor Namier has analyzed this system.[19] Each party, but more particularly the Whig party under Walpole and Pelham (1715–1760) sought to secure for itself a solid majority in Parliament; for such a majority greatly facilitated the realization of policies and the enactment of necessary legislation. Walpole proceeded to secure such a parliamentary majority for himself and his cabinet by a carefully worked-out system which to his contemporaries, more especially the leader of the opposition, Lord Bolingbroke, appeared to be a system of corruption. Wraxall tells us in his *Memoirs* that the government under Pelham handed each of its partisans in Parliament from five hundred to eight hundred pounds at the end of a session, the amount varying according to the services rendered. These payments were official enough to be entered on a record kept in the Treasury (which has enabled recent researchers to elucidate the actual practice of corruption involved). These investigations have shown that the Whigs had worked out a very elaborate system of governmental favors, ranging from direct payments to voters and members of Parliament, to patronage and the various favors available in foreign trade and the privileged trading companies. All this is well enough known, and was intimately bound up with what caused the Americans to rebel. If they had been better informed, they would have attacked this corruption rather than King George in their Declaration of Independence. In fact, Walpole once remarked that he and Lord Townsend constituted the "firm" to which the king had entrusted the government of the country.[20]

The argument of Bolingbroke and his friends that this system constituted corruption of the old constitution was, of course, sound. It was radically disfunctional in one sense, but in another it actually helped a system which had become antiquated to function and to be transformed into a preferable one. An economist might say that a kind of market of the services of government officials had been substituted for monocratic (monopolistic) control. Such an arrangement was at variance with the requirements of a responsible public service, a rational bureaucracy in which ideally the official is paid from the public treasury for precisely defined legal duties, and must not have any other interests.[21] In Germany, all attempts at bribery on the part of private persons or groups are made crimes and punished. Such bribery is considered the most pernicious crime, an attack upon the very foundations of the state, and comparable to treason, in fact a form of treason. These are views by no means restricted to Germany,[22] but are found also in Switzerland, the Low Countries, and Scandinavia. They are logical consequences of the rationalized bureaucracy as developed in modern government and economics. For a large business concern will just as rigorously insist upon this approach to personal favors as will a responsible government.

Corruption, then, has become a particular form of political pathology rather than a global degeneration. As such it can be defined in behavioral terms, and the activities objected to can be outlawed. Institutions like the Comptroller's Office can be and have been set up in all advanced countries to watch the expenditure of public funds, and civil service commissions and the like have been established to inhibit and prevent patronage outside the official merit system. In this sense, modern bureaucracy spells the end of aristocratic privilege. Under absolutism, it was quite common that offices could be bought and sold. But to speak here of corruption is anachronistic, for the kings were not subject to any legal rules. Such sales were regulated and the proceeds went to the public treasury to be employed for such purposes as the king and his council decided upon. Thus, the sale of public offices was considered a "check on corruption" because it benefited the public weal, instead of some personal favorites of the king.[23] Reform-minded writers, such as Montesquieu and Bentham, openly advocated the buying and selling of offices because the service would thereby be improved. It is remarkable that Bentham of all thinkers should have taken this position: for it was the Utilitarians and the reform movement they sparked which put an end to the venality of public offices in Britain. In fact, the process by which the British pulled themselves out of the morass of corruption which had made a Burke defend the "rotten borough"[24] as a sound political institution and developed what is, in the opinion of many, the most thoroughly honest public service ever organized is little short of miraculous. It shows that pathological phenomena are not necessarily destined to go from bad to worse and the corrective for them is often quite readily at hand. By the second half of the nineteenth century what had been considered "normal behavior" had become corruption sharply condemned by the majority of Britons.[25] Similar, though less dramatic, reforms were achieved in Prussia, Bavaria, and France; in all of which a properly trained bureaucracy, a responsible public service, was developed in this period.[26] It is not here possible to explore the problem of "bureaucracy" and its development, to which this transformation in the concept of corruption is linked.[27] The socialist movement, and more especially Marxism, developed their revolutionary ideology without any stress on the corruption of the social and political order they proposed to supersede. Only in recent years have the rulers of the Soviet Union and other socialist states had to acknowledge the growth of corruption in their own regimes, and to seek to combat it by vigorous countermeasures, not especially successfully. In view of the corrupt behavior of the Tsarist bureaucracy, notorious at the turn of the century, the original thrust was in the direction of developing an honest public service, thereby catching up with the bourgeois societies of the West. In this connection, these regimes have added yet another dimension to the unfolding concept of corruption. As mentioned above, their conceit is that most corruption in socialist countries is traceable to a preceding ideological corruption of which it is the result. The total bureaucratization which the socialist ideology has tended to promote in practice has made the problem of corruption particularly central to these regimes, and each case is apt to appear as a flagrant case of betrayal of the trust that had been placed in the offending functionary. Thus treason and corruption become intertwined and the language of the Soviet criminal code demonstrates it.[28]

The foregoing discussion has made it plain that the conception of corruption has evolved in close relationship with the ideas on government and the state. It is therefore not to be wondered at that the expansion of Western politics into countries with very different cultures has produced a novel set of issues. Colonial administrators had long been familiar with these problems, of course, and the difficulties facing anyone seeking to superimpose Western standards of probity in public administration upon peoples who accepted the fact that public officials exploited their position for personal gain, as well as for the benefit of their families, kin groups, and other groups.[29] Foreign aid administrators ran into the unwelcome discovery that such aid had a tendency to disappear into the pockets of the native rulers, rather than being employed for the purposes of economic development for which it had been destined.[30] It is small consolation to acknowledge that "there is some corruption in all governments and in the public services of all countries."[31] For, in keeping with our analysis of political pathology, how much corruption there is makes a vital difference. In some cases corruption has been found to be so widespread that it has become a major obstacle to economic and other development. Therefore, in spite of the tolerant rhetoric, derived from anthropological relativism, about local cultures and the respect due them, it has proved practically necessary to combat such culturally conditioned corruption.[32] But this is easier said than done; for who is to set the standard of rectitude? Is there a universally valid standard, derivable from the rational requirements of modern technology? If so, by whose say-so?

As has been pointed out, widespread corruption will produce certain ascertainable evils: (1) inefficiency, (2) mistrust of the government, (3) waste of public resources, (4) discouragement of enterprise and of foreign capital, and (5) political instability.[33] Comments on all of these evils would lead far afield; suffice it to note that all of them interfere with the workings of a developed industrial system. If therefore these evils are to be avoided, it follows that corruption must be uprooted and eliminated as was done in European societies emerging from feudal and post-feudal absolutism. For, in a sense, corruption results when an official, like a feudal lord, regards his position as his property with which he can do as he wishes and which he can exploit for his own private benefit. Nor is it necessary to apply a rigid legal standard of Western derivation. The common understanding is that an official is corrupt when he accepts monetary or other reward from someone under his jurisdiction for something he should or should not do anyway, or exercises the discretion entrusted to him so as to favor his corruptor.[34] These are ways of behaving which may be prohibited and which have been prohibited and punished. Yet, an impatient developer may feel that it would be more functional to accept the corrupt behavior and work with and through it. One of these men has written: "Given the continued desire by the governments of the West African countries for rapid economic development and general modernisation, conflicts fruitful of corruption will continue and are indeed almost certain to increase. . . ." Frankly facing the possibility of a function of corruption: ". . . although damaging . . . it is clearly not a subversive or revolutionary phenomenon. It is rather an emollient, softening conflict and reducing friction. At a high level it throws a bridge between those who hold political power and those who control wealth enabling the two classes . . . to assimilate each other."[35] And another has added that "in most cultures it [corruption] seems to be most prevalent during the most intense phases of modernization."[36] All this has led to a view of corruption that conceives it as highly functional under conditions of rapid social and political change, when new conceptions are superimposed upon a recalcitrant society, when laws multiply, when one class replaces another as the ruling one—in all these and similar situations corruption facilitates the transformation, it provides oil, so to speak, on the clashing gears, or, if you prefer, on the turbulent waters. Actually, it is now recognized by students of the modernization of developing countries as a recurrent phenomenon of the past; in ancient Rome and China as well as in Britain, Prussia, and elsewhere, the well-to-do achieved a measure of participation in the political system by buying themselves into positions of power and authority. Local conditions may vary, and a particular pattern of corruption may become the customary and accepted way of politics, and in such situations it may well be political suicide to go against the established folkways. When Christ drove the traders out of the Temple, he was enacting the typical role of the moral reformer, indignant at the corruption which had become customary. It is not difficult to imagine some of the traders in the mob who shouted for his crucifixion rather than Barabbas' when the Roman magistrate asked the multitude to indicate their preference. Nor is it hard to believe that the priests who no doubt received a "kickback" for their permission to let the traders trade were eager to rid themselves and the community of so annoying an antagonist of corruption.[37] Such an excursion into the familiar background of the Christian West may help to vivify the persistence of an anti-corruption mentality in the West. It has its parallel in Luther's indignation at the absolution sales which sparked the Reformation. The corruption of the Church at that time had become so notorious and so generally accepted that even high-minded sympathizers of the reform like Erasmus did not hesitate to participate in its more civilized forms, such as accepting benefices for propaganda services rendered.[38]

The theorizing about corruption on the part of philosophers and students of politics has produced a plethora of schemes for its elimination. Beyond the rhetoric of sermonizing, these theories vary depending upon what kind of corruption is to be combated. Machiavelli's concern with the global kind led him to believe that only a heroic leader who would infuse the citizenry with his virtue would be capable of inspiring a morality that would eliminate corruption. It is interesting that this moral aspect still finds its place in contemporary programs of how to deal with partial corruption.[39] Such nostrums are at times stated in a form which renders them utopian. Thus we read that "the first and by far the most important corrective is that of common acceptance by the total society of standards of governmental morality." It is the kind of proposal that American folk wit has mocked at as "when hell freezes over." Other

plans resemble the old Tammany suggestion of distinguishing between "honest" and "dishonest" graft—"honest" is graft that has become part of the folkways and is acceptable to the community.[40] But it is a dubious distinction. In some developing countries, notably India, governmental morality has been embodied in Codes of Conduct, such as the Code of the Conduct of Ministers and the Code of Conduct of Public Servants.[41] But these moral sermons apart, certain proposals for reducing corruption have been developed which include items like a merit system for appointment, legislative supervision, pride in work, administrative courts and accounting procedures, as well as the ombudsman system for public complaints.[42] These programs of reform often overlook the function which corruption may have in a rapidly developing society. But they are commendable because they serve the function of limiting this particular phenomenon, and thereby preventing it from becoming pathological and requiring radical cures, such as the military dictatorships which the military and the technocrats propose to provide in propounding a technically motivated kind of puritanism and austerity.[43] This may even be ideologically reinforced. The other side to this matter is an adequate salary which would enable a public servant to live without needing additional outside income. It is a matter that has been much discussed and argued about in the West, and while it possesses a certain validity, it is hardly the panacea which some would have us believe.

Corruption in the historical perspective appears to be ever present where power is wielded. It bears a close relationship to betrayal—the corrupt official betrays his trust—and to violence. These pathologies appear to be interacting and mutually reinforcing. It may be instructive to analyze some cases of recent date and the arguments which they have precipitated in sophisticated political circles, before seeking to arrive at any general conclusions.

CHAPTER

9

CASES OF CORRUPTION

NO MONETARY corruption was involved in the case of Profumo, the British Minister of Defense in the Tory Cabinet in the fifties. There were no loyalties bought or sold.[1] But then, as pointed out before, monetary corruption is the least serious form, or at any rate the politically least interesting, as is the case with monetary treason or betrayal. In the Profumo case, three issues were so closely intertwined that it is difficult to disentangle them: there was first the security risk involved, second the problem of sex morals, and third the issue of "constitutional ethics." We shall not be concerned here with the third, but the first and second are part of that case which involve corruption.

Stephen Ward, a good osteopath and a gifted artist was, in a sense, the prime corruptor. He seduced girls, then furnished them to others and spent some of the money that came from such prostitution. One of the girls he had picked up was Christine Keeler, with whom he had relations off and on for two or three years. He handed her to other persons for monetary reward, but it is questionable how important this was to him, since he was well-off as a professional osteopath and an artist.

Stephen Ward became a friend of Eugene Ivanov, the assistant Soviet naval attaché at the embassy in London. The British Security Service discovered that he was also a Soviet intelligence officer. He had established a strong influence over Ward, but it is believed that Ward did not consciously betray Britain. He lacked discretion. It was out of friendship for Ivanov that he secured "secrets" for him.

Lord Astor was a patient, friend, benefactor, and possibly also a beneficiary of Ward. Lord Astor as tenant of a great country house let a cottage to Ward on the estate. One of his visitors was John Profumo, a man of great wealth, and married to a well-known actress; he had a fine war record and had held several parliamentary offices. Profumo met Christine Keeler at the Astor estate, was attracted to her, and visited her at Ward's house. This acquaintance led to sexual relations with her.

This was the setting which offered to Ivanov his chance to learn state secrets. Specifically, he asked Ward when the United States would be giving nuclear weapons to the Federal Republic of Germany. Ward asked Miss Keeler to try and find out from Profumo. She did not do so, nor did she presumably learn any other secret information from Profumo. It appears that the British Secret Service knew about the relations between Ward and Ivanov, and hence warned Profumo about the risk of Ward's picking up information for the Soviets.

On the day of this warning, Profumo wrote a letter to Miss Keeler in which he addressed her as "darling" and expressed his sorrow about not being able to see her the next day and suggested "some time in the future." As a result, the relations between Profumo and Miss Keeler remained unknown.

During the Berlin Crisis of September, 1961, Ivanov asked Ward about British intentions in this crisis, and Ward tried to get information from Lord Astor and other men in high position. When Lord Astor suggested to the Foreign Office that they might want to use Ward's services, he was refused, because the Foreign

Office considered Ward dangerous because a Communist sympathizer. At that time, Miss Keeler became involved in brawls between some Jamaicans, and when this became public, she spoke to a Labour MP who in turn informed the Security Service. At that point, Miss Keeler was persuaded to sell her life story to the press. Thereupon, Ward tried to get the story stopped, Ivanov fled, and Profumo denied the story.

So far the story of corruption. What followed was essentially the story of Profumo's trying to talk himself out of it, and by not telling the truth to his cabinet colleagues, and misinforming the House of Commons, he violated "constitutional ethics," which led to his fall. It is the considered opinion of knowledgeable Britishers that he would have fallen even if he had not misinformed the House, because of the violation of morals which his conduct constituted. Since Miss Keeler had intimate relations with a British minister and with a Soviet agent at the same time, a serious security risk was created. The Security Service took a narrow view of this risk. The warning they gave to Mr. Profumo was by many regarded as not sufficient, considering the key position Profumo occupied. It is puzzling that the Prime Minister should not himself have taken the matter up with Profumo. One suspects that the setting had become sufficiently corrupt so that Profumo's conduct was not considered anything but his private affair, until his statements involved him in misrepresentations. It is apparent that it becomes decisive what degree of tolerance for corrupt conduct a society is inclined to permit. Widespread private corruption will necessarily affect public life. Very often, such corruption occurring more or less behind closed doors remains hidden from the public, and hence may provide the setting for a sudden outbreak of indignation when one such case becomes known and the perpetrator is victimized. It very often happens by way of the efforts of opposition elements who thus "reveal" the rottenness of the regime. Francis Bacon was a victim of this kind of situation.[2]

The history of the Third Republic is studded with scandals over corruption, the most famous being the Dreyfus case. But it became involved with the issue of anti-Semitism, and is really primarily a case of treason, alleged and not proved. The repeated financial scandals which rocked the public life of the Third Republic proved highly disfunctional; they undermined its legitimacy and contributed to its eventual downfall. They offered a ready butt for the attack of rightist and of Communist critical commentators.[3] As far as the Communists were concerned, such recurrent scandals were merely the outward signs of a "financial feudalism" in which and through which all the key positions in government and politics were occupied by members of a caste of interrelated families, the two hundred families[4] who controlled the levers of the capitalist economy. In this view, the administration is their fortress from which they direct the political and economic life of the nation. They identify their class interest with the national or general interest.[5] Diplomats and high administrators (in France usually *inspecteurs des finances*) are seen as the hired agents of the great capitalists and more especially the bankers, who operate from behind the scenes and who have their parallels among university professors and the press.[6] Impressive lists of names have been compiled to show how this intermingling actually worked under the Third Republic. It is even possible to see some of the actual scandals in this perspective as "shows" by which the inroads of unrelated outsiders are exposed to prove the integrity of the system, and of its exponents and defenders. A striking instance is provided by the Stavisky scandal of 1934. It shook the Republic to its foundation. Serge Alexandre Stavisky has been described as "a cosmopolitan crook," a "frenzied financier," a debonair swindler repeatedly convicted. He, like Casanova two and a half centuries earlier,[7] managed to engage in all kinds of dishonest practices through protection in high places, that is through corruption. He finally issued bonds, on a large scale, on the basis of a Bayonne

Municipal Pawn Shop. He eventually committed suicide, in 1934, whereupon the police "discovered" him. The most sinister feature of the case was that the prosecuting attorney of state who had repeatedly failed to secure Stavisky's arrest was the brother-in-law of Camille Chautemps, at the time Prime Minister. The general political atmosphere in France at the time was so charged —political intellectuals were anticipating a revolution[8] and a general perplexity and exasperation reigned—that the scandal ignited a great demonstration. On the Place de la Concorde, in front of the Chamber of Deputies, a vast crowd assembled on February 6, 1934, which had no common purpose, no sense of direction, and no leadership. Fascist agitators, such as Colonel de la Roque, of the Croix de Feu, did not have any idea what to do with the angry crowds, and the moment passed without any decisive action and with relatively little violence. Hence it would be possible to claim that the corruption served a system-maintaining purpose in that it provided a safety valve for the manifestation of public indignation under conditions of extreme tension. But such a claim seems rather far fetched; the beforementioned function of obscuring the general corruption which is involved when class interest is identified with the public interest would seem a more correct interpretation of this and comparable events.

The Weimar Republic, too, suffered from corruption and the Communist and Nazi propaganda was full of violent accusations and the promise to "clean up" after the takeover. We have already in the previous chapter referred to the vast corruption which actually characterized the Hitler regime. As a result of that—and of the not very impressive record of the military occupation regimes in the several zones of postwar Germany[9]— German public opinion has become rather sensitive to accusations of corruption and they have become fairly frequent. They are at times pushed to rather fine points and the case of Koennecke, the then general director of the Mercedes-Benz automobile works, may serve as an illustration. It involved primarily the "lending" of automobiles to friendly officials over a considerable period of time.[10]

The very skillful defending counsel pointed out that the Federal Republic was in a very special situation in facing the Communist world. He said: "The Eastern world reacts in a particular way, when accusations are brought against leading businessmen, especially accusations of corruption; for it is inclined to conclude that Germany is a corrupt state, that corruption extends to the government, and indeed its highest functionaries." Hence he thought that the attorney of state had to be particularly alert. But he pleaded for seeing the activities complained of within the context of the relations between state and business and that the attorney of state had failed to do so. Business he thought is a part of political life *(des staatlichen Lebens)*. After alluding to the amazing reconstruction of Germany in which government and business cooperated he said that it was wrong to be suspicious of all human contacts between governing personnel and business personnel and he spoke of a "bribery psychosis." He mocked at the tendency to look upon any dinner that a businessman might have with an official as an attempt at bribery. This kind of psychosis is well known in the United States, where in the early days of the anti-lobby movement a similar tendency appeared. Finally even a cup of coffee may be seen as an attempt at bribery.[11] The attorney vigorously attacked the attorney of state for the very extensive searches and seizures that were made in the central offices of Daimler-Benz (near Stuttgart) and in their local offices. Everywhere it was a question of sales under price or "lending" the cars and no convictions were the result. He then complained about the amount of publicity generated by frequent releases from the attorney of state's office. This "trial by public opinion" as it has been called in the U.S. he felt placed the defense attorneys in a very difficult position, since they could not effectively reply to these often hypothetical releases, which were directed against quite innocent men, he thought. Hence they were "powerless." Continental European criminal procedure provides for a "process of inquiry" *(Ermittlungsverfahren)* in which a special judge seeks to ascertain the facts. This procedure weakens the defense and exposes the accused in such a case as corruption to slanderous defamation. The defense attorney declared that it hit Mr. Koennecke as a man, the Daimler-Benz works, the automobile industry, and all of German business. Koennecke appeared as "the greatest car lender of Germany." He became a butt of mockery in the night clubs and in the carnival parades. And the Communists seized the case as proof of the corruption of capitalism in Germany.

It seems that a good deal of intimidation was practiced by the investigators for the attorney of state general. It went so far that many witnesses refused to testify for fear of self-incrimination. The case was further complicated by the fact that it was linked by the attorney of state with another case, the Kilb case, in which a government official was accused of corruption because he had accepted a number of cars on loan over a number of years—he was cleared of the accusation. And so was Dr. Koennecke. Even so, there is plenty of evidence to suggest that both officials and businessmen have become much more cautious in what they do, and how they carry on their relations. The case raises a basic issue of a democratic industrial society in which business is carried on competitively and government is involved in a great deal of business.

Before turning to a case in the United States, it might be well to look at India. It has been remarked, perhaps somewhat exaggerating, that "corruption in the public services was the greatest single threat to democracy in India."[12] The president of India, Radhakrishnan, had earlier remarked that "corruption is an evil which must be fought on all fronts and at all levels."[13] Charges of corruption against members of the Congress party are a familiar story in India. They extend back into the thirties, when popular government was instituted in the provinces. Indians have enacted comprehensive anti-corruption legislation which embody very high standards that are the obverse of actual practice. It has been remarked that they also make indiscriminate accusation easy.[14] Two of Nehru's chief ministers were accused of corruption and after parliamentary investigation were dismissed; many others were accused, as they have been under Mrs. Gandhi. There has been a natural tendency to use administrative discretion in the allocation of resources and patronage to favor the governing party. How could it be otherwise in a "developing" country confronting such vast difficulties as does India? No matter what decision is made, it will seem corrupt to him who is not favored by it. It is just the same arguable that "in a poor country like India, with limited financial resources, and yet ambitious national planning, with a view to increasing the living standards of the people, the restriction of corruption to the lowest limits becomes a national and not merely an ethical necessity."[15] One may discern in that approach, especially when it is implemented by legislation, a view which does not appreciate the possible function of corruption in a country subject to rapid social change such as India. Yet, the approach of India has been in such terms, as can be seen from the Report of the Committee on the Prevention of Corruption, known as the Santhaham Committee. Whether the report will prove a landmark remains to be seen; it was thus hailed at the time. It is at any rate a report which spells out the range of the problem in India and can serve as the basis for this case here.[16] Its statistical data are, of course, merely estimates, but they reveal something of the magnitude of the problem. Many licenses were obtained by fraud. It is common knowledge that each license is worth a multiple of its face value in the open market. Customs seemed to be a racket involving many customs officials[17] and many departments of the government appear to be regularly accused of corrupt practices, including Railways, Finance, Defense, Transport and Communications, Works, Housing, Post and Telegraph, Rehabilitation, Home Affairs, Commerce and Industry, and Food and Agriculture.[18] The committee stated that "corruption is not confined to the lower ranks of public servants. . . ."[19]

It seems there "is no social sanction against taking bribes" according to an Indian scholar[20] who compares it to the offering of bribes to a deity. But the only remedy he sees is exhortation and education. Low salaries and large families appear to be another source of corruption, and hence an increase in salaries and birth control appear as remedies for corruption. In the Report of the Santhaham Committee, this matter is even directly related to the extent of discretion that a particular official has, and it is argued "that officials who exercise considerable discretion in the fields of taxation, licenses and permits, etc. should be given special attention regarding status and emoluments."[21] It is difficult to see how that is going to be possible, and the skeptical conclusion is probably justified that as long as India remains poor "the problem of corruption in the administrative services will continue to remain in acute form."[22] If, as is often the case, the bribe or other corrupt practice is primarily directed toward expediting a decision, toward getting the administration to move, it is a striking case of functional corruption. It might be better for the administration to move with due dispatch without such added inducement, but if it does not, the corruption may help considerably. In the granting of licenses, it may be a matter of life or death for the particular business, and in India one speaks of "speed money" for this kind of corruption. Now it is true that an improvement in administrative procedure may bring about the required speed-up, but the likelihood is that such devices will rarely work if they deprive the official of needed or desired income.[23] Altogether, as already indicated, it is dubious that a significant improvement can be achieved by elaborating laws and rules. Corruption, an endemic evil in rapidly changing societies, is more likely to be reduced by removing the opportunities for it, by not charging the government with all kinds of tasks involving economically valuable discretionary power. This conclusion is reinforced by the inspection of an American case, the Billie Sol Estes case, which we shall examine next. A thorough democratization with effective opposition interested in bringing to light any corrupt practices is another contextual preventive device. But our concern here is not with the practical problem of how to deal with corruption, but to demonstrate that there are situations in which it has a definite function to perform. This function is, judging by the case of India, which stands paradigmatically for all developing countries, to make a government function more satisfactorily from an economic viewpoint than it otherwise would or could.[24]

In the United States, lobbying has been developed into an elaborate operation, and it is an accepted fact of political life that one of the main functions of the large lobbies operating in every major field of interest is to participate in the legislative process through advice and pressure. Indeed, that is why the interest groups have come to be known as "pressure groups." Their function of expediting public business, of seeing that important pieces of legislation do not "die" in the legislature but are promptly adopted, is universally recognized indeed almost as part of the system, that is to say systemic in itself. There was a time when this function became disfunctional, however, when the energy and enthusiasm carried the lobbyists way beyond what can be accepted as functional in the proper sense. A statement made in the Congress some years ago will illustrate the point; one of the methods was "to furnish sumptuous free meals without number, and great quantities of intoxicating liquors to legislators." Another was "to let the persons to be influenced win large sums of money in card games." Still another was "to debase them morally by procuring for their entertainment lascivious women who were on the payroll of lobbyists and who were willing to run the whole gamut, so to speak, of immorality." V. O. Key opined that these were lurid folklore, and that it will remain a matter of conjecture how accurate such stories were.[25] In any case, he agrees that the extent of such techniques of corruption has declined over the past half century and that they survive chiefly in some state legislatures. He rightly notes that outright monetary corruption is found in relatively small groups interested in legislation that involves matters of great and immediate monetary value, such as small loan companies, public utilities, racetrack operators, contractors, gambling syndicates, and the like. It may take the form of contributions to party treasuries and campaign funds.[26] Key observes that "the distinction between a campaign contribution and a bribe cannot always be made with certainty." He cites a case that occurred in connection with a natural gas bill where an agent for Superior Oil Company distributed gifts of $2,500 which were later described as contributions to senatorial campaign funds, unrelated to any votes on the bill. Many wondered.

It has been customary in some quarters to distinguish between administrative, legislative, and judicial corruption (see next chapter), but such a division, while pragmatically justifiable in terms of the availability of material, is not significant in terms of what is done. Because the Congress and state legislatures were the key decision-makers in America's past, lobbyists addressed themselves primarily to these legislators. In other countries, where the bureaucracy held the central position, much corruption occurred on this level (France, Germany, the developing countries as well and more especially the dictatorships), and so it stands to reason that where the judges have wide discretionary power, corruption will attack the courts. This was the case of Bacon, and there has been a certain amount of judicial corruption in the United States, though rather limited in scope. In a recent study of the corrupt judge,[27] some cases of corruption in federal courts are examined. Rightly the author observes at the outset that "the office is customarily, legally, and almost instinctively regarded as sacrosanct."[28] And he adds, "A judge is the epitome of honor among men, the highest personage of the law." There follow a number of highly normative statements such as Chief Justice John Marshall's statement that a judge must be "perfectly and completely independent with nothing to influence or control him but God and his conscience." The political skeptic may well ask whether there is any such person as a completely independent one. Is not everybody bound to be influenced by his social and class position, and the more so the less he realizes it? It may be true that "to deviate from the most rigid honesty and impartiality is to betray the integrity of the law," but then such betrayal seems to be the rule rather than the exception. Yet, the more specific kind of influence which expresses itself in bribes is another matter. Here the United States has seen the emergence of a code, The Canons of Judicial Ethics, which was formulated in 1922–1924 by a committee headed by Chief Justice Taft. It was adopted by the American Bar Association and embodies "what the people have a right to expect from judges." By these Canons, a judge may not accept from a lawyer an inadequately secured loan, he may not appear on a commercially sponsored radio program on which legal advice is given, nor may he conduct a newspaper column. He may not accept presents or favors from a lawyer, litigant, or their friends. He may not be the director of lending institutions such as banks, insurance, or mortgage companies. The recent case of Supreme Court Justice Fortas involved the violation of some of these standards and he was obliged to resign from the Court.[29]

Corruption is relatively rare in the judiciary of the United States, but by no means absent. A list[30] of federal judges whose official conduct has been the subject of Congressional inquiry contains fifty-four names extending over the entire history of the Republic; more names have been added since the list was compiled. Federal judges have often been engaged in business activities, and the assertion that "there are absolutely no facts which would indicate that any of these judges ever permitted their private business obligations to interfere with the integrity of the judicial process"[31] does not prove the soundness of such a tradition; for the mere fact that these business activities are a matter of public record tells little about it. In any case, such an arrangement would involve judges in the mentality of business and that may warp their judgment in matters of social policy. The well-known and often-commented-upon conservatism of the bench may well be related to such an arrangement. The countercase of Mr. Justice Douglas of the U.S. Supreme Court is hardly reassuring. A recent study of three flagrant cases of corrupt judges —Martin T. Manton, J. Warren Davis, and Albert W. Johnson —which occurred in the thirties concluded that "unsettled economic conditions, particularly those associated with the depression, coupled with a deteriorating state of a judge's financial condition, produce a climate in which judicial corruption can flourish." No discernible functionality attaches to these cases, and in view of the fact that the functioning of the judiciary depends upon its integrity, it is hard to see how it could be otherwise. The crucial function of the judiciary in maintaining and enforcing the law would seem to suggest that only where such corruption might mitigate the formal rigidity of the law in an autocratic regime could such functionality develop through its softening effect.

In the United States and other advanced welfare state orders corruption may, however, take the form of prejudicial discretion where the legal provisions are equivocal. The expansion of governmental activities into every nook and cranny of a people's economic affairs produces many situations in which corruption can easily develop through favorites and the misuse of discretionary authority on the part of administrative officials, induced by such activities on the part of the corrupter as campaign contributions, gifts, and the like. Regulatory commissions which possess the power of life and death through the granting or denial of licenses are easily a prey. Here the corruptions may not involve money payments, but career opportunities and the intermeshing of jobs. Some commissions of this type in the United States are largely staffed by men whose careers were in the industry or business to be regulated; it is natural that such commissioners should be thinking in terms prejudiced in favor of corporations highly successful in the field.[32] Not only regulatory commissions but administrative services are involved in such temptations.

A striking case—one of quite a few—occurred in the United States recently, involving a department which had enjoyed a high reputation for integrity in spite of its involvement in the business which it regulated, namely the United States Department of Agriculture. The Billie Sol Estes case (1962) involved a skillful operator who had taken full advantage of the law, and eventually had stretched it to amass a fortune in connection with manipulating subventions, credits, and discretionary grants made in conjunction with fertilizer programs, cotton allotments, and grain storage facilities. It would serve no useful purpose to go into the rather complex operations as revealed by the eventual investigations.[33] The case which eventually landed the corrupter in jail for fifteen years involved the misuse of public funds and gifts to individuals and party coffers, including election campaigns. One student of the affair concluded that "it is questionable whether or not, in this case, corruption served a useful purpose." The hope that it might lead to a reevaluation of the policy of subventions has not been fulfilled.[34] So the only purpose the case served was to alert administrators and legislators to the potentiality of corruption. The case also provided a conservative opposition with a welcome occasion for discrediting politicians and administrators whom they hoped to defeat. It is no doubt true that "whether they lead to the truth or to false accusations, the political and personal motives are often the strongest inducements to exposing political corruption." But that does not make the corruption functional, except in a very hyperbolic sense. When it came to light that the personal assistant of President Eisenhower, Mr. Sherman Adams, had been the recipient of valuable presents from a businessman who expected to benefit from his personal intervention, it may have been no more than a case of speeding up governmental action that should have been taken anyhow.[35] But it was a case illustrating what has come to be known as the rule of "Caesar's wife," who must not only be virtuous, but must appear to be so. Unfortunately, a strong emphasis on appearance may have the effect of making it seem more important that appearances be preserved than that the substance be achieved. Also, certain kinds of system-related "corruptions" may be part of the system's functioning. A good many of the present indictments of men in authority for being related to "the establishment" suffer from this paradox. A revolutionary's notion of public benefit may be and usually will be radically at variance with the system's inherent make-believe. It will be our task in the next chapter to attempt a clarification of this complex issue, and thereby relate the pathology of corruption to those of violence and betrayal.

CHAPTER
10

THE FUNCTIONALITY OF CORRUPTION

ED BANFIELD, a few years ago, undertook to show in a study of political influence in Chicago municipal politics that corruption often is highly functional. The argument is essentially focused on the type of situation in which a rigid and/or antiquated political system can only be made to work by circumventing the legally required processes or by making men do what the promoter wants them to do by handouts of one kind and another. This situation is not, of course, unique, but quite common in established political orders; such long-lasting structures as the Chinese and Russian empires were notorious for their corruption; an ill-paid government service extracted from the public illicit payments for doing things which they were supposed to do anyhow, or for not doing such things as collecting taxes and customs duties or punishing offenders against the law. While such massive corruption eventually contributed to the collapse of these systems, it helped to maintain and operate them for long periods of time. But such is not limited to autocratic orders; it is equally true of republican and democratic ones. Besides the United States, the Roman Republic comes to mind, which eventually became so thoroughly corrupt that it collapsed.

The Roman system was extremely complicated, and in the absence of any attempt at effective constitutional codification, the mass of laws and customs by which the Roman political order worked was full of contradictions and offered many opportunities of conflict and even deadlock. This is not the place to enter into the details of this complex system.[1] Several kinds of legislative assemblies overlapped with each other, administrative officials likewise had conflicting and overlapping duties and functions, and to complete the difficulty of effective movement, the tribunes of the people had, as a check on aristocratic power, an almost unlimited right of obstructing the acts of other power wielders.

The widespread corruption in Rome seems to have been the consequence of an unwieldy electoral system which derived from history. The steady expansion of the Roman electorate through conquest and the absorption of many of the conquered towns into Roman citizenship opened the door wide to all kinds of manipulations, especially since the actual voting continued to be done at Rome so that an ever larger part of the electorate had to travel long distances and had to be induced to do so by candidates. There was also the problem of which one of the "tribes" they were to be included in, though eventually new tribes were admitted, which led to further maneuvers since the voting was by tribes.[2] Eventually, toward the end of the Republic, men like Crassus spent huge sums to bribe the electorate, as did certain factions of nobles as well as ascendant groups.[3] All in all, it can be concluded that the changing economic and social conditions which Rome's expansion had engendered made it increasingly impossible for the traditional system to function effectively.

At the same time the expansion and colonial acquisitions of Rome throughout the Mediterranean world offered ever larger opportunities for the kind of corruption that is often associated with colonial administration; the posts in these provinces beyond

Italy were looked upon as opportunities for self-enrichment, and some of the records of the great cases of such corruption are reasonably well known because men of lasting fame, especially Cicero, were involved in trying them. The funds spent in electoral and legislative corruption were thus gathered and a subsystem of corrupt relationships developed, which consisted in "investing money" to secure colonial posts which were then expected to repay with large interest what had been thus invested. As with the tax farmers of the later Empire and the French monarchy in the days of absolutism corruption served to substitute a market economy for a managed one, as we shall discuss below. If corruption had not, under such conditions, served a sustaining function, it is hard to believe that it would have lasted.

This system was closely linked with the ascendancy of the Senate. From the time of the Gracchi (120 B.C.) onward, several men arose who challenged this predominance of the Senate and stood up to the oligarchy which had manipulated the elections and the votes in elected assemblies. After the Gracchi there were Cinna, Pompey, Caesar, Catiline, as well as Marius. These leaders called Populares, usually of noble birth themselves, might well have been quite satisfied if the Senate had been willing to endorse what they considered needed measures, but when it proved impossible they adopted methods which involved them in corruption on a large scale. Although claiming to do so for the public benefit ("the people") they appear mostly to have been motivated by ambition and the pursuit of power.

Corruption arose therefore from the aspirations of individuals for high office and controlling power, including that of leading Rome's armies and achieving military glory. Thus the conclusion is in line with Montesquieu's reflections that the empire was the decisive corrupting influence through the enormous spoils that it provided. A recent historian has rightly concluded that "in the last analysis, the whole constitutional development of

Rome is seen to be a faithful reflection of her external history."[4] That external history was one of ruthless conquest and domination. There was no such ideological sentimentality as that of the "White Man's Burden" or the "rights of man" to disturb the exploitative rapacity of the Roman victors. "The idea of power without responsibility, of profit without service, which was dominant in the foreign administration, came at last to pervade the whole life of the people and there was a complete breakdown of political morality." The same critic adds: "The most remarkable thing about the situation is not the prevalence of corruption but the easy toleration of it."[5] Remarkable perhaps in the perspective of a Christian conscience, but not so in light of a pagan mentality. The provinces were "farms" of the Roman people to be enjoyed to the best of one's ability.

The Roman situation after the Punic Wars may be compared with that of Britain in the eighteenth century. In both places, during these periods, politics was the in-fighting of prepotent individuals without much of a program, within the limited circle of an aristocracy.[6] Since it was all "within the family," a certain amount of corruption was not realized to be such: in England the pocket boroughs were seen as functionally related to the system, as Burke argued in a famous defense of the system,[7] and similarly in Rome the client-system provided a way for acquiring votes under conditions of an expanding *urbs,* a city spread over a good part of the peninsula.

It may have been the hope of some that all this corruption, which had become necessary to make the ancient Republic function as the heart of an empire, would cease when the imperial organization became openly recognized in the generations after Augustus. But it did not work out that way. The struggle against corruption was a continuous one during the long ages of imperial rule; in fact it to some extent institutionalized corruption of a sort in the way in which the Pretorian guards exploited their emperor-making power for the securing of private gain.[8] The Roman story is by no means unique; other bureaucratic empires have shown the same propensity.[9] In a sense, the protracted efforts at coping with corruption are part of the history of bureaucracy: the constant tendency of officials to convert their offices into private gain, and the counter-effort to maintain them as administered for the public benefit.[10]

If one looks at corruption in historical perspective, its tendency to become regularized as an essential part of the functioning of a political system—and the more autocratic the more so—is incompatible with public service based upon merit. As merit has become associated with technical qualifications (including legal technicalities), corruption appears in subtler forms than before. It may be the kind of corruption that reserves the first choice to members of certain families or oligarchic groups. It may be the kind of corruption by which individuals manage to by-pass the tests set up for entrance by corrupting the examiners, as was widely done in China over many generations. Or advancement in the hierarchy may be secured through a variety of corrupt practices, ranging from contributions to party chests (explicitly outlawed in the United States)[11] to flattery of a superior or his relatives, or catering to his personal hobbies. Corruption may take such "subtle" forms as coddling students in order to induce them into one's classes because the salary is tied to the number of students by a fee system, as was the case in Germany until quite recently. Interlocking systems of corrupt influence have been built up by partisans of particular approaches to public policy, such as New Dealers (U.S.A.), Gaullists (France), or Stalinists (socialist dictatorships). The line is often hard to draw, because the causes to which these partisans were attached were by them seen as "in the public interest" and therefore anything done to promote them might escape the label of corruption. (This is the reason why certain analysts have tried to define corruption without reference to the public interest, but it does not work.[12]) This circumstance accounts for the theoretical possibility of a political order without any corruption, and it has been alleged that such a system actually functioned as the Inca state. To follow a recent summary, "here all the resources of the country were claimed for an economic plan that served the glorification of the ruler and the sun cult. Since there were no productive factors left untapped [a questionable assumption], it was impossible for civil servants to divert more revenues than were already allocated to them by the king in the economic plan. The incomes of civil servants and the people were precisely determined according to social position. This even affected nutrition patterns, number of wives, and the quality of clothes that were distributed. . . . Thus everyone received an appropriate income and to claim more constituted an offense against the Sapa Inca (Emperor) and the sun cult."[13] The last sentence shows that the preceding ones are normative and may be violated. What we have is a description of how the Inca state was supposed to function, and not how it actually functioned. Such a description might easily be made of the Hitler regime, if only certain kinds of statements contained in schoolbooks of the regime are consulted. In theory, that is to say as an abstract model, a corruptionless political order would have to be a completely static one, so that there were no emergent forces interested in breaking through the systemic armor of the order. It is, as Plato put it, "laid up in heaven," perhaps, but the function of corruption is so persistent in all dynamic orders that it can only be prevented from getting out of hand.

How this process of corruption reasserted itself in spite of vigorous efforts at stopping it is well illustrated in the case of Emperor Charles V.[14] Shortly after the conquest, the conquistadores, like their Roman predecessors, sought to convert the colonies into personal estates, known as *encomiendas*. Charles sought to stop it, but an uprising of the Pizarro brothers stopped this effort. Charles now sought to prevent new land from becoming similarly appropriated by putting it in charge of civil servants, known as *corregidores*. But these officials in their turn appropriated what the natives paid in the form of tribute. When Charles to stop this sent treasury officials to the colonies in 1550, they in turn became part of the system of exploiting proprietors which his successor, Philip II, accepted as the system of colonial administration: only with such corrupt practices could the formal control of Spain be maintained. One suspects that similar conditions flourished under the Incas, as they did in the Middle Ages. The issue of how to control the great church dignitaries never ceased in spite of recurrent waves of reform which served to stop the corruption from getting out of hand. But church benefices remained so rich a source of private gain that eventually the issue became one between the secular rulers and the church who would bestow these benefices. In general, the state won out as long as the secular corruption continued. Only by a long process of self-epuration could the ecclesiastical control be recaptured.[15]

We are here face to face with one of the key conditions of corruption, especially visible in the totalitarian orders of our day, namely the tying of public office to some kind of belief or faith. For the testing of such belief or faith is at best fraught with uncertainties. It remains very much a matter of judgment, and for that reason can easily be corrupted. If the possession of such ideological qualifications is linked with considerable economic benefits, the temptation for corruption is great, but is usually disfunctional to the extent that the belief system is vital to the maintenance of the power system. In a sense one can generalize by saying that the economic values assert their superior strength as motivating forces, superior especially to all ideal motivations. This assertion brings the discussion face to face with the economics of corruption.

It is generally assumed that corruption is on balance unprofitable; that it is a waste. But in recent years, and especially in the light of experience with economic development, another view has been gaining ground, namely that corruption has positive effects. It has been argued that it serves to overcome the indifference and hostility of government to economic progress. "Graft can have beneficial effects," we are told[16] for it can persuade the bureaucracy to understand the needs of business enterprisers, and to give them greater freedom to engage in private initiative. Hence, secondly, graft may serve to get the government to act where action is required for "getting things moving," as was pointed out before. Because of these and related reasons, capital will be attracted; for its possessors are more likely to have confidence in the future. In developing countries the uncertainties of government seem to be the most severe handicap.[17] "By enabling enterprisers to predict and at times even control governmental action, which affects so many factors in a more or less planned economy, corruption helps to make investment of foreign capital possible. It has even been argued that corruption provides a field of operation for competition, since the highest bidder usually receives the license or whatever other factor is at the discretionary control of the government and its bureaucracy. Innovators will be able to break down resistance of entrenched interests. Corruption will provide a "hedge" against ill-conceived economic policy, since it can help to soften its impact. It is like an insurance against an otherwise incalculable risk. It has been argued that the corruption and carelessness of British government aided the country's economic development, while the efficiency and integrity of the French bureaucrats handicapped that of France, in spite of all of Colbert's interventions.[18] In short, in relation to the economy, corruption would appear functional, up to a point, though beyond it, the negative effects would outweigh such positive advantages and gains. In essence, the argument turns on the possibility or even the probability of the government of a new nation being more interested in other goals than economic development, more particularly its own entrenchment and enrichment, while it is at the same time assumed that business enterprisers are by their very function preoccupied with economic growth through their concern with the prosperity of their own enterprises. This may or may not be the case. In Puerto Rico the main impetus for economic development came from the government, which through its agencies, notably the Economic Development Administration, fostered the establishment of new enterprises. The integrity of the government's operations was a crucial condition of this "Operation Bootstrap." It would seem doubtful that any such development would have resulted from corrupting an indifferent administration. In other words, corruption may be a short-cut substitute for a government committed to economic development as a prime goal, from the viewpoint of one to whom this goal possesses priority, but even he would be better off with a government and a public committed to this goal. Where the government is popular, corruption in favor of economic development when other goals appear to the majority of the people more urgent is dysfunctional; it falsifies the democratic and electoral process.[19] Any argument that defends such falsification out of preoccupation with economic development would politically imply a revolutionary transformation of the government into one accepting the author's views and prepared to put them through dictatorially, if necessary.[20] This is actually the story behind many of the military coups in which military security technicians combine with economic development technicians to set aside democratic machinery, denounced as corrupt. From the businessman's viewpoint, such a change may recommend itself as "cheaper" than the corruption he had to practice to deflect the administrators from the course of action prescribed by popular or party decision. Even in highly developed countries, this may be a persuasive argument to many businessmen, as the rise of General de Gaulle could be said to prove; such a development cannot be excluded from the alternatives which the United States faces in the future. In a sense, and allowing for a different historical context, this may be said to have been the outlook of the urban middle class in supporting absolute monarchy in Europe in the seventeenth century; in France, in Austria, and in a number of German principalities, notably Prussia and Bavaria, voices which spoke thus were numerous.[21]

But it is an illusion to think that corruption disappears when it can no longer be aired in public, and as we have pointed out before, the more autocratic the regime, the more functional are varieties of corruption. In contemporary America with its mature democracy, even very illusive forms of corruption, such as those involved in the Sherman Adams case, will from time to time be exposed to the glare of publicity. That a man in an especially influential position may be corrupting the government's operations merely by making strategic telephone calls was "discovered" by Adams through such criticism. As he himself put it in his memoirs, it occurred to Mr. Adams rather late in the game; he wrote: "I was not sufficiently aware of the added importance that I might be giving to these inquiries [such, e.g., as calling the chairman of a regulatory commission] by handling them myself. A call or inquiry from the Assistant to the President was much more likely to cause interference than a call from a less prominent White House staff executive. If I had been alert to that fact at the time, I might have saved myself later embarrassment."[22] The mocking comment that "Mr. Adams' insight into the power of his position was astoundingly slow in coming" misses the point of functionality. Generally speaking the system of regulatory commissions has been corrupted to the point where its functioning is subject to the complaint of a concerned Senator that "it seems almost invariably to happen that when Congress attempts to regulate some group, the intended regulatees wind up doing the regulating."[23] This situation has given rise to demands for constitutional amendments which would more firmly institutionalize these bodies; the obvious "solution" would be to incorporate them under civil service into the executive establishment, as far as their administrative functions are concerned, and to establish an administrative court for their quasi-judicial functions, reinforcing it by strict professional requirements for its staffing.[24] The present functionality of corruption would thereby be reduced very substantially.

It is often maintained that the chances of such institutional reform are so poor, or at any rate its prospects so remote, that corruption has to be accepted as an intermediary solution. This seems to be the implication of Edward Banfield's study on *Political Influence*.[25] He argues that the wider the distribution of authority, the larger the stock of power that is required if proposals are to be adopted.[26] In a context like the city of Chicago, the number of autonomous actors who are involved in the adoption of needed proposals is quite large; quite a few of them can be brought into line only by corruption. If this were not done, many projects which are in the public interest would remain unaccomplished. Such an argument may be readily supported by individual cases such as those which Banfield describes, but it would not cover the many cases in which corruption prevented the adoption of perhaps more urgent proposals, or even their consideration. Banfield shows that the value judgment "there should be no corruption" clashes with a wide distribution of power and indeed the democratic requirement that all actors should be autonomous,[27] in other words that there would have to be accomplished a centralization of power and a reduction of autonomy of individuals and groups of actors. As long as such changes cannot be brought about, corruption will remain. It is endemic to the political structure. It may, however, become so all-pervasive that an effort at institutional reform will have to be made, if the political order is not to become so static as to generate explosive revolutionary ferment, with the consequent violence and betrayal of its underlying belief systems and institutional core. It can be seen at such a juncture that corruption is closely linked with the other pathologies, especially violence and betrayal.

Corruption may, therefore, afflict a society in its ideatic core. These kinds of corruptions, though of great political effect, often go unobserved or unchallenged. The totalitarian dictatorships have shown a considerable concern over them, as have religious regimes, such as the medieval European order. It may be very difficult to cope with. In a recent article I pointed out the subtly corrupting influence which foundations and other sources of funds may have. Student rebels have highlighted the risks involved in financing of research by the military, although the claims advanced in this connection are often rather extreme, bordering on the absurd.[28] What foundations need to face is that they form part of the "power structure," or more accurately of the political order. As such they must allow themselves to be subjected to the controls which all power wielders are under in a reasonable free society or democracy. The dictum of Lord Acton that "all power tends to corrupt" applies to them also, but a most troublesome kind of corruption it is, much more insidious than the crude criminal types. The life of the mind is a very tender plant, easily thwarted by an ill wind. Claims and counterclaims have been made, and several Congressional investigations have been undertaken, each concerned over an issue which turned out to be unreal: the Walsh Committee (1912), which sought to prove that foundations were distorting things in a conservative direction, the Cox Committee and the Reece Committee (1952 and 1953), which sought to establish that the foundations were promoters of "radicalism," and the more recent Patman investigations (1962–1964), which linked foundations to the concentration and abuse of economic power. Mutually contradictory to some extent, they did not focus on the crucial issue of intellectual corruptions; they were sparked by a false "political" issue. The main concern needs to be the disturbing and disorienting impact which foundations are capable of exercising in sensitive areas of scholarship and learning, as well as public policy. On the assumption that the greatest benefit accrues to the public from a free science and scholarship, such influences are apt to reduce this benefit. The testimony of the respective beneficiaries proves little in this connection.[29] Nor has the point much to do with the individual foundation executive's integrity and good will. It is however conceivable that such administrators, even though responsible to no one except their superiors in the organization, may have a better notion as to what is in the public interest. This is particularly possible where they channel the science of highly developed countries into less developed areas.[30] Here we would in our terminology have cases of functional corruption; it may of course happen in any context. A detailed study would probably reveal a number of cases of intellectual corruption that proved highly functional in America, as well as in Europe, but it would take us too far afield to try to enter into these cases. Still, a key foundation executive has written that "it is almost inevitable that primary concern, even loyalty, tends to attach to the source of main financial support. . . . These unhealthy disturbances within a university are not, I believe, as likely to result from philanthropic foundation activities as they are from activities of the federal government."[31] It is the point where corruption can and does occur, even if only through "anticipating the reactions" of key foundation executives.[32]

In terms of political theory, the argument relates to the hoary discussion about the corrupting impact of despotism. John Stuart Mill has written perhaps the most balanced refutation of the notion of "good despotism"—popular from Plato through the Enlightenment to contemporary totalitarians. There is here the root of the basic paradox of this field of political pathology: the total control advocated for eliminating corruption in its more specific and tawdry forms is itself likely to involve the total corruption which has been so eloquently described by men like the Soviet scientist Sakharov. When speaking on this corruption, Sakharov focuses on "censorship." He writes: "We are all familiar with the passionate and closely argued appeal against censorship by the outstanding Soviet writer A. Solzhenitsyn. He as well as other writers . . . have clearly shown how incompetent censorship *destroys the living soul* of Soviet literature; but the same applies of course to all other manifestations of social thought, causing stagnation and dullness and preventing fresh and deep ideas." In his prefatory note, Salisbury adds that Sakharov "emphasizes the debilitating effect of the censorship on Soviet literature and on Soviet creative thinking," thereby emphasizing the disfunctional effect of that kind of intellectual corruption. Its agency is a special office, the Chief Literary Administration (Gavlit), and Solzhenitsyn in his famous letter of protest suggested that magazines and publishers reject manuscripts because they anticipate a negative judgment of Gavlit. Hence Solzhenitsyn demanded its abolition as unconstitutional. It is well known that the Goebbels ministry of propaganda under Hitler engaged in parallel activities. Thus, at this point, the problems of the next part, dealing with propaganda, heave into view. For the corruption of the mind is the most serious disfunctionality of propaganda and secrecy. Both are ubiquitous phenomena of politics.

Let me conclude by asserting that not only is propaganda corrupting, but every corrupt act is a betrayal; it does violence to the political order. The question of its functionality is closely linked to that of these other pathologies. Where it helps to adapt an antiquated or obsolete political order to changing conditions and givens, social, technological, convictional, it can be said to be functional. It is impossible to be more specific and precise, because these conditions vary greatly, as do the political orders that need adapting. The main conclusion therefore is that *it may be functional.* The other is that corruption may be reduced, but it is not likely ever to disappear. Like other utopian projects, the attempt to make it disappear is apt to wreck the political order and to generate an autocratic one which is more apt to be corrupt than the one it replaces, due to the rule we found that corruption increases with the rigidity and autocracy of such an order. Therefore one might, as Walter Goodman counsels, "temper indignation with philosophy." He cites Mr. Dooley: "The trouble with this house [the house of politics] is that it is occupied entirely by human bein's. If twas a vacant house, it cud aisily be kept clean." Though said about American politics at the turn of the century, it applies to all politics everywhere. But such gently cynical resignation carries the danger that the reduction of political corruption, which is a never-ending task precisely because of its ubiquity, is neglected. For such corruption may well be functional; it is kept so by the efforts to get rid of it.[33]

PART IV

Secrecy and Propaganda

CHAPTER

11

NATURE AND FUNCTION OF SECRECY AND PROPAGANDA

SECRECY is, as we saw, cleary related to betrayal and corruption. For betrayal is often the betrayal of a secret, and corruption is usually secreted and ceases to be corruption when openly engaged in. Secrecy is for many a pejorative term, and hence some philosophers, notably Bentham and Kant, have been inclined to make it the hallmark of immoral action. Action which must shun the light of day must be bad, they thought. Bentham more particularly was insistent that the proceedings of representative assemblies must be public. He thought that the objections to complete publicity, that is to say the arguments for secrecy, could be summed up in one proposition, that the public is incompetent to judge fairly the proceedings of a political assembly. Presumably the same kind of argument would apply to other governmental functions. There is no recognition in Bentham that secrecy may have a distinct function to perform.[1] Such a view reflects Bentham's primitive psychology; he would no doubt have been rather unresponsive to the subtle reflections of a Georg Simmel when he explores the functions of secrecy in human relations.[2] Even so, the function of secrecy is more generally recognized and understood than that of treason or corruption or even that of violence, at least non-governmental violence. We shall presently explore the reasons for this fact further.

Propaganda is, like secrecy, a tampering with communications; it seems to conflict with the norm of candor and sincerity, which are considered ethically good. But whereas secrecy withholds information, propaganda distorts information or even adds misinformation. The popular view of propaganda is simply that it consists of lies. But while lying may at times be a method of propagandists, it often is not. An inspection of the propagandist's activities shows that he is a person who hands out information in order to gain benefits (material or ideal advantages) for himself or the group he is acting for. More specifically he seeks to persuade people to take or not to take particular actions which benefit the group he is acting for. Ordinarily the group will pay for the service. Hence it is usually important to ascertain who pays for the propaganda.[3] The crucial function, then, of both political propaganda and secrecy is to manipulate men in relation to the political order, to make them support it, at least not to oppose it, whether these men be citizens or foreigners, more especially rulers of other political orders.

As a consequence of the function of manipulation, both secrecy and propaganda will increase with the number of persons who have to be manipulated. Political and governmental secrecy consists of the process of secreting information about political entities, especially when that information has significant implications for rival entities of the general public. It is part of the topic to discuss efforts made by such rival organizations to break the secret, more especially espionage. We have had occasion to touch upon the subject when dealing with treason, which as mentioned consists so often in betraying secrets, but shall devote more detailed attention to it in Chapter 13.

Where secrecy cannot be preserved or where it is decided to prefer publicity, propaganda steps in to manipulate by positive misinformation and thus to swamp the channels; jamming in international broadcasting is its modern technical form.

There was a time when the presumption was altogether in favor of secrecy. At the time of the emergence of the modern state, the doctrine of the *arcana imperii*, the secrets of rule, which dominated the early modern period, taught that these "mysteries of state," as James I used to call them, are not for persons outside the narrow circle of power wielders.[4] It is not generally realized that even the proceedings of Parliament were supposed to be a closely guarded secret well into the eighteenth century.[5] There was, then, legislative as well as administrative secrecy. It was often broken by shrewd journalists, such as Dr. Johnson, a Drew Pearson of his day. But legally such a breach was treated and prosecuted as "treason."

In both legislative and administrative secrecy it was largely a matter of secreting the proceedings; but the results, such as laws, ordinances, taxes, and so on were of course public. On the other hand, in foreign and military matters, the decisions arrived at as well as the process of arriving at them were usually subject to strictest secrecy, and all modern states have, usually by law, sought to protect official secrets.[6] These enactments clearly show that a good deal of secrecy is considered functional, and that its breach is dangerous. However, there is a good deal of such breaking of official secrecy, and the more democratic the political order, the more so.[7] For all such secrecy conflicts with the principle of popular control, and the related freedom of the press and generally of expression. There is also the function of the secret ballot. It became a battle cry of liberal politics as it was claimed to be necessary to protect the anti-establishment voter against the pressure of his patron, especially in rural districts. A very striking description of such pressure was recently offered for the Cumberlands of the Kentucky coal fields. Related to this problem is the importance of secret ballots in party conclaves and conventions which has always been stressed.[8] Secrecy constitutes a basic paradox of democratic politics which no amount of subtle disputation can eliminate.[9]

Students of the legislative process in modern democratic states have shown that a measure of secrecy is needed for the achieving of satisfactory results.[10] Indeed, so strong is the need for secrecy that any effort to do away with it, such as radical reforms, has merely had the result of shifting the scene for the important decision making: from plenary sessions into committees, from committees into party caucuses, and so forth. The extravagant demands for publicity in academic proceedings which are being voiced at the present time usually overlook the force of this law of politics; they forget that if faculty proceedings are made public, men who do not believe it desirable that their deliberations be made public can gather into private conclaves and make their decisions *in clausuro*. An interesting illustration was provided in the Weimar Republic when the Communist party became strong enough to claim representation on the Committee on Foreign Affairs. Since it was known that the Communists would communicate what they learned to their friends in Moscow, it became customary for the Foreign Minister to communicate with a selected group which did not include the Communist party, and then meet again with the full committee to communicate what it was safe to tell the Communists.[11]

Generally speaking, administrative process is more secret than legislative process, and judicial process is usually divided into a public procedure, the trial, and a strictly secret procedure by which the court arrives at its decision.[12] Even here, a breach has developed in the form of the dissenting opinion, practiced in Britain and the United States, as well as the Dominions, but only recently considered on the Continent, where the German Constitutional Court (but not the Supreme Judicial Court) has after bitter controversy allowed a dissenting opinion to be voiced.[13] In passing it may be noted that jury deliberations are also traditionally surrounded with the strictest secrecy. It is a matter of excluding undue influence and exploitation by an often sensationalist press. But breaches do at times occur, when jurymen "tell," as happened in the Hiss case and other cases of great public interest. Opinion is greatly divided on how to evaluate such breaches. But in general secrecy is considered functional, in the sense that the function of the jury, itself under serious attack for many years, can be maintained only with the employment of secrecy.

In short, secrecy is eminently functional in many government operations. And if the functionality of secrecy is clear in so-called free political orders, it is even more patent in autocratic ones, especially in the totalitarian systems of our time. In these regimes the all-pervading secretiveness epitomized in the operations of the secret police becomes linked with the monopolization and extension of propaganda to be taken up later. The disfunctional excesses of this secretiveness are in these regimes at times quite marked. It is a characteristic of autocracy through the ages. A striking example of excessive and hence disfunctional secretiveness is furnished by Philip II of Spain, the absolutist ruler of the sixteenth century. "Even to the Ministers in whom Philip appeared most to confide, he often gave but half his confidence. Instead of frankly furnishing them with a full statement of facts, he sometimes made so imperfect a disclosure, that, when his measures came to be taken, his counsellors were surprised to find of how much they had been kept in ignorance. When he communicated to them any foreign dispatches, he would not scruple to alter the original, striking out some passages and inserting others, so as best to serve his purpose. The copy in this garbled form was given to the council."[14]

Autocracy likewise causes the invasion of privacy, that is to say the secrecy of the private sphere. There has been a corresponding trend in free societies to break into the private sphere where the public interest of security seems to require it. An illustration is provided by Congress's legislating that the membership in the Communist party is to be a matter of public record.[15] The excesses to which such an approach may be carried are manifest in totalitarian regimes when they encourage children to report remarks uttered in the family circle to the police, if such remarks disclose a hostility to the regime or its rulers.[16] Constitutional democracies have, with considerable variations in detail, provided privacy, that is to say functional secrecy, where such privacy serves the process of democracy, as in the case of the secret ballot, but also where it does not impinge upon the public sphere—freedom of religion is a case in point. Again, even these regimes have been invading the private sphere when the safety and security of the political order are thought to require it, as in wiretapping.[17] Such tendencies may be reinforced or obstructed by particular religious beliefs and cultural traditions, but such special deviants must not be allowed to obscure the inherent logic of the standard of public interest, vague as it is,[18] as the yardstick for striking a balance between too much and too little privacy (private secrecy). The dignity of the individual has been held so crucial a constituent element of the democratic belief system that it calls for recognition except in a clear case of disfunctional secrecy, such as hiding a fugitive from justice or betraying official secrets.

In his study on secrecy, Edward Shils has depicted some of these dilemmas and his conclusion seems right that

> Ideological extremism is the enemy of the privacy and publicity which support our liberties. It is the progenitor of the combination of symbolic

secrecy and universal publicity.[19] The pluralistic society is the society of privacy and publicity. Privacy and publicity are the parallels in the focus of knowledge and sensitivity, of autonomy and cooperation based on affinity.[20]

Perhaps the principal merit of this significant study is its introduction of the concept of privacy into the usually oversimplified dichotomy of secrecy vs. publicity. The concept of privacy renders the notion of functional secrecy more subtle. Functional secrecy, of which allowable privacy is an important part, by definition is system-maintaining. It is obviously the crux of the argument in support of secrecy in diplomacy and military policy.[21] Woodrow Wilson once asserted, in his *Congressional Government,* that "there is not any legitimate privacy about matters of government. Government must," he continued, "if it is to be pure and correct in its processes, *be absolutely public in everything* that affects it."[22] Such propositions are a radical overstatement of the disfunctionality of secrecy. The sound core of it is that secrecy (privacy) should be avoided as possibly disfunctional in the democratic process, unless a convincing case can be made out for its functionality.[23] Robert Luce, in his detailed work on legislative procedure, after citing Wilson, asserts that "the complete justification of privacy is that its absence would inure to the injury of public business." Luce is preoccupied with the functioning of the legislature. He found five functions of secrecy in committee work of the American Congress; they presumably hold *ceteris paribus* for other legislatures. There is first the function of securing information from persons who might hesitate or even refuse to talk in public. Second, there is the function of facilitating legislation by avoiding public stands on issues which would make compromise difficult. Third, purely private matters should be protected. Fourth, one should avoid assisting a common enemy, as in war. His fifth point may seem less conclusive, for he argues that party caucuses are entitled to privacy and such privacy should therefore be protected. It has been authoritatively stated that Congress, "although opposing secrecy as a principle of government or diplomacy, in fact attempts to accommodate its behavior to the existing situation by establishing whatever control it can over certain areas of secrecy."[24] We shall deal below (Chapter 13) with the particular problems created for Congress by the need for secrecy in exercising its control over foreign and military affairs as well as the work of intelligence agencies.[25]

Here we shall concentrate on the problems of privacy in the context of the contemporary "meritocracy"—a bureaucracy based on technical competence. Such meritocracy depends upon the possibility of a supervisor or superior being able to speak with complete frankness in reporting on his subordinates. If his views are not kept confidential, he will not be able to do so, since he has to maintain a satisfactory working relationship with them. Again, all investigatory work requires secrecy for its effectiveness. Unfortunately, such operations have a way of expanding beyond what is functional, because of their secrecy. Privacy is needlessly invaded, and the secrecy becomes disfunctional, as became painfully evident in the practices of Senator Joseph McCarthy and the Un-American Activities Committee.[26]

One feature of such proliferation of secrecy (and privacy) is that matters are considered secret which are or could be known to everyone. When such secretiveness takes the form of forbidding high officials of the government to express in print their critical views of matters of grave public concern, it becomes disfunctional in a democracy, because the system depends for its functioning upon an adequately informed public opinion. The much-discussed "credibility gap" on the federal level in the U.S. under Johnson was to some extent due to this tradition, but of course also to the breaking of it; men who had served under Kennedy and continued to serve under Johnson felt free to criticize the latter without restraint, often to the great detriment of the country and its war effort. This situation became possible because for a long time it was not officially acknowledged that the U.S. was engaged in war, the reason being the lack of a formal declaration of one. Even so, in response to vital need many data were withheld, and when information reached the public through other channels the disillusionment was great. The allegations of atrocities have found widespread belief among a disaffected public which was inclined to feel that anything might be true since they had not been told. The government's rejoinder that much of this information would have given "aid and comfort to the enemy" (the traditional formula for defining treason under the U.S. constitution) aggravated the difficulty. The bitter disagreement between the government, the Congress, the mass media, and the public was largely a disagreement over the functionality or disfunctionality of secrecy.

At such a point, secrecy and propaganda may be closely linked. For not only may the withholding of important information be a part of a propaganda campaign, but certain lines of propaganda may presuppose secrecy, such as the withholding of information about reverses.[27] All these problems are found in an aggravated form in totalitarian regimes, and the credibility gap may actually develop into a vacuum.[28] In general it may be said that the inclination of officials and party functionaries to include information on issues of public policy under the classification of "official secrets" is both widespread and harmful. Such information cannot be compared with information about strictly private matters which a doctor or a lawyer is obligated to secrete although such analogies are often made. The tendency under the party system to "privatize" policy deliberations by withdrawing the drafting into the secrecy of the upper echelons of the party bureaucracy threatens the well-functioning of the democratic system. On the other hand the demand, now often heard in connection with "democratizing" the parties, is largely unsound, because it would be disfunctional to have internal conflicts broadcast through sensationalist mass media, thus forestalling compromise. Even more mistaken is the demand, now frequently advanced by rebellious elements and backed by a "publicistic"[29] press, that the proceedings of internal organs of private or semiprivate institutions, such as the boards of business enterprises and the faculties of universities, should be publicized. Thus in response to such demands the Harvard faculty meetings are now broadcast to outsiders over the radio with the result that certain opinions are muffled and demagogic appeals are heard; for such publicity is a disfunctional invasion of privacy. It is disfunctional because privacy is a condition of the effectivness of such bodies. So great is the functional value of such secrecy that separate informal bodies are formed for the purpose of arriving at the consensus which decision-making requires. History shows that bodies have often been "defunctionalized" by publicity, as happened to the House of Commons mentioned before, and to the plenary sessions of Congress. Members increasingly talk to the outside—to publicity media and to "the galleries," as the old phrase goes, instead of to their colleagues. Many important points cannot be stated in the limelight of such publicity, while irrelevant rhetoric takes their place. In the two instances just mentioned, the party leadership in caucus or the committee (in the U.S.A.) will enable those responsible for policy decisions to maintain the necessary secrecy. The sphere of secrecy depends upon the task in hand and the setting within which it must be executed, with a presumption in favor of publicity under democratic conditions.

This presumption does not, however, hold where the individual is entitled to his private sphere. Here democracy presumes in favor of privacy and against publicity. George Orwell has, in *1984*, painted a distressing picture of the almost total lack of privacy in a fully developed and technologically advanced totalitarian regime. Through the tapping of all walls in private dwellings the secret police is put in position to ascertain what people say to each other in the intimacy of the home. This culmination of a widespread trend, to which wiretapping for the detection of crime, postal censorship in the armed forces of many countries for the alleged purpose of detecting traitors, defectors, and just indiscretions and the like belong, is an accepted feature of such totalitarian regimes; it is a radical abandonment of individualism; for the idea of the sacredness of privacy (of the home!) grew with the growth of individualism, and the notion of the sacredness of private property was intimately related to it.[30] We are not here concerned with the private, individual aspect of this privacy, nor with the normativity of these norms, but with the political interest and functionality involved. Has such privacy a distinctive function in particular political orders? The privacy of property clearly has in a competitive economy of advanced industrialism. For it serves the very competition; this is demonstrated by the length to which industrial firms will go in protecting their innovations as automobile manufacturers do in regard to their car designs. The vastly complicated system of legally protected patents serves this purpose[31] and is a striking instance of functional secrecy. But this range of issues is not my concern here. The privacy of the home, of correspondence and the like, is protected in democratic systems and the individual's private sphere surrounded by secrecy. What value has such an arrangement for the political order? The classical writers on politics, notably Plato and Aristotle, had little interest in or use for it. In many of the underdeveloped countries and their ancient civilizations it is not considered important or even valuable. The secrecy associated with it appears disfunctional. To get a perspective on its functionality, one has to ask about the role of the individual. His primary function is that of the independent voter.

The secrecy of the ballot illustrates the point. The function here is to insure that each voter is genuinely free to express his or her preference on persons and policies, that neither community pressures nor other forms of intimidation, such as losing one's job or the esteem of one's neighbors, should interfere with an individual's freedom of choice. There is a curious paradox involved in this outlook; for it seems contradictory to provide for the secreting of an individual's views on *public* issues. The traditional American saying "Stand up and be counted" relates to an older and less individualistic conception of democracy. It has therefore been argued that the secret ballot is surviving from the time when liberal groups in Europe were struggling against an autocratic monarchical state as happened in many parts of continental Europe during the first half of the nineteenth century. A truly democratic community, so the collectivist argument runs, would not need such secrecy. The argument is unrealistic; for the pressure of interest groups continues and is becoming more decisive in a pluralistic society. Hence the functionality of such secrecy is likely to increase rather than diminish in a fully democratized community and will have to be achieved in underdeveloped countries.

From the privacy of a man's political convictions, the argument leads to other facets of the individual's convictions, more especially in religious matters. By implication, these also are functional to a democratic order. Religion in turn shapes a man's personal conduct and habits, more particularly in matters of family and sex. The argument is essentially always the same: only an individual free to shape his own life and that of his immediate human relations is capable of fulfilling the crucial function of a citizen in a democratic community, and thereby the secrecy that is privacy becomes functional in a democracy.[32]

Thus the security needs of the community, requiring disclosure of some aspects of a man's attachments, may come to clash with his personal freedom and produce the torments of secrecy of which Shils has written so persuasively.[33] The ancient doctrine of "reason of state" is no great help in this dilemma, because a destruction of individual independence undermines the very order which reason of state thinking seeks to maintain.[34] This dimension illustrates anew that the balance between secrecy, publicity, and privacy is a delicate one which needs to be oriented toward the functionality of secrecy as the penultimate test.

The functionality of privacy and secrecy is inversely related to betrayal and treason, as we mentioned at the outset. For when in a certain situation the secreting of an act or of an item of information becomes disfunctional, betrayal becomes thereby functional. The airing of such public policy issues may be vital to the country's survival. Dramatic instances, such as that of Admiral Sims's criticism of United States naval policy, or Billy Mitchell's attack on air policy,[35] not to mention the more recent case of atomic submarines, illustrate the need to set aside discretion when the issue is of sufficient importance. But the extent to which such airing of official secrets can be considered functional presents a very difficult problem. Generally speaking, the revealers of secrets have usually had to pay for their boldness by the loss of their positions, or at least of promotion. How far this sort of thing can go is illustrated by the case of a British member of Parliament, Duncan Sandys, the son-in-law of Winston Churchill. He in 1939 found out from a military officer the questionable disposition of guns around London and complained to the Ministry of Defense about the inadequate protection of the city. Thereupon the Ministry threatened to prosecute him for violating the Official Secrets Act, presumably in case he should make this information public. The *Spiegel* affair in postwar Germany[36] offers another illustration of how far the official view of the disfunctionality of the revealing of secrets may go.

In psychological terms, it may be true, as Simmel has argued, that the lure of secrecy consists for the possessor of a secret partly in the possibility of betraying it.[37] It gives the possessor of a secret a certain sense of exclusivity whereby he is set apart from ordinary mortals; every one of us has at some point smiled at eager young diplomats clutching their brief cases carefully locked and containing—the morning newspaper! This psychology may in turn be the cause of the proliferation of secret societies and of fraternal orders with secret rituals in a democratic, egalitarian society where potentially everything is public. The privacy in such groups and organizations is restricted, however, to the group itself. Between the individual members there is often a marked lack of privacy.[38] Another scholar has argued that the publicity and equality prevalent in a democratic society are typically counterbalanced by the ubiquity of clubs and other kinds of exclusive groupings.[39] Simmel on the other hand insists that secret groupings are the characteristic of aristocratic and oligarchic societies; he cites in support of this proposition the fact that in Venice the state inquisitors were unknown, and that in certain Swiss towns in the aristocratic days some of the most important officers were known as "secret ones."[40] Neither of these "proofs" proves more than that secrecy plays a role in oligarchic societies as well as others, which no one would deny, since it is ubiquitous; whether there is more or less of it than in democratic or monarchical societies would be difficult to ascertain and necessitate a rather farflung comparison.

Georg Simmel has formulated another general hypothesis concerning privacy (secrecy) relating it to the degree of civilization. "It seems," he suggests, "that with increasing cultural utility [*Zweckmaessigkeit*] public affairs become steadily more public, while the affairs of individuals become more secret."[41] It seems to me that this development is related to democratization rather than to civilization in general. For no such trend is recorded for imperial China and Rome. The "progress" of culture and civilization did not cause any increasing publicity of public affairs, but rather the opposite as Rome turned from the Republic into an Empire. The prevailing mood is epitomized in the Chinese saying: "Those who talk do not know; those who know do not talk." When Simmel writes that "politics, administration and courts lost their secrecy while the individual gained the chance of ever greater withdrawal," it seems in the perspective of the political analyst that both of these trends are the response to democratization; for secrecy loses systemic functionality in a democracy, in the public sector, while it gains it in the private sector, especially if the economy is a competitive market economy. It is not the historical development as such, as Simmel is inclined to surmise, but the growth of participation in politics under increasingly democratic conditions, which causes that "what is in its very nature public and concerns all, becomes . . . increasingly publicized; and what has according to its inner meaning a separate being [*Fuersichsein*], the personal affairs of each individual, become increasingly private."[42] In the totalitarianism of the present century a sharp reaction in the opposite direction has occurred, which Simmel and men of his generation did not anticipate, much less take into account. What concerns all has become increasingly again a secret of rule *(arcana imperii)*, as it had been under absolutism, as noted above. At the same time the affairs of individuals are being deprivatized and made part of public records and thereby subject to official inspection.[43] These regimes are inclined to view as functional without limits practically all secrecy.

In sum it may be said at this point in our analysis that the manipulation of the ruled by the ruler, through secreting and through propaganda, is endemic in all political orders, and hence in all politics. But the functionality of both are dependent upon the system of which they form a part, and hence their evaluation must vary. We have shown how this differentiation presents itself in the case of secrecy; we shall in the next chapter deal with propaganda. Here it remains to observe that secrecy also acts as an important factor between systems rivaling with or influencing each other. In recent years the destruction of privacy and the expansion of official secrecy, indeed the whole apparatus of the secret police state, have forced other states to adapt to the world of totalitarianism, to meet their competition with analogous weapons and thus to increase official secrecy and reduce privacy by the institution of police and investigatory methods. Thereby these other states have endangered their systemic order and hence their internal security. The functionality of secrecy is often too readily assumed without adequate proof. Many of the matters secreted by such agencies as the CIA and the FBI could just as well be a matter of public record, and other such matters subject to scrutiny by Congress and other administrative agencies. This problem is by no means restricted to the United States. It has led to bitter conflicts in Britain, France, and Germany in recent years. These problems of intelligence will be dealt with further in the last chapter.

CHAPTER

12

PROPAGANDA, MASS COMMUNICATIONS, AND THEIR PATHOLOGY[1]

MUCH of the pro-democracy oratory with which the market place is filled is little more than hypocrisy. Freedom may still be a cause, but it is unlikely to be served by offering up incense at the altar of bygone views—views begotten in a day when no methods of mass communication, controlled by huge corporate enterprises, had been placed in the position of manipulating the mind and morals of the citizen, the common man. The Northcliffes and Beaverbrooks, the Springers and Cotys, the Hearsts and Howards, the Sarnoffs and Paleys and Luces are as champions of liberty quite different from Benjamin Franklin and John Stuart Mill. The cynic might say that the anguished cry "Give me liberty or give me death" has been converted into "Give me liberty *and* give me profits!" In defining propaganda above we spoke of it as a tampering with communications, and said that the popular view of propaganda is simply that it consists of lies. The response to this naïve proposition was at a time: propaganda analysis. A group of well-meaning pedagogues thought that you could combat the massive propaganda of government and mass communications by an educational effort.[2] Such an initiative was bound to fail in the premises; for to succeed it would have to be able to muster propaganda campaigns as massive as those it wished to combat—a utopian enterprise.

The pathology in this area of politics is inherent in the very premises of popular government. For, on the one hand, it is intended to be a government *by* the people. What this means is that the people are supposed to be a self-propelled, independent, free-willing entity and composed of persons of like character. On the other hand, a popular government depends upon and guarantees the freedom of the press, which has come to mean the freedom of mass communications.[3] This freedom is seen as expressed in the freedom of the proprietors of the technical apparatus required for such communications. They are free, therefore, to engage in propaganda, and many of them do so, while others practice to a greater or lesser degree a measure of self-restraint. Governmental operation of such means of mass communication, as is common in Europe (BBC, ORTF, and the regional stations in Germany, such as Westfunk), substitutes merely another, party-oriented manipulator, though regulatory devices, by parliaments and the like, have been instituted to moderate the more obvious kinds of propaganda.[4]

In spite of all these forces, the public is not a phantom, as was alleged many years ago,[5] nor can it be said to have disappeared;[6] it merely has turned out not to be the prime mover, the independent variable, in the political process that early democratic theorizing and ideology was ready to assert. When Lincoln wrote to a friend: "Remember, Dick, to keep close to the people —they are always right and will mislead no one," he overstated what has remained a good point,[7] namely the decisive role of the public in the democratic system. The role of mass communications has become fatal whenever they distort this seismograph of the system to the point where its gyrations are the result of special propaganda unchecked by effective counter-propaganda. It has been said with a good deal of sense that the only cure for propaganda is counterpropaganda. Hence several channels are better than one, several newspapers better than one, several radio and television stations and networks better than one. Better not in a moral sense, but in the sense of checking the pathological propensity of propaganda to get out of hand.

The mass communications media have produced one of the most dangerous tensions in modern constitutional democracies.[8] At the same time, they have become a prime instrumentality of the dictatorships.[9] They have played an important role in whipping up mass hysteria in critical situations. They have helped to plunge countries into wars;[10] they have magnified the hate reactions after wars and contributed to the difficulties of organizing peace.[11] The sensationalism of the tabloids, the distortions of radio and television have become so generally known that it seems almost tedious to mention their deleterious effects. The electorate has, in course of time, developed a certain measure of skepticism concerning all this distorted information. Increasingly, as careful researches have brought to light, people vote and form their political opinion regardless of, and often contrary to, the newspapers they read.[12] The elections of Truman and Kennedy, of Harold Wilson and Willy Brandt have been won in the face of sharp and at times vicious press campaigns against them.

We have dealt in the previous chapter with the question of what is to be understood by propaganda (Chapter 11, p. 176). It is the behavior, conduct, or action of a propagandist—a person who hands out information in order to gain benefits, material or nonmaterial advantages, for himself or more typically for the group he is acting for. We noted that ordinarily the group will pay for the service. Thus characterized, it is clear that it is not a novel phenomenon, but as old as politics, though many assume it to be. Some have interpreted it as caused by the very workings of a democratic industrial society; others see it as an evil machination of wicked men. These are emotional reactions rather than analytical judgments based upon facts. Even a casual inspection of the propagandist and his tasks shows that several communications processes need to be distinguished in the work of a propagandist. There is government propaganda, there is party propaganda, there is interest group propaganda, and there is the propaganda for "causes." All these involve the employment of communications for the purpose of persuading people to take actions which will benefit the group for whom the propagandist works. This propagandizing by the propagander of the propageese (if these terms may be allowed for simplicity's sake[13]) may be a continuous process, or it may take the form of a distinctive campaign, or the process may be composed of a succession of campaigns. The activities of political parties consist largely of this process; they are accepted as part of the democratic process, although they are in fact equally significant for the political process in totalitarian and other autocratic regimes. The difference is that in the latter the party or the government possesses a monopoly over mass communications, whereas parties are competitive and so are interest groups and causes in a popular regime.

Besides being the work of a propagandist, now often called the public-relations man,[14] propaganda of a kind is often produced by educational and cultural activities. But it is propaganda in effect rather than in the more limited sense of a distinctive action of a propagandist as just described. It is rather important to bear this propagandistic effect in mind when discussing the pathology of propaganda. But it should not be confused with propaganda in the true sense. Many news items in press and radio-television have such a propagandistic effect, though they are not issued by propagandists. News editors often are unaware of the unintended propagandistic effect of their news, which springs from their unexplained subconscious premises. The same is true of many teachers. Their communications to students may be shot through with propagandistic effects, especially in the social sciences (including law) and history, but unless they are controlled from a propagandist center, as happens at times under totalitarianism, such communications are not propaganda in the true sense.

At this point, it is necessary to face the issue of so-called civic education. The education of citizens has been a key concern of philosophers and pedagogues since the days of Plato. Charles Merriam sponsored a broad comparative inquiry of which he undertook to summarize the findings in a basic volume[15] on the making of citizens. The process is an important part of any functioning political order; this proposition runs like a red thread through the history of political thought and philosophy. Merriam's volume is basically concerned with civic training. On the basis of the comparative study of the techniques of such civic training he noted a trend toward ever greater formal organization. He differentiated between learning to value political order as such, accepting a particular regime, such as the United States or the Soviet Union, and cherishing a country or other basis of a regime. I doubt that these learning processes can ever be sharply separated from each other. A young American in the process of growing up learns all three together and in their interdependence. Merriam's inclination to view these processes in terms of "the making of citizens" suffers from an overemphasis on the collective. The same may be said of the more recently fashionable way of looking at these goings-on as "socialization." This term has achieved popularity as an alternative to education, which is seen as "formal." But the true difference is that education seems to focus on the individual to be educated, whereas socialization focuses on the collective into which a person is integrated to a greater or lesser degree. Whether one or the other of these foci is preferred, it is clear that the propaganda involved in these processes is believed to be functional to the political order. It would not otherwise be undertaken! To return to the main point, whatever may be the particular embodiment of the human values to be transmitted, whether they be rational principles, rituals, felt preferences, or customs and folkways, civic education will be concerned with them.[16] It is one of the interesting features of a mature democratic society that it takes propaganda in its stride. All information has a potential propagandistic effect, and the crucial task is to organize communications in such a way that different sides get a hearing in public.[17] Even very deviant viewpoints and their propagandistic dispersion are functional in such a community, as they relate to critical problems.

Actually, a great deal of political propaganda is directed toward one of two objectives: to get people to vote for someone or to join his organization (party) even if only for the vote, or financially to support an organization. This is the hard core of the work of the propagandist, and around it cluster the more general activities which develop in people a disposition to do these things. Let it be remarked at this point that any rational effort to carry on propaganda and any successful propaganda campaign involves a calculation of cost, relating it to the expected benefit. Cost-benefit analysis is here, as in other fields of activity, very necessary. No propagandist (and no advertiser—a specialized kind of propagandist) will spend a thousand dollars to gain five hundred. That is, only if $\frac{b}{c} \geqq 1$ (where *b* stands for benefit and *c* for cost) will a propaganda campaign be undertaken. The difficulty in applying this simple formula is that benefit is often quite difficult to state in quantitative terms. In politics especially the benefit may be so paramount, such as a victory in a major election, that any expenditure, any cost, would seem to those engaged in the fight to be worthwhile. The only limit then would be their available resources. This is incidentally one of the reasons why public expenditures for propaganda have had a tendency to soar in wartime. The winning of victory appears so paramount, and the public's enlistment in the cause so vital that the cost of propaganda is assimilated to the cost of weapons. At this point the rational calculation of cost in relation to gain breaks down.

Cost-benefit analysis of propaganda activities and campaigns is closely related to the problem of functionality. Generally speaking, it can be said that where the cost-benefit analysis gives a positive ratio, the propaganda is functional, or at least appears so to the political bosses who decide upon it. It may in practice turn out to have been a faulty analysis, but that does not alter the fact that it is important to attempt it. In view of the increasing alertness and skepticism of the propageese, the cost is likely to rise. The shaping of public opinion is not so much a result of spontaneous response and thought, but is rather the result of the directed impact of manipulative forces.[18] The techniques employed for such manipulation are numerous; they include repetition, exaggeration, identification, false association (name calling), and the bandwagon appeal, to mention only a few.[19] An Institute of Propaganda Analysis at Columbia University at one time distinguished six "devices" which may also be properly called techniques: name calling, glittering generalities, transfer, testimonial, plain folks appeal, and card stacking. For our present purpose, there is no need to go into these issues, which I have dealt with elsewhere.[20] These techniques do not determine the functionality or disfunctionality of propaganda. Nor should this issue be confused with the extended debate over good and bad propaganda. One of those concerned with this moral distinction has said that "bad propaganda is distinguished by a disregard for the welfare of those to whom it is directed."[21] It seems a dubious approach; for Hitler's propaganda would thereby seem not bad, while all propaganda directed toward foreign countries would appear to be bad. The writer who made this statement did not see it this way. He later adds that Hitler's is the prime example of bad propaganda, and he cites him as saying that "mental confusion, contradiction of feeling, indecision, panic—these are our weapons." It would appear from this that the badness of propaganda must be seen in the methods employed rather than the end sought. He then proceeds to define good propaganda as "reversing all of the directions of Hitler's prescription." Reverence for the individual addressed, desire to clarify his mind, an effort to create harmony and eliminate conflict, to create faith, to engender self-reliance and a confidence in others—these high-minded tasks, if they define good propaganda, suggest that there is very little of it. It shows that such an approach differs radically from one that asks what kind of propaganda is functional, that is to say which serves the function of those who engage in propaganda, when it is defined as organized persuasion.

It would seem that a great deal of electioneering propaganda is of this kind. Though it may corrupt the electorate, it is obvious that without it the electorate would not be in a position to exercise its "sovereign" right of choosing between candidates.[22] In a very able study on political television, a political scientist has shown how such propaganda is being handled in the United States in one particular medium, namely television.[23] Election studies of recent years have developed a good deal of additional material, all of which goes to show that propaganda, whether televised or not, has a decisive function in the working of democracy. That such propaganda may distort the "independent," that is to say the more meandering, reflections of many voters there can be, in light of the evidence, little doubt. That the Nixon-Kennedy debates influenced the outcome of the election is now generally conceded. Whether one thinks that was a good thing depends upon one's partisanship in this instance. As far as techniques were involved, all those identified above can be shown to have been employed by both candidates. They were not properly speaking debates at all, as Reston observed, but press conferences, with a limited number of skilled reporters who chose the issues, and thereby manipulated the impact. It was therefore afterward recommended that the issues should be selected by the candidates.[24] These so-called debates attracted a very large audience. Estimates had it that seventy-five million people watched the first debate, and the second and third debate still had audiences variously estimated to have been over fifty to over sixty million. The last of them was believed to have been seen and heard by between forty-eight and seventy million.[25] As Theodore White commented in *The Making of the President,* "The TV debates did little to advance the reasonable discussion of issues. . . ." But one may ask: was that their function? Or was it rather to enable the electorate to assess the two candidates, both new, and choose the one that seemed better as a leader of the nation? Need the audience remain totally passive as it did in these debates? Or would modern electronic techniques make it possible to have the audience participate? And if so, would this enhance the functionality or reduce it?[26]

This is also a serious question in connection with the broadcasting facilities in various countries, but especially in the U.S. "Some major reform is necessary," one scholar has written, "to offset the financial problem that faces aspirants to all public offices in this country" (U.S.). On the eve of election day, 1964, *Broadcasting* magazine compiled an estimate of the television and radio costs of the election from the convention days through to November 3; it was found that costs had jumped almost three times above the 1960 expenditures—from $14.2 million in 1960 to the record total of approximately $40 million in 1964.

"Half was for the presidential, and the other half for broadcasting on state and local levels."[27] That these facilities should not be made available for the public's business seems grotesque and disfunctional and contrasts sharply with practice elsewhere. However, there then arises the perplexing question of how to divide the available time between candidates and parties.[28] It has been argued that television has changed the conventions for its arrival has brought it about that speeches and demonstrations are mainly directed to the national audience and only secondarily to the men and women actually at the convention. After the violence at the Democratic convention at Chicago in 1968, staged with a view to television, the feeling was widespread that such conventions had outlived their usefulness, i.e., had become disfunctional and should be discontinued.[29]

Similarly television's highlighting of student rebellions has produced a feeling of revulsion at this sort of propaganda. It has been felt that at times these rebellions were in fact undertaken with a view to their impact through television. There have been reports about overeager photographers actually inciting violence for the sake of what can be done with the dramatic pictures, and university authorities have made appeals for playing down these incidents, rather than highlighting them.[30] In the case of ORTF (Paris) a fierce controversy developed between some of the broadcasting personnel and the government, which felt betrayed; it led to wholesale dismissals after the student strike and rebellion ended.[31] There seems to be every indication that propaganda as broadcast, and more especially the revolutionary oratory of Cohn-Bendit and his friends, was disfunctional as far as de Gaulle's regime was concerned. Mass communications had become a vehicle of the propaganda of violence.

What the students have grasped is the technique of the propaganda of the act. Television has enormously increased the potentialities of such propaganda, though it is an old and often tried device. It is quite important, in considering propaganda, to avoid the common error of considering only propaganda of the word. Considering the amounts of propaganda spewed forth by governments, parties, interest groups, and causes, not to mention all the commercial advertising, every propagandist knows that one act is worth many thousand words, when it comes to publicity, to getting the public's attention. At a time when the skills of propagandists were not yet as highly developed as they are now, the promoters of causes instinctively realized the attention-arresting quality of the active challenge. The women's suffrage movement is a striking case in point. The fact that women were willing to undergo such ordeals as they did had a cumulative effect upon the male public. In recent years, the same may be said of Negroes and other cultural minorities, peasants and students. Demonstrations and confrontations with the established authorities, in the form of the occupation of buildings, blocking of motor traffic, and dumping of food, all activities which are sensational and thus arouse the mass communication media to report and often to overdramatize them, have served the purpose of calling a particular situation and its badness to the attention of the public. These acts are rapidly becoming dysfunctional. The white backlash is endangering the civil rights progress which was in process of being made, universities are being deprived of the funds they desperately need for the reforms called for, and so on.

Propaganda of the act, if multiplied beyond a certain limit, also creates an atmosphere of total emergency, not merely crisis, which readies the public for an autocratic takeover by the military or by some totalitarian movement, be it Communist or Fascist. Each individual "act" seems harmless enough, but in their quantity they cause the average citizen to feel that the political order is breaking down, that it has ceased to *function* by not providing him with the security which in the eyes of most people is the only persuasive reason for the existence and acceptance of government. This result may, of course, be the ultimate purpose of such propagandists of the act and their masters. When Black Panthers, French and German students, and assorted other groups openly assert that they are revolutionaries, and that they wish to destroy the "establishment," often without any indication as to what is to replace it, then the reaction of the common man is flight to protective authoritarianism and it is quite natural (see above, Chapter 3). It means that such propaganda is highly disfunctional to the established order, while not even being functional to an emergent new order. For a long time, skillful propagandists will stage acts, if they do not occur spontaneously, and publicize them to the fullest. From the standpoint of the non-involved, such acts may lack the implications the propagandist expects. A striking illustration is provided by the Reichstag fire, which the Nazis are believed to have staged; it impressed none but their own party followers for any length of time, but it perhaps served a useful purpose at the time in confusing the public just prior to the election which gave Hitler the mandate he was seeking in March 1933.[32] In recent years, some of the occurrences during the student rebellions are said to have been staged, but the largest part of them were without doubt a spontaneous response. Much propaganda of the act always will be a natural part of any great movement, as well as of the very process of history, especially in politics, where the main actors are moving upon a very visible stage and through their encounters and decisions provide themselves with most impressive propaganda of the act.

Within the context of competitive politics, much propaganda is met by counterpropaganda, and the thrust of one campaign is blunted by the counter campaign of an opposing camp. The equilibrium of interests may be such that the total effect is nil, because the contending forces are a match to each other. This was the situation prior to Pearl Harbor, when the Committee to Defend America (William Allen White) and the America First Committee battled with each other for the mind and heart of America. They spent about the same amount of money, operated organizations of about the same size, and probably kept each other from having any marked effect. They merely heightened the tension by arousing violent feelings.[33] Yet it would have been no argument against supporting the campaign with those who felt strongly on either side of the issue.

Such an equilibrium, in this case destroyed by the Pearl Harbor attack, is not necessarily to be found. If no serious disadvantage corresponds to the advantage sought by the campaign, no opposing campaign will be undertaken. This is not infrequently the situation in government campaigns; for these are often directed toward securing the public's response to an action program which springs from an approved public policy, such as the Social Security Act or the U.S. Savings Bonds.[34] Counterpropaganda may also fail to develop or be ineffective when the persons adversely affected by the actions advocated are widely dispersed, so that each person's disadvantage is small as compared with the benefit the propaganda is serving. It is often the situation in which opponents of governmental activities find themselves. The persons who are adversely affected by a decree of the U.S. Food and Drug Administration apart from drug companies will be individuals who are deprived of some remedy they like and trust, but their chance of combating the propaganda campaign of the administration in publicizing their view of the matter is very small indeed. Thus the highlighting of rather dubious experiments with mice in feeding them what would in the same ratio to body weight be huge quantities of cyclamate, if consumed by human beings, led to an adoption of a policy of outlawing cyclamate-sweetened drinks, which typically placed the consumer at the mercy of government propagandists and their doings. The idea of "saving" people from their own folly is itself a propaganda slogan which rests upon a public philosophy which some people—individualists by conviction—may reject, as did John Stuart Mill in his classic *On Liberty*.

The extent to which a particular propaganda campaign receives financial support from private individuals or the government is not necessarily a gauge of the effectiveness of a campaign; for dedication to a cause opposed to the campaign and a willingness to make other kinds of sacrifices may provide an effective counter to such a campaign. The student rebels of recent years have provided a striking illustration of how, especially through the propaganda of the act, dedicated followers of a cause or movement may outmaneuver or at least check even very powerful and financially well-supported propagandists. The extent to which such operations are functional depends upon the circumstances.

The relation of the government to mass communication media has been the subject of large-scale inquiries in a number of countries.[35] While providing good summaries, they rarely contain any startling revelations of new truths. They are, however, even without thinking or saying so, usually occupied with the problem of the functionality of these media. The crux of the problem of mass communications in contemporary society is their deleterious effect upon the beliefs which these societies are based upon, and the consequent corrosion of the values constitutive of these societies. There is a vicious circle implied in much that was discussed in this chapter, by which every new technique begets a new set of troubles. The so-called crisis of democracy is largely the result of the developments in these fields.

Liberals, fettered by their almost fanatical commitment to

freedom of the press, are greatly handicapped in assessing the functionality of some of these developments. In an important report in this field, the opinion is stated that "the government" cannot "make the press better."[36] Maybe not; but it is difficult to see why the combating of undue concentration of power may not be functional in the sense of maintaining a strong competition in this field as in any other. The empires which have been built, while not perhaps constituting a monopoly, are surely limitable. And when the same report questions "whether law can impose more than a low minimum of fairness and decency upon the instrumentalities and frame reasonable regulations for the flow of their output through the channels of communication to citizens,"[37] and therefore all a political system of liberal politics can do is to depend upon the maintenance of professional ethics, one may doubt whether this is all that can be said on a prescription for making the press "better" than it has become in recent years. The refusal of the U.S. Congress to face the problem of program content of American broadcasting, or to allow the Federal Communications Commission to do so for it, is in line with such timidity. Pious wishes that "it may be that profits may come to play a smaller part in the life of an established newspaper" or indeed an established broadcasting enterprise are not likely to secure such reduction in the profit motive in a business "affected with a public interest." What is more, the history of the press in most countries does not bear out such optimism. On the contrary, the decline in quality is directly linked to mass production and maximization of profits. At the same time, there is a decline in effective competition. A small-town newspaper may nobly proclaim that it considers its monopoly a responsibility rather than a privilege, but it has a monopoly just the same and the power that goes with it. The situation in broadcasting is not markedly different, except in countries which, like Britain and France, have accepted the inherent trend toward monopoly by establishing a government monopoly and then trying to work out an effective control which will ensure a measure of competition for rival political programs and movements; but it cannot be said that these efforts have been overly successful, although the BBC (British Broadcasting Corporation) has proved a better instrumentality than the ORTF (Office Radio-Télévision Française) in achieving a degree of functionality.

It is not the task of a pathologist to devise methods for the practitioner of medicine, and we shall here abstain from entering the fascinating field of remedial proposals, and restrict ourselves to the task of functional analysis. What has been discussed, inadequate as it is, demonstrates clearly that modern mass communication media have introduced into industrial mass societies very dangerous potentialities of pathology, that is of disfunctionality resulting from the limitless potentialities of propaganda, both on the part of the government and other groups. The government and the press may well be "associates in the joint enterprise of making the great society work" as the above-mentioned report puts it,[38] but a good part of the time they seem to be antagonists rather than associates. The oratory of men like Vice President Spiro Agnew has highlighted such antagonism. He may be right and he may be wrong—he is in my opinion both from time to time—but he has in any case succeeded in bringing out into the open the pathological dangers in this field. There is no such thing as a modern government outside of mass communications, nor can mass communications be conceived except within the rules of the game which are set by modern government. Not only radio broadcasting but the press depends upon them for their operations, as press laws in all these regimes clearly show. Most assuredly therefore such governments and the people acting through them could put a stop to the "empires," the huge trusts of opinion falsifiers, if they would. Unfortunately the pathology has already gone so far that it is doubtful that anyone who tried to do this could ever get to first base about it. For with the controllers in charge of all propaganda channels, where would they get the information? Certainly not from the purveyors of most opinion on public issues, the mass communication manipulators. The frustration of modern man and with it the disfunctionality of propaganda are nowhere more completely confining than in the field of mass communication. The feeble and unconvincing responses of these media to Agnew's massive attacks showed the weakness of their position, in terms of the underlying issues, but they have nonetheless all but blotted out the impact of the challenge of this high official. The media could not suppress his views, because his statements had almost the impact of the propaganda of the act, but they could dissipate its impact by indignant oratory about the freedom of the press (and of the air) which was precisely what these criticisms called for.

It remains to consider briefly the role of these propaganda media in the field of international relations. All modern governments have adopted a policy of employing these media for the purpose of influencing foreign opinion. The Voice of America for example is part of this babel of "voices."[39] Under pressure from a suspicious Congressional control, these voices are forced to adopt a more or less nationalist line of argument. It may be the beauties of socialism which Moscow peddles to all listeners and readers, or those of a "free society" which Washington and its friends proclaim. In the market place of world public opinion, so-called—for it may be doubted that such a thing exists—one propaganda campaign and continuous propaganda lines "jam" the other, and yet no one of the participants can afford to stop, lest the other become predominant. A particularly striking instance is provided by Radio Free Europe, which for many years now has broadcast into the lands beyond the iron curtain news and views by refugees from them, with controversial effects. Cases like the campaigns in connection with the civil war in Nigeria and the Mideast conflict are only striking because of their extreme and radical forms of propaganda. They resemble the struggle of the soap manufacturers for the housewife's dollar. Their functionality may well be doubted, since like the soaps they only differ in their color. The promised perfection of their "solutions" exists not even in the minds of their progenitors. But they are disfunctional, because foreign policy is increasingly made with a view to its propaganda appeal. Such an imaginative initiative as Chancellor Brandt's effort at reducing East-West tensions is constantly threatened by the chorus of voices in the mass media and from official propaganda offices seeking to "interpret" what is being done, for or against, with a maximum effect. The conduct of foreign policy has become well-nigh impossible under these conditions, and the relations between nations continue to deteriorate, tensions mount, and the threat of armed conflict increases (see Chapter 4). At the same time, the patient, steady effort in the agencies of the United Nations remains largely unknown to the mass audiences, except when some dramatic act or event arouses the mass media to take notice. Developments like the steady growth of community sentiment within the European community are overshadowed by the occasional "crises" on the official level, when the impending collapse of this important development is announced from the housetops by press and broadcasting in all the world, either as an impending disaster or a to-be-expected consequence of mistaken notions.[40] Actually, the community sentiment continues to grow, because of the inherent forces at work. Propaganda is, of course, also carried on by the European Economic Commission at Brussels; its Information Directorate, under able leadership, tries to counteract these hostile critics, as well as the over-enthusiastic partisans of a sudden and miraculous "unification."

But the resources at its disposal cannot possibly balance, let alone rival, the vast output of government and press in all the countries affected by this development, which is thus condemned to struggle on in its uphill fight for progress.

The role of propaganda in international relations must therefore be considered largely disfunctional. The skeptical observer is forced to the conclusion that democracy is virtually incapable of handling these relations effectively. A large part of the reason is the disfunctional propaganda which modern mass communication media provide, without whose participation it is even so inconceivable that the mass publics of contemporary political regimes could possibly have the necessary information for participating effectively in the process, as democratic theory requires. The disastrous course of the debate on the United States' involvement in Vietnam is only the most recent illustration of disfunctional propaganda certain to be followed by other similar campaigns and pathological disturbances.[41] The response to all this noise on the part of those responsible for international relations has been an increasing secretiveness in their operations, to which we shall return in the next chapter to complete the analysis begun in the preceding one.

CHAPTER
13

INTELLIGENCE AND ESPIONAGE

INTELLIGENCE is the technical term of governments to describe all the necessary information, both overt and secret, which it needs for fashioning its policies and doing its work. Espionage is the effort to secure clandestine information about foreign governments and politics, more especially their military resources and weapons; it is a particular way of securing some of the information which is needed. Both are therefore specific operational aspects of the problem of political secrecy, and the issue of functionality presents itself; in view of the costs involved in espionage and intelligence, it is important; disfunctional intelligence is worse than no intelligence, and poor espionage may have a high cost in loss of mutual confidence and the capacity to negotiate besides. "Intelligence is the knowledge which our highly placed civilians and military men must have to safeguard the national welfare," wrote one of the best writers on the subject in America some years ago.[1] Some intelligence, described as "strategic," is considered "knowledge vital for national survival." It is evident, therefore, that some of it is clearly functional, if that statement is correct. It has been considered so for long ages.

We are here obviously not concerned with every kind of intelligence, but with that part related to secrecy and directed toward overcoming secrecy of the other party (not only enemies, but friends as well!), while buttressing the secrecy of one's own. Such intelligence is required for decision-making in foreign and military policy, and espionage serves to secure the information which the other party seeks to secrete. As such it has existed ever since the dawn of organized politics, and like the other phenomena here under consideration, it is endemic to the political process.[2] Intelligence of this sort is often confused with espionage which is only one of the many methods for collecting the needed information, and often by no means the best or most reliable. Indeed, espionage may readily become the source of very misleading information, and thus become disfunctional to a high degree, as will be elaborated below.

The understanding of functionality in intelligence and espionage would greatly gain from a more extended knowledge of historical experience. Which policies were correctly fashioned because of good intelligence? Which battles were won because of it? Unfortunately the very secrecy of these operations, the destruction of evidence, and the vainglory of military commanders and statesmen who prefer to have the success and victory appear to be the result of their superhuman qualities, wisdom, and insight have combined to obscure most of the record. We know that the remarkable successes of the Mongols were at least in part due to their extensive preparatory espionage; we know that the medieval church maintained an elaborate system of secret intelligence agents, sometimes said to have been linked to the confessional, and by this means succeeded in surviving with relatively little raw power in a hostile political world. The Mogul Emperor Akbar is said to have maintained as many as four thousand spies, scavengers presumably like the legendary concierges of Paris and similar agents of oppressive regimes elsewhere. The Roman Empire in its later oppressive stages developed an elaborate secret police system, which became a source of invisible disturbance on account of the power it acquired.[3] In our own time, glimpses of such operations have become available in instances like the Hiss case, discussed above (Chapter 6) and the revelations of Nazi and Soviet secret police agents, such as Penkovskiy,[4] and the studies on Himmler.[5] Frederick the Great of Prussia has been described as the "inventor" of an organized system of espionage to reinforce his less than adequate military establishment.[6] If he did, he followed the French, who had been skillful in the employment of spies for many a generation; the most famous of these secret agents under Richelieu was Père Joseph, the "grey eminence" who presumably contributed vitally to Richelieu's diplomatic and military successes.[7] These practices had already been skillfully employed in the Italian city-states, which may well have been the faithful students of the Holy See in this as in so many other practices of government and politics.[8] Machiavelli speaks of spies as a necessary instrument of the art of war and of foreign policy, especially one of expansion.[9] But the most extraordinary system of intelligence in those early modern times was probably that of the Republic of Venice. Its ambassadorial reports served as the basis of the great historian Ranke's reevaluation of the history of European nations.[10] Again it was a case of reinforcing intrinsic weakness by "intelligence." For the Republic of Venice succeeded in maintaining its independence for many centuries by the skill with which it was able to anticipate developments in other countries. This latter capacity may be of particular importance in a revolutionary age, especially if the siding with the revolutionaries assists a power in dealing with friends and adversaries. This aspect of the matter in turn links foreign to domestic intelligence, and in turn to counter-intelligence. For if a regime is faced with substantial internal opposition, it may become vital for its survival whether it knows in advance what these elements may be planning to do. Infiltrating their organizations and similar activities, including wiretapping and various forms of censorship, fall under this heading. There is no need here to go in any detail into the complex matter of techniques employed in such secret intelligence work. But their conflict with certain basic rights, fought over and won in the struggle of liberal constitutionalism against monarchical absolutism, is apparent. The recent proposal to establish a "data bank" for all "important" Americans was, of course, motivated by the desire to secure adequate surveillance; its invasion of privacy seemed unacceptable to a majority of Congress. A similar fate struck down some years ago a suggestion that all Americans be fingerprinted. We are here entering the borderline of the functionality of intelligence work. It may be desirable to have such information, but the cost in terms of the regime's value system may be too high. What may be accepted temporarily during war may appear unjustifiable in times of peace. Putting the matter thus brings out what is probably the underlying ground of the difference of opinion: some will consider a time of peace what to others appears clearly a time of war, cold or other, and hence permitting intelligence activities which in genuine peacetime would be out of the question.[11]

There can be no doubt that the rise of totalitarian dictatorships in this century has, in combination with an advanced technology, very much promoted intelligence work of all kinds. Reference to nuclear weapons highlights the obvious; but a vast network of more or less secret agents has grown up in the course of the so-called cold war, which has not been so cold as the oratory on the subject often implies. It may well be doubted, however, that the American Presidents responsible for the country's involvement in Vietnam would have adopted such a policy had their intelligence service been able to forecast correctly the nature of the warlike activities in which the country became involved. No one except insiders knows what the intelligence actually was on the subject. Similar critical observations would seem in order for the Bay of Pigs misadventure, as well as several other failures in American foreign policy of recent years. The controversies over these failures have brought out how inadequate was the intelligence, or at least its communication to the decision- and policy-makers. It had been so earlier, in the days before Pearl Harbor, when American officers in their concern to secrete their success in breaking the Japanese secret code prevented their secret information from reaching the top echelons.[12] We have similar evidence to the effect that the very realistic reporting within Himmler's secret police on the disaffection of the mass of the German population never reached top decision-makers, especially Hitler. Presumably something similar occurred in Stalin's Russia, as revealed by Khrushchev's famous secret speech. This is the vacuum phenomenon which was briefly discussed above (Chapter 11).

The pathology of intelligence and espionage is in part the result of too much (sic!) and too late. Students of intelligence have been in agreement that whereas the gathering of the data is the first step in intelligence work, and its coordination highly important, much the most important and the most difficult is the interpretation of the data. You may have six reports on the same subject, five of which take one line and one another. Yet the lone dissenter may be the correct one. How are you to know, sitting at the center of a large intelligence operation? Various techniques have been developed to deal with credibility, reliability, and the rest, but these techniques have produced as many failures as successes, or at least quite a few. In the case of the Cuban missile crisis some of the lower echelons in the Navy were convinced much earlier than their superiors, let alone the

President; it was only at the last minute, so to speak, that they succeeded in persuading the President[13] of the dangers in the situation.

In the writer's own experience, very erroneous information estimates as to the behavior of the Germans after their defeat, including an overestimation of their loyalty to the Hitler regime, led to a series of mistaken policies and actions in military government during the occupation, which have since occasioned excessive and misdirected criticism.[14]

The problem of how to evaluate popular support for a dictatorial regime seems to present particular difficulties to political intelligence; for it is generally agreed that the mistaken estimate of the popular attitude in Cuba prior to the Bay of Pigs attempt at an invasion was very serious; the expectation of a popular uprising was not at all fulfilled.[15] In fact, as already noted, these totalitarian regimes have themselves very great difficulties in securing reliable information on this score. It is, of course, very risky to rely on refugee enemies of such a regime,[16] who have a natural inclination to overestimate the degree of internal opposition; the wish is the father of the thought. But it is equally risky to rely upon the party supporters of such a regime, because they have the opposite tendency of underestimating the degree of disaffection. And since such regimes, out of their passion for consensus, even for unanimity one might say,[17] are ready to suppress any signs of popular discontent, and punish harshly even the harmless griping of ordinary people, the intelligence man who reports such dissent is apt to encounter the displeasure of his superiors. The proverbial 99 percent support which such regimes get in plebiscites is expressive of this situation and provides no reliable guide to popular attitudes, although often mistakenly considered to do so—at least abroad.

Students of totalitarianism have been in considerable disagreement on this score. The inclination of these regimes to expand the roster of the "enemies of the people" more or less at will has, in combination with their insistence upon consensus, produced a bewildering picture. Perhaps the most extreme case is offered by the Stalinist regime. Stalin, a typical paranoiac, saw the world teeming with his (the Soviet people's) enemies. The entire capitalist order and all its hangers-on were seen in this light. It supposedly organized successive encirclements and plots, ringing the Soviet Union with air bases and military establishments, planning war and destruction of the socialist motherland. The developments in Czechoslovakia are only the latest in these formidable undertakings, and what appears to the distant observer as world revolutionary undertakings of the Soviet Union are to a considerable extent moves to counter the machinations of others and to uncover and destroy their plots.[18] The work of secret service agents and spies plays an important part in this image. Since these regimes are themselves engaged in large-scale operations of this kind, as has been convincingly described by some defectors, such as Oleg Penkovskiy, it is not surprising that allegations of similar activities by their enemies find ready credence. And since there is more than a kernel of truth in these reports, the entire system works to create an atmosphere of intense suspicion and distrust which is destructive of any belief in the statements of top leaders, and hence destroys or at least severely handicaps the efforts of well-meaning persons to develop more peaceful relations between the powers. It is likely that here lies the most dangerous disfunctionality of intelligence and espionage work. Although intended to aid rational policy- and decision-making in international relations, it actually corrodes the basis of such rational decision-making, by generating an atmosphere of universal, indeed total distrust.

This development, while significantly related to the outbreak of the Second World War, intensified after it, owing to the presence of nuclear and other weapons of total destruction.

Hence the United States, until then rather indifferent toward intelligence operations, proceeded to organize the Central Intelligence Agency under the National Security Act of 1947, which also created the National Security Council and other structures. This CIA was not to monopolize intelligence functions, as some were inclined to advocate, but was to coordinate them. It became the central element of the "intelligence community," responsible for coordinating the intelligence activities of the various branches of the administration. All these different entities are spoken of as "the intelligence community," that is to say rather euphemistically the community of all those engaged in intelligence activities, notably the Department of State's Bureau of Intelligence and Research, the Defense Intelligence Agency of the Armed Forces, the National Security Agency, the separate intelligence units of the Army, the Navy and the Air Force, and to some extent the Atomic Energy Commission, and where counter-intelligence is involved the Federal Bureau of Investigation.[19]

The Central Intelligence Agency was, unfortunately, also given the task of intervening covertly in the affairs of other nations, when so directed. This function should not be combined with those of (1) gathering information, by public as well as secret (*overt* and *covert* are the technical terms usually employed) agents and (2) collating the information it collects itself with that of other agencies, to analyze and evaluate it, and to present it to the policy-makers. The Bay of Pigs incident revealed the disfunctionality of combining these intelligence functions with "cloak-and-dagger" projects; for the commitment to and involvement in the latter makes the CIA an advocate, even a propagandist, in the presentation of intelligence bearing upon such projects in supporting them and developing arguments for them. This judgment is not shared by some observers and participants in these activities. Some of the arguments are rather weak, or purely agency-oriented ("power of the director" and that sort of thing), others plainly mistaken, such as that "operators and analysts each benefit from the other's substantive knowledge and experience," for such an argument would undercut the existence of a separate intelligence agency altogether, and is sometimes heard from advocates of a particular intelligence office in a specialized service.[20] It has been rightly pointed out that those who decided for the establishment of the CIA felt "that the task of providing much of the information needed by the government should rest with men who had no direct policy responsibilities and thus no position to support, no interest to defend."[21] It is to give the policy-makers adequate and well-digested information as to what the situation in specific areas is at any particular time, as well as estimates concerning the probable future and the policy implications thereof. To do this well, the intelligence gatherer ought to be informed as to policy alternatives that might be under consideration. It has been said that "the U.S. intelligence community has become one of the largest consumers and producers of information in the world today. . . ."[22] Here lies one of many dangers of pathology and disfunctionality. The masses of facts that are being gathered, including the rumors and guesses of all the world's politically engaged persons, constitutes an undertaking that is intrinsically threatened by "overload."

The effort to cope with it by careful subdivisions leads to excessive bureaucratization, and a consequent breakdown of effective communication. Information, like any other input into government, can only be absorbed at a limited rate; if that rate is exceeded, breakdown is the result. For this reason, much is to be said for the British preference in intelligence work for less coverage, but more intensive coverage by fewer but abler minds. An intelligence agency must compete with other consumers of intellectual ability, and hence the larger it gets, the lower will be the average quality of the minds engaged in it. A single report from a top-notch security agent about the state of a foreign nation may be better, and usually is better, than two dozen reports from mediocre observers, contradicting each other and leaving the final analysts in a state of bewilderment. It has been said that "the great danger is that the intelligence officer . . . will come to feel completely cut off from the policy-making process." The same observer adds that "there have been more failures . . . and more mediocrity than the United States should be willing to accept."[22a] If sound judgment is the crucial element in producing functional intelligence, then assuredly an agency with thousands of employees cannot give it. As in the other phenomena here under consideration, intelligence too becomes disfunctional when it exceeds a certain limited amount, namely the amount that can be effectively digested and applied. In light of the constant increase in complexity of the political world, the solution is not an ever-expanding intelligence apparatus as some seem to think, but on the contrary a smaller one staffed by superior talent trained as well as possible. Subtlety of thought is assuredly not "the most noteworthy trait of any large organization" and it is therefore very true for any intelligence apparatus that "special efforts will constantly be necessary to see that thoughtful, unorthodox views and individual insights are encouraged rather than stifled by the system." Reduction in size is the first requirement!

The covert information gathering which is ordinarily referred to as spying is subject to several other pathologies, and there are those who would deny its functionality altogether. A rigorous moral approach to politics, such as Kant's, has no use for espionage, [23] just as it advocates complete publicity. But if secrecy is acknowledged as endemic in the political process, then efforts to break the secret and learn what is being withheld are equally so. Hence the history of espionage is as long as that of organized government, as was noted before. Its pathology is related to its moral condemnation. The term *spy* carries a pejorative connotation which is not shared by its synonyms, such as *scouting*, *patrolling*, and the like. In law, espionage is a violation of a state's territorial integrity and as such unlawful. Hence, governments usually repudiate a spy, if he is caught, although defending his activity in general. In the heyday of liberal constitutionalism, countries like Britain and the United States prided themselves on their very limited use of espionage. But there was an outburst of it all over Europe prior to the First World War which followed upon the presumably successful use of it by the Prussians in their war against France (1870–1871).[24] The presumed initiator of this Prussian enterprise was a man named Stieber, who claimed that he had thousands of secret agents in Eastern France prior to the decisive French defeats. Since France was defeated, the accepted inference at the time was that the defeat was at least in part due to Stieber's activities. It seems in retrospect rather doubtful, and during the First World War the functionality of this kind of large-scale espionage, while filling the sensationalist press, proved in fact illusory. One of the best students of these problems has commented that "before the end of the war in 1918 neither the agents of the Allies nor of the Germans and Austrians were doing any significant amount of spying."[25] Bureaucratic skepticism was perhaps carried too far, and some real successes were missed because of it, but "if everything reported by spies, informers and hysterical civilians had been recklessly acted upon, massacre and chaos would have resulted." This judgment holds true for the Second World War as well; the disfunctionality of such suspicions is particularly great in countries with mixed nationalities, such as the United States. The fear of universal treason is, as we saw, very dangerous to a political community.

Since the Second World War, espionage has enormously increased; largely because of the increase in the destructiveness of weapons and the consequent arms race, the arguments in support of it have become very persuasive even to the most reluctant. Technology of an advanced kind has become the servant of these espionage activities. The so-called U-2 incident by which it was revealed that the United States was flying reconnaissance planes over the Soviet Union in an effort to be forewarned against any military adventure by the U.S.S.R. against the United States in connection with a then impending summit conference highlighted this development. The secrecy of these operations had been so great that key members of the U.S. Senate were unaware of them, and the U.S. President became involved in embarrassing contradictions by denying and then admitting them. "The record suggests the shocking fact that neither the President, the Secretary of State, nor the Secretary of Defense knew on May 1, 1960, that our U-2 pilot was in the air over the Soviet Union. The U-2 reconnaissance project was operated by CIA, using the Lockheed Aircraft Corporation, the Air Weather Service of the Air Force, and the National Aeronautics and Space Administration as 'cover.' "[26] Even so, the President had a general acquaintance with this program, through an *ad hoc* group of advisers representing State, Defense, and his own staff. The general outburst of moral indignation, both here and abroad, was highly hypocritical, especially on the part of the Soviet Union, whose espionage activities are very large, as revealed by their own agents.[27] The only sensible answer was given by the British, who when queried by the press invariably returned a Sphinx-like "No comment." For while democratic governments dislike and morally disapprove espionage, they are engaged in it on a considerable scale because of "necessity." The so-called "cold war" is a war of espionage as well as of ideologies. Propagandists and spies have taken the place of soldiers. Satellites are being developed for the purpose of more extensive espionage, and the high seas as well as the air are swarming with these invisible fighters for democracy and freedom, or democracy and socialism, or whatever the banners might be. That the U-2 at that particular moment proved distinctly disfunctional few would now doubt, and Eisenhower has recorded his opinion to that effect by saying that he would not authorize such flights at such a moment. But similar activity proved distinctly functional in the case of the Cuban missile crisis, where it proved crucial in providing the advance information which enabled President Kennedy to take decisive and effective countermeasures to stop the emplacement in Cuba of middle-range missiles within the reach of major centers in the U.S.[28]

Intelligence and espionage clearly demonstrate that secrecy has a distinctive function in the body politic. The condemnation which moral philosophers like Kant and Bentham have heaped upon it is apolitical. If all men were of good will, the argument would hold, but even then serious difficulties would arise from the non-observance of a measure of discretion in communicating with others. The French have a very wise saying: *ce n'est pas que la vérité qui offense*—the very truth of a certain saying is what makes it offensive. Antagonisms would be magnified; between states as well as between parties the inherent tensions of their relations would be greatly increased. Hence, the manipulation of communication by withholding certain informations serves the public interest. And so does its obverse, namely the multiplication and exaggeration of certain informations, indeed their distortion, by propaganda. Propaganda is by no means merely lies, but it is impossible to imagine group life, and more especially party activity, without a good deal of positive manipulation by propaganda. Whenever men are engaged in persuading others to take or not to take particular actions which benefit a group politically, to join, to contribute, or to vote, they are engaged in propaganda—a most important function in democratic politics. Yet we have seen that both propaganda and secrecy may easily go beyond the limits and become disfunctional. If every communication is looked upon as propaganda, people cease to communicate with each other and politics becomes impossible; the vacuum surrounding the totalitarian leader is an extreme form of this communal breakdown. And similarly, if secrets are suspected on all sides, confidence vanishes and political life becomes a nightmare of terrorized suspicions. The cold war gave a taste of it, and so have the operations of secret police agents in autocratic regimes of our time. It is obvious then that limits exist within which the functionality of propaganda and secrecy is enclosed. But it has not proved possible to fix these limits with any degree of accuracy. Probably the range of tolerance is considerable, but generally speaking it might be said that where distrust becomes widespread, that is to say where a considerable percentage, and certainly where a majority are inclined to disbelieve what communications they receive, that limit has been exceeded. The hesitation of democratic governments to call their official information agencies by their correct name, propaganda ministries, is a sign of this problem. For hypocrisy renders homage to virtue by pretending it. The totalitarians in Orwell's *1984* no longer operate a ministry of propaganda, but instead possess a ministry of truth. In this imaginary outfit even history is being rewritten to suit the changing cliques. Such a façade is a striking symbol of the functionality as well as the disfunctionality of secrecy and propaganda.

CHAPTER

14

SUMMARY AND CONCLUSION

Two conclusions stand out from the analysis of the preceding chapters dealing with violence, corruption, betrayal, secrecy, and propaganda. One is that all these forms of political conduct have several functions, notably that of facilitating the adaptation of a system or regime to changing conditions occurring either in the system or in the social substructure, or in the outside environment. The other conclusion is that these phenomena are interdependent; they tend to entail each other and to reinforce each other. If violence spreads, treason (betrayal) tends to become more frequent, as persons shift their allegiance between groups, out of fear and other motives. If betrayal increases, violence is apt to multiply, as men indignant about their betrayers revenge themselves. Both phenomena may, indeed will, invite corruption—to escape violence, to combat betrayal. And again *vice versa* corruption often engenders betrayal, and indeed violence, both official and unofficial. Secrecy is obviously called for by these practices, since their moral shadiness will induce their perpetrators to try to hide them from public view. Yet, the secreting of them becomes the basis of much propaganda, as indeed is true of all these phenomena; propaganda may seek to justify them or at least to let them appear in a tolerable light, or on the contrary may cause propagandistic attacks upon the system by men disaffected by these goings-on.

In view of these links between the potentially pathological phenomena, it is understandable that political philosophers in the past have lumped them all together under the heading of corruption. A polity in which these forms of conduct flourish seems to be "corrupt" in the sense of being generally rotten. Historians such as Tacitus and Machiavelli have given vivid descriptions of this kind of general decay. Montesquieu in his *Considérations sur les Causes de la Grandeur des Romains et de leur Décadence* sought to explain the decadence of the Romans in the later Republic by the dissolution of their morals resulting from the spread of Empire. It seemed a paradox: their military prowess had given them the Empire which gave them the riches which corrupted them and the Empire! Yet, in keeping with this preoccupation with the spiritual source of corruption —a recurrent notion as we noted earlier—he declares at the outset of his discussion of corruption that he believes it was Epicurus and his sect, the Epicureans, who contributed much to "spoil the heart and the spirit of the Romans." He notes that the Greeks had been so corrupted earlier and recalls Polybius's comments in contrasting the rectitude and religiosity of the Romans with the unreliability and faithlessness of the Greeks. It is well known that Polybius stressed the religious foundations of the greatness of Rome; it was natural to argue that the decline in religious belief corroded the basis upon which Roman greatness rested. After discussing Sylla, Pompey, and Caesar and describing sketchily their several contributions to the downfall of the Republic, Montesquieu then proceeds to show how corruption grew under the empire until its final downfall. It is a sad story and it was told to his contemporaries as a warning of what might befall France, where corruption was rife and all the phenomena we analyzed flourished in excess. His warning went unheeded, as it almost always does when the pathology has far advanced. There is a sage observation concerning the beginning of the reign of Augustus: "Augustus established order, that is to say a durable servitude. For when in a free state someone usurps the sovereignty (supreme rulership) one calls order all that may establish a limitless authority of one, and one calls trouble, dissension and bad government all that might maintain the true liberty of the subjects." The pathology is not cured, but covered up; secrecy spreads its mantle over violence, corruption, and betrayals, and official propaganda interprets as rebirth what is actually the end of a political system.

Such preoccupation with the "decline and fall" yielded in the nineteenth century to one with revolution and the "birth" of new orders. The shrillest voice was that of Karl Marx. In a striking passage from the preface to *A Contribution to the Critique of Political Economy* he states the case of such violent transformations. "In considering such transformations the distinction should always be made between the material transformations of the economic conditions of production, which can be determined with the precision of natural science, and the legal, political, religious, aesthetic, or philosophic—in short ideological—forms in which men become conscious of this conflict and fight it out." The "contradictions of material life" explain all the other transformations; they generate the stresses and strains in other spheres, more particularly in politics. The pathological potential arises which we have explored and each one of them may be employed to adapt the system to the new "conditions of production." Marx surely did not seem to expect such palliatives to work, but the non-revolutionary socialists of the next generation, Bernstein, Kautsky, and the rest, inclined toward the notion that a parliamentary, and more particularly a democratic, system could be made to develop a socialist order. But of course they did not dwell on the phenomena here considered, although it is clear how much they were involved when one considers the cries of treason hurled at these evolutionists by the "orthodox" Marxists; in the bitter controversies that rent, for example, the French socialists, the readiness of some men to take over cabinet posts when they had the votes to support them was roundly denounced as corruption by those who rejected such gradualist maneuvers. That the rise of these radical movements considerably increased violence, both on their part and in the establishments' defense against them, is obvious; the high point may be said to have been the Paris Commune of 1871, greeted by Marx as an exemplary display of proletarian virtue—a theme which was to be elaborated by George Sorel as we have seen. The glorification of violence on ideological grounds has pushed it beyond the limits of functionality, except in terms of the revolutionary new order itself. The functionality of all forms of violence may always be asserted, and has been so asserted by the totalist ideologies of this century. The very fact of their totalist thrust leads to this conclusion. We saw that therefore even the establishment of effective world government is no panacea for the elimination of all violence; on the contrary the problem of more violence will have to be faced. Small wars, in the nature of police actions, will be necessary from time to time to subordinate recalcitrant members of the world community. Such wars would be functional to the world community.

Having shown that police action and war are forms of political violence which are employed on behalf of a political order, we saw that as such they may or may not be systemically functional, but they are presumed to be so under ordinary circumstances. The violence employed by resisters may also prove to be functional. Violent resistance and revolution are endemic in any political order though they are often effectively controlled. The means of avoiding resistance (and revolution) and preventing it from occurring is to combine enforcement with broad consensus to governmental activities, including its procedures. The old saying of substituting ballots for bullets makes little sense when the consensus to what ballots achieve—namely a government—is lacking. It may be impossible to construct a statistical measuring rod that will enable rulers to predict the impending revolution or when it will occur. But a potentially revolutionary situation can be gauged. Every political order is subject to change, and unless means are provided for adaptations of the institutions and processes to such changes as occur in the substructure, such change will generate violence, sporadic and eventually all-engulfing. The process of revolution, we saw, is the marginal extreme; revolution when successful manifests the death of one political order and the emergence of a new one. The violence accompanying such a revolution is therefore necessarily two-faced in its functionality; it is disfunctional to the dying order and functional to the new and emergent one.

We concluded that the widespread employment of violence in this century has frequently and under varying circumstances gone beyond the limit of functionality, when seen in the perspective of the established order. Bombs have become substitutes for arguments. The advancing technology has provided the necessary means for sporadic violence and unusual opportunities for escape. But wiretapping and various new weapons have in turn strengthened the hand of the established powers, which have been increasingly inclined to employ discretion without the sanction of law in their struggle with violence. In these combats the functional limits of violence have been left far behind by both sides. A continuous escalation on the part of both sides of these scattered civil wars has been such that many law-abiding citizens despair of ever seeing public order restored. Hence a flight into utopian anarchism.

The conclusions on betrayal relate closely to those on violence. Through the examination of a number of cases and the writings on them, we came to the conclusion that motivations and causes suggest different forms of betrayal and treason, but they are not sharply separable from each other. Betrayal multiplies where revolutionary mass movements appear on the scene, and the violence which they beget is accompanied by much betrayal and treason. The material showed that betrayal and treason are widely practiced in spite of their moral ill-repute. The reason is that betraying has important functions in the political process. But when treason (betrayal) becomes very widespread, when everyone must fear being betrayed, treason's functionality declines very rapidly. The betrayal of ideals is a common concomitant of this our situation. It is bitter mockery when Ignazio Silone lets a former socialist who has made his peace with the Fascists explain to a young man who is trying to persuade him to make some sacrifice for his old ideal that he has made the greatest of all sacrifices: "I have sacrificed my convictions!" The number of such cases is very great, and by no means only under Fascism. The American ideals of freedom and democracy have become dubious to many young Americans, because they are so generally betrayed. Can they function, if they are so generally betrayed? is countered by: Can they function, if they are not so generally betrayed? These two desperate questions highlight the perplexities of any inquiry into treason's functionality. In summary we showed that it might be said that functionality of treason is the purposive rationality of what treason counsels in the civil war constellations in many contemporary political communities. Such reasoning clashes with the contemporary tendency to impute *manna*, a divine and sacred quality, to the nation and to treat any hostile thought or word as treasonable and by implication as disfunctional.

Corruption, like the other potential pathologies, appears in historical perspective to be ever-present where power is wielded. It bears a close relationship to betrayal, as the corrupt official or group leader betrays his trust. It also is closely linked to violence as mentioned before. Certain kinds of system-related corruption may be part of the system's functioning. A revolutionary's notion of public benefit may be and usually will be radically different from the system's rationale and make-believe. Not only is propaganda corrupting, but every corrupt act is a betrayal. It threatens the political order. Its functionality usually derives from its helping to adapt an antiquated or obsolete political order (and other orders too) to changing conditions and givens, social, technological, or convictional. It proved impossible to be more precise, because these conditions vary greatly on account of the orders that need to be adapted. The main conclusion is that corruption under such conditions is apt to be functional. The other conclusion is that corruption may be reduced—and has in various regimes been reduced from time to time (Britain, Prussia, India, for example). But it is not likely to disappear. The recurrent efforts, so well-known from American city politics, of "cleaning up" are utopian, if conceived in radical terms. An attempt to make corruption disappear entirely is apt to endanger the political order and to bring in an autocratic one. Unfortunately, such an autocratic regime is likely to be more corrupt than the one it replaces. This is due to the rule we discovered that corruption increases with the rigidity and arbitrariness of a regime. The precise ratios cannot at present be determined. It is important, however, for the well-being of the body politic to be forever on the alert. A gentle resignation will not do. Like the job of housecleaning, de-corrupting is never done for good. The reduction of corruption is a never-ending task. Corruption is kept functional by the efforts to get rid of it.

The conclusions we reached on secrecy and propaganda—the two ways of manipulating the ruled by the ruler and of influencing the ruler by the ruled—are similar to those on the other pathologies. They are endemic to all political orders, to all politics. The functionality of both depends upon the system of which they form a part. The greater a regime's autocratic decision-making, the greater will be the secrecy with which the processes are surrounded by which decisions are made. The totalitarian dictatorships of our time present extreme cases of this sort; the doctrine of state secrets, of *arcana imperii,* arose in the age of absolutism: 1550–1789. The Official Secrets Act of Britain still reflects the somewhat authoritarian order of British aristocratic rule. Secrecy is also increased where orders or systems rival each other. In recent years, the totalitarian apparatus of the secret police state has forced other states to adapt to their world by increasing police and security measures. The functionality of such secrecy is often too readily assumed without adequate evidence. Since such methods endanger the systemic order of relatively free democratic systems, they should be adopted with great caution. This problem is found in most Western states, notably in Britain, France, and Germany, as well as the United States.

Curiously enough, much secrecy is accompanied by much propaganda. They both spring from the same desire to manipulate the public, that is to say the ruled. Yet propaganda can no more be eliminated than secrecy. It is inconceivable that the mass publics of today could have the necessary information for participating effectively in the political process as democratic ideology requires. This massive propaganda elicits counter-propaganda of all sorts, and hence requires the secreting of the most essential information. Examples such as those provided by the Vietnam War are plentiful. It has proved exceedingly difficult under these modern conditions to keep both secrecy and propaganda within functional limits. Indeed they represent at the present time probably the most serious pathology, at least in free democratic systems. The pleas and counter-pleas in terms of more publicity or more freedom of the press do little to clarify the crucial issues of functionality. We were able to show that intelligence and espionage continue to be vital to the survival of political regimes, just as propaganda both for and against the establishment is vital to its maintenance and its effective (and objectively necessary) change. Propaganda (and in a measure secrecy) are preferable substitutes for violence and corruption, though violence is often employed for the propaganda of the act, and secrecy assists the corrupters in playing their dubious game.

Our analysis has, I hope, shown that politics needs all these dubious practices; it cannot be managed without violence, betrayal, corruption, secrecy, and propaganda. The moralist will be asking in vain for a moral politics, but he may reasonably ask for *a more moral* politics. If he does, he plays himself a vital role. When acting thus, the moralist is highly functional. For it is through his challenge that these practices are kept within the limits within which they are functional, as aids to constructive change and necessary transformation. It is the problem of politics, both theoretical and practical, to find and maintain that middle course which Aristotle strove for when he pleaded for *mesotes*, the mean between two extremes. It is not a golden mean perhaps, but it is a necessary mean. The moderate man is the only one who can prevent the functional instrumentalities we have dealt with from becoming poisons endangering the political order, while at the same time avoiding the destruction of the order in the effort to get rid of them. And the theorist of such moderate politics will seek to find that same mean in analyzing these phenomena. It is hoped that the present effort succeeds in this task. Politics is a hard thing, said the Romans *(politica est res dura)*, and they meant that it is a dangerous enterprise not suited for the sentimentalist and romantic. For the well-being of the political community is the necessary condition for all other human endeavors. That is why Aristotle thought that the science of politics was the highest of all the sciences; highest in the sense of most needed, and not in that of most certain.

NOTES

1 Introduction: Politics and Morals

1. See my *Constitutional Reason of State: The Survival of the Constitutional Order*, 1957, ch. 1, as well as Martin Hillenbrand, *Power and Morals*, 1949; Benedetto Croce, *Politics and Morals*, 1945; Reinhold Niebuhr, *Christianity and Power Politics*, 1940; H. Butterfield, *Christianity and History*, 1949; Ludwig Freund, *Politik und Ethik*, Frankfurt, 1955. The distinguished German historian Gerhard Ritter tried in *Die Daemonie der Macht*, 5th ed., 1947, a commentary on Thomas More's *Utopia*, to resolve the conflict in terms of the "demonic." But this is no more a resolution than is Friedrich Meinecke's celebrated escape into the esthetic by talking about the "tragedy" of the conflict, in his *Machiavellism*, 1957 (a poor translation of his original title now given in the subtitle as *The Doctrine of Raison d'Etat and Its Place in Modern History*).

2. *The God That Failed*, ed. Richard Crossman, 1950, with contributions André Gide, Arthur Koestler, Ignazio Silone, and others.

3. Thucydides, *History*, Book V, ch. 89.

4. Gabriel and Daniel Cohn-Bendit have in their broadside against established Communism, in the work cited in note 49 of ch. 4, revived an old argument of the anarchists, notably Bakunin, against Marx. Mao's opinion is candidly expressed in his *Problems of War and Strategy:* "The central task and the highest form of the revolution is to seize power by force of arms and to settle the question by war" (my own translation from the German ed.).

5. In his searching discussion of the organic (*Critique of Judgment*, 1793, paragraphs 64–65) Kant at one point, in contrasting organic and mechanical beings, says: "An organic being, therefore, is not a mere machine. For a machine has solely the *power of motion*, whereas an organic being possesses a formative or *creative power* [*bildende Kraft*]. It is a power which it can impart to materials which do not possess it; it is a power of recreating, of self-propagating itself which cannot be explained by the capacity of motion (a mechanism) alone."

6. Talcott Parsons, *Essays in Sociological Theory*, 1954, p. 217.

7. Robert K. Merton, *Social Theory and Social Structure*, 1949 (and later), pp. 115–121 in the new enlarged edition of 1968.

8. A. W. Eister, in his article on function in *A Dictionary of the Social Sciences* (ed. Gould and Kolb), 1964, p. 279.

9. See my *Man and His Government*, 1963, note 1 "Some Thoughts on System Analysis," pp. 24 ff., for further elaboration of the points alluded to in the text.

10. I am writing d*i*sfunctional deliberately, although it has, unfortunately, been widely written as dysfunctional. *Dys* is the Greek prefix for indicating a negative implication, whereas the Latin form is *dis*. *Functio* is a Latin term, and hence good linguistics requires that the word be spelled *disfunctional*, like *dispersion, dispensation*, and so on.

11. See J. R. M. Butler, *The Passing of the Great Reform Bill*, 1914, and E. L. Woodward, *The Age of Reform, 1815–1870*, 1938.

12. My *op. cit.* (note 9, above) ch. 24.

13. "Cited in note 12" pp. 1–2.

14. On these reforms see the works cited in note 11. For a thoroughly conservative critique of a foreigner, cf. Hegel's "The English Reform Bill," tr. in *Hegel's Political Writings*, ed. Z. A. Pelszynski, Oxford, 1964.

15. On justice cf. my *Transcendent Justice: The Religious Dimension of Constitutionalism*, 1964; on the categorical imperative, Immanuel Kant, *Critique of Practical Reason*, 1788, and the searching commentary by H. J. Paton, *The Categorical Imperative*, 1948, and Max Scheler, *Der Formalismus in der Ethik und die materiale Wertethik*, 1916.

16. Frank Popper has recently developed the challenging proposition that poverty is functional and cannot be eliminated from society; what is needed is to limit it.

17. I. Kant, "Ueber ein vermeintliches Recht aus Menschenliebe zu luegen," 1797.

18. A thesis is being written by Frank Nebelung on corruption in the Hitler regime; general works contain some data.

19. Cf. my *op. cit.* note 1 and Meinecke, *op. cit.* (note 1, above).

2 The Problem of Political Violence

1. Carl J. Friedrich, *Man and His Government,* 1963, pp. 232 ff.
2. My *op. cit.*, ch. 34.
3. Carl J. Friedrich, *War: The Causes, Effects and Control of International Violence* (Washington, D.C.: The National Council for the Social Studies of the National Education Association, 1944); Stanley Hoffmann, *The State of War: Essays in the Theory and Practice of International Politics,* 1965; Raymond Aron, *Paix et Guerre entre les Nations,* 1962.
4. Quincy Wright *et al., A Study of War,* 2 vols., 1943.
5. Carl J. Friedrich, "War as a Problem of Government" in Robert Ginsberg, ed., *The Critique of War* (1969), pp. 163–184. This volume contains several other valuable contributions.
6. Governor's Commission on the Los Angeles Riots, *Violence in the City: An End or a Beginning?*, December, 1965 (first called the McCone Commission Report), pp. 27 ff. Cf. also Timothy D. Naegele, "Civilian Complaints against Police" in Renatus Hartogs and Ric Artzt, *Violence: Causes and Solutions,* 1970, 383 ff.
7. Carl J. Friedrich, *Constitutional Government and Democracy,* 4th ed., 1968, ch. V.
8. Eli F. Heckscher, *Mercantilism,* 1935, vol. II, pp. 1 ff.
9. Carl J. Friedrich, *The Age of the Baroque,* 1952, p. 16, where I cite Pietro A. Canonhiero, *Dell'introduzione alle politica, al ragion di stato . . .*, 1614, Book X, where this definition is found: *La ragione di stato e un necessario eccesso del guire commune per fine di publica utilità.*
10. Friedrich, *op. cit.*, p. 220.
11. Jean Bodin, *De la République,* 1576; Latin edition, 1586; cf. also Kenneth McRae's edition of Knolles's English translation of 1606, Cambridge, Mass., 1962.
12. *Op. cit.* (note 1, above), ch. 13.
13. Lewis Mumford, *The City in History,* 1961.
14. David J. Dodd, "Police Mentality and Behavior" in Hartogs and Artzt, *op. cit.* (note 6, above), pp. 153 ff. See also James Q. Wilson, *Varieties of Police Behavior,* 1968, ch. 7.
15. *Ibid.*, p. 151.
16. Edward C. Banfield, *Political Influence,* 1961; Charles E. Merriam, *Political Power: Its Composition and Incidence,* 1934; contrast the view expressed in James Bryce, *The American Commonwealth,* 1888, 1924.
17. David J. Bordua, "Police" in *International Encyclopedia of the Social Sciences,* 1968, p. 174. See also his, ed., *The Police: Six Sociologi-*

cal Essays, 1967, and O. W. Wilson, *Police Administration*, 1950. The British system is described in James Cramer, *The World's Police*, 1964. For a recent reassessment of the situation in the U.S.A. cf. *Task Force Report—The Police* of the President's Commission on Law Enforcement and Administration of Justice, 1967.

18. David J. Bordua and Albert J. Reiss, Jr., "Command, Control and Charisma: Reflections on Police Bureaucracy," *The American Journal of Sociology*, vol. 72, 1966, 68–76; and John P. Clark, "Isolation of the Police: A Comparison of the British and American Situations," *Journal of Criminal Law, Criminology and Police Science*, vol. 56, 1965, pp. 307–319. Clark concludes that "a considerable similarity between the two situations exists." The policemen in both countries feel isolated, a point also stressed in Dodd's article, *op. cit.* (note 14, above).

19. *Final Report—Royal Commission on the Police*, May, 1962, Cmnd. 1728, p. 140.

20. *Ibid.*, Appendix V. Cf. also D. C. Rowat, ed., *The Ombudsman—Citizen's Defender*, 1965, which contains interesting descriptive accounts.

21. *Report, op. cit.* (note 19, above), p. 141.

22. See for this *Report, op. cit.* (note 19, above), pp. 22 ff., 34 ff. and throughout.

23. R. Dogherty, "The Case for the Cop," in Hartogs and Artzt, *op. cit.* (note 6, above).

24. *Ibid.*, p. 180.

25. For Britain and the map, see the *Report, op. cit.* (note 19, above). For the U.S. see the *Task Force Report, op. cit.* (note 17, above), pp. 7–9. For France see Henry Buisson, *La Police: Son histoire*, 1958. For Germany cf. James Cramer, *The World's Police* (1964).

26. Carl J. Friedrich and Z. Brzezinski, *Totalitarian Dictatorship and Autocracy* (2d ed., 1965), chs. 13 and 14.

27. E. V. Walter, "Violence and the Process of Terror," *American Sociological Review*, vol. 29, 1964, 248 ff., suggested this useful term to distinguish "areas of terror" from a "system of terror," but when considered in isolation, such "areas" appear as systems, of course, and can be so considered.

28. Leonard Schapiro, *The Communist Party of the Soviet Union*, London, 1960, p. 431.

29. William A. Westley, "Violence and the Police," *The American Journal of Sociology*, vol. 59, 1953, 34–41. In arguing that "the policeman uses violence illegally because such usage is seen as just, acceptable, and at times expected by his colleague group," he implies that no objective ground, more especially the functionality of such violence in terms of systems maintenance, might be involved. It is a common error among "liberals" to argue this.

30. On justice, cf. the various perspectives developed in *Nomos,* vol. VI: *Justice* (1963); and my *op. cit.* (note 1, above), ch. 14.

31. The writings on war are legion. A recent comprehensive survey was offered by Raymond Aron, *op. cit.* (note 3, above). Cf. also the earlier encylopedic work by Quincy Wright, *op. cit.* (note 4, above), and Hoffmann's collection of essays, *op. cit.* (note 3, above).

32. Cf. my *op. cit.* (note 5, above).

33. Such glorification of war is found throughout the history of political thought. Among modern writers, Hegel is particularly blatant as he relates war to his philosophy of history; the contrary view was maintained by Kant; for the background of the notion of an everlasting peace see my *Inevitable Peace,* 1948, 1969.

34. Cf. the works cited in notes 3 and 4, above. In Wright, note especially pp. 74 ff. and 131 ff.

35. These terms are employed by Q. Wright, *op. cit.* (note 4, above).

36. A radically skeptical view was set forth by Sigmund Freud, *Beyond the Pleasure Principle,* 1920, and *Civilization and Its Discontents,* 1930. These and similar views were rejected in Gardner Murphy, ed., *Human Nature and Enduring Peace,* 1945. The argument has continued ever since, and was given a new dimension by Konrad Lorenz' biological work, *On Aggression,* 1966 [German original, 1963]; cf. also his *King Solomon's Ring,* 1952. Cf. for a broad review of the controversy, including the frustration-aggression syndrome, the article by L. Berkowitz in *The International Encylopedia of the Social Sciences,* 1968, entitled "Aggression."

37. See the recent article by Arthur Maass, "Public Investment Planning in the United States: Analysis and Critique," *Public Policy,* vol. XVIII, 1970, pp. 211 ff., with valuable references.

38. M. M. Bober, *Karl Marx's Interpretation of History,* 1948. More recent works include Robert C. Tucker, *The Marxian Revolutionary Idea,* 1969, ch. 7; James A. Gregor, *A Survey of Marxism: Problems in Philosophy and the Theory of History,* 1965, part II; and Shlomo Avineri, *The Social and Political Thought of Karl Marx,* 1968, especially ch. 6.

39. Pitirim Sorokin, *Social and Cultural Dynamics,* 1937, vol. III, ch. 2, Tables 15 and 17 (combined by me).

40. Cf. my *op. cit.* (note 33, above), and the recent pamphlet by J. H. C. Creyghton, *Emergency World Government,* The Hague, 1969, as well as the last chapter of my *Man and His Government,* 1963.

41. An interesting attempt to relate the violence of war to that of revolution is made in John W. Spanier, *World Politics in an Age of Revolution,* 1967; however, the problem of violence is not a central concern of this interesting study.

3 Resistance and Revolution

1. Harry Eckstein, ed., *Internal War: Problems and Approaches*, 1964. Carl J. Friedrich, *Man and His Government*, 1963; ch. 34 gives the systematic context for the problems of resistance and war as features of politics.

2. Friedrich, *op. cit.* (note 1, above), ch. 19.

3. Emile Durkheim, *De la Division de Travail*, 1893, 1932, Book III, ch. 1, para. 3.

4. Basic is Karl Renner, *Der Kampf der oesterreichischen Nationen um den Staat*, 1907, and *Nation und Staat* . . . , 1918; and R. Johannet, *Le Principe des Nationalités*, 1923; and Karl Deutsch, *Nationalism and Social Communication*, 1953. In none of these works is the problem of violent resistance given the central place it deserves.

5. Henry Wells, *The Modernization of Puerto Rico: A Political Study of Changing Values and Institutions*, 1969.

6. Carl J. Friedrich, *Puerto Rico: Middle Road to Freedom—Fuero Fundamental*, 1959.

7. John Calhoun, *Works* (1853), vol. I, pp. 12 ff. and 38. Calhoun was, in a way, harking back to the resistance notions of the feudal order. He put them into stipulative terms, but they might be made into a working hypothesis for a descriptive analysis.

8. Paul Friedrich, "Language and Politics in India," *Daedalus*, Summer, 1962, pp. 543 ff. Cf. my *Trends of Federalism in Theory and Practice*, 1969, ch. 18. There are also some figures on the quantitative distribution of languages. The riots are mentioned on page 139.

9. Charles E. Merriam, *Political Power: Its Composition and Incidence*, 1934, where the cited passage is found on page 159. An interesting overview of the problems of *Civil Disobedience* is contained in the pamphlet of the Center for the Study of Democratic Institutions, an occasional paper of April, 1966. Cf. also M. Q. Sibley, *Quiet Battle: Writings on the Theory and Practice of Non-Violence*, 1963.

10. On this and especially on the form Gandhi gave it, Erik Erikson's psychoanalytic speculations are very suggestive (Erik H. Erikson, *Gandhi's Truth: On the Origin of Militant Nonviolence*, 1969). See also Lloyd I. and Susanne H. Rudolph, *The Modernity of Tradition*, 1967, part II, pp. 155 ff. Gandhi's own views are given in M. K. Gandhi, *Gandhi's Autobiography: The Story of My Experiments with Truth*, 1948, and *The Gandhi Reader*, H. A. Jack, ed., 1956.

11. Cf., for example, the Winter, 1968, issue of *Daedalus*, entitled "Students in Politics," where many instances are found, beginning with Seymour Martin Lipset's "Students and Politics in Comparative Per-

spective." Cf. also Morris B. Abram, "Reflections on the University in the New Revolution," *Daedalus,* Winter, 1970, issue entitled "The Embattled University," pp. 122 ff.

12. Hans Rothfels, *The German Opposition to Hitler: An Appraisal,* 2d ed., 1948; Gerhard Ritter, *Carl Goerdeler . . . ,* 1954; Constantine FitzGibbon, *20 July,* 1956. The moral note is particularly striking in Dietrich Bonhoeffer, *Letters and Papers from Prison,* Bethge, ed., 1953. Compare with it Saul Friedlaender, *Kurt Gerstein: The Ambiguity of Good,* 1969, and Annedore Leber, *Das Gewissen steht auf* (1954) [English edition, *Conscience in Revolt* (1957)], which gives personal sketches of the men and women involved in the resistance; striking is the case of von Tresckow, who had answered his wife's plea that the enterprise was bound to fail by saying that it (the killing of Hitler) must be done not because of the prospect of success, but because of the likelihood of failure; for thus it would be a witness to the moral cause of overthrowing evil. Count Moltke did not agree; at one point he argued on the question of violence that it was a manifestation of "the beast in man" and that violence bred violence. See Paul Kekskemeti, *The Unexpected Revolution: Social Forces in the Hungarian Uprising,* 1961; for the predominantly national sentiments of Vlassov's enterprise, held however with religious fervor, cf. George Fischer, *Soviet Opposition to Stalin: A Case Study in World War II,* 1953. Cf. also the work cited in note 18, below.

13. Cf. Erikson, *op. cit.* (note 10, above); for Moltke, see Ernst Wolf, "Zum Verhaeltnis der politischen und moralischen Motive in der deutschen Widerstandsbewegung" in *Der Deutsche Widerstand gegen Hitler,* Schmitthenner and Buchheim, eds., 1967, and the there-cited monograph by Ger van Room, *Neuordnung im Widerstand—Der Kreisauer Kreis,* 1961.

14. My *op. cit.* (note 1, above), pp. 637 ff. See also my *Transcendent Justice,* 1964, and *Constitutional Reason of State,* 1957.

15. Oscar Jaszi and John D. Lewis, *Against the Tyrant: The Tradition and Theory of Tyrannicide,* 1957. Cf. also Kurt Woltzendorf, *Staatsrecht und Naturrecht in der Lehre vom Widerstandsrecht des Volkes,* 1916. Note also the *locus classicus* in Thomas Aquinas, *Summa Theologica,* II. II. q. 42, art. 2. See also introduction to Johannes Althusius' *Politica Methodice Digesta,* 1933.

16. Earl Latham, ed., *The Meaning of McCarthyism,* 1965. Cf. also *Investigations of Senators: Joseph R. McCarthy and William Benton,* pursuant to S. Res. 187 and 304, Report of the Subcommittee on Privileges and Elections to the Committee on Rules and Administration, U.S. Government Printing Office, 1952. This report is inspired by a critical

sentiment, intensified by McCarthy's abusive refusal to testify, calling the committee's members Communist agents and the resolution a Communist smear.

17. Jaszi and Lewis, *op. cit.* (note 15, above), ch. 20, quote on p. 233.

18. Cf. the works cited in note 12, above, and Harold C. Deutsch, *The Conspiracy Against Hitler in the Twilight War,* 1968.

19. Andrei D. Sakharov, *Progress, Coexistence and Intellectual Freedom,* with introduction and notes by Harrison E. Salisbury (New York Times, 1968), is perhaps the best statement of the issue. Cf. also the striking recent argument by Andrei Amalrik in *Will the Soviet Union Survive until 1984?,* 1970.

20. See ch. 21 of my *Totalitarian Dictatorship and Autocracy,* with Z. Brzezinski, 2d ed., 1965, and the entire part VI, where resistance under and against totalitarian regimes is extensively and comparatively analyzed.

21. Acute observations are found in B. Moore, Jr., *Terror and Progress U.S.S.R.: Some Sources of Change and Stability in the Soviet Union,* 1954, ch. 5.

22. C. J. Friedrich, ed., *Nomos,* vol. VIII: *Revolution,* 1966, offers many contrasting views. Cf. also Hannah Arendt's much discussed *On Revolution,* 1963, in which she argues that revolutions have become the prime political factor, because of the nuclear stalemate, which has been sharply and interestingly criticized by Chalmers Johnson in *Revolutionary Change* (1966) as "too restricted." The problem is set in methodological perspective by George A. Kelly and Linda B. Miller, *Internal War and International Systems: Perspectives on Method,* Occasional Papers in International Affairs, Harvard University, August, 1969.

23. Alfred G. Meyer, *Marxism: The Unity of Theory and Praxis,* 1954. He gives many references to writers on this issue.

24. John H. Kautsky, *The Political Thought of Karl Kautsky: A Theory of Democratic, Anti-Communist Marxism,* 1951. Cf. also Karl Kautsky's own *Parlamentarismus und Demokratie,* 3d ed., Stuttgart, 1920, and Lenin's violent attacks in his *State and Revolution* in *Selected Works,* vol. VII, as discussed in Alfred G. Meyer's *Leninism,* 1957.

25. Arthur Bauer, *Essai sur les Révolutions,* 1908, p. 11, defines revolution as follows: "*Les révolutions sont les changements tentés ou réalisés par la force dans la constitution des sociétés.*" The same view is also stated by Arendt, *op. cit.* (note 22, above), p. 10, but in her last chapter she seems to be taking a different view. Sheldon Wolin in his introduction to the Johnson volume, *op. cit.* (note 22, above), also takes this position; and on page ix he speaks of "widespread use of violence."

26. Leon Trotsky, *My Life,* 1930, p. 320.

27. For further comments on "suddenness" see my *op. cit.* (note 1, above), pp. 642–643.

28. On the *coup d'état,* cf. my *op. cit.* (note 1, above), p. 642, and Curzio Malaparte, *Coup d'Etat: The Technique of Revolution,* 1932; V. Gueli, "Colpo di Stato" in *Enciclopedia del diritto,* 1960; and A. L. Goodspeed, *The Conspirators: A Study of the Coup d'Etat,* 1962.

29. E. Rosenstock-Huessy has gone so far as to link these unlimited revolutions to the evolution of Western culture. See his *Out of Revolution* (1938) [a revised English version of his *Die Europaeischen Revolutionen* (1931)]. According to him, each of the great European revolutions has been made by one of the major nations of Europe, which in its course has developed its own life style.

30. Cf. Arnold S. Feldman, "Violence and Volatility of Revolution" in Eckstein, *op. cit.* (note 1, above), pp. 211 ff. Feldman stresses the difficulty of estimating "revolutionary potential," cf. esp. p. 126.

31. A striking recent example is Truman Nelson, *The Right of Revolution,* 1968, who openly appeals to the Declaration of Independence and cites John Q. Adams at length, who himself in 1842 launched such an appeal in Congress as discussed by Nelson in ch. 7. See also his ch. 8, which begins: "John Quincy Adams was not the only American to say yes to the right of revolution." He then shows how the abolitionists had "no hesitation in breaking the law . . . mostly by violence."

32. Aristotle's well-known discussion is found in Book V of the *Politics,* but the stasis (change) which he discusses is not only a revolution in the usual sense, but any kind of overturn, such as may result from an election. The matter is further complicated by the broad meaning of *aitia* which is not only the efficient cause of modern parlance.

33. Besides Rosenstock-Huessy, *op. cit.* (note 29, above), see Crane Brinton, *The Anatomy of Revolution* (1938); R. B. Merriman, *Six Contemporaneous Revolutions, 1640–1660,* 1938. Cf. also the works cited by Arendt, *op. cit.* (note 22, above); Pettee, *op. cit.* (note 34, below); and Pitirim Sorokin, *The Sociology of Revolutions* (1925).

34. George S. Pettee, *The Process of Revolution* (1938), and the restatement of his position twenty years later "Revolution—Typology and Process" in *Nomos,* vol. VIII: *Revolution* (1966), pp. 10 ff. His penetrating analysis has been unfairly neglected beside the more flashy one of Brinton.

35. Karl Deutsch, "External Involvement in Internal War," in Eckstein, *op. cit.* (note 1, above), pp. 100 ff., gives some interesting statistics on recruitment and attrition, pp. 104 ff. Cf. also Kelly and Miller as cited in note 22, above, who on p. 13 state that "both international systems and domestic systems may be analyzed as potential *war* systems."

36. Hermann Mosler, *Die Intervention im Voelkerrecht* (Berlin,

1937). Cf. also "Intervention and World Politics," a special issue of *Journal of International Affairs* (vol. XXII, no. 2, 1968). Soviet scholars have taken a very conventional view, in spite of actions by the Soviet Union in Finland and Hungary, not to mention Czechoslovakia. Cf. M. M. Boguslavsky, *Staatliche Immunitaet,* 1965 [from the Russian] in which a radical doctrine of absolute sovereignty is made the basis of the argumentation; by implication, intervention is excluded. This position has been modified since Brezhnev's proclamation of the solidarity of all socialist countries, at the Soviet Union's discretion. See for this complex of questions Edward McWhinney, "Soviet Bloc Publicists and the East-West Legal Debate," *The Canadian Yearbook of International Law,* 1964, pp. 172 ff., and the same author's "Soviet and Western International Law and the Cold War in the Era of Bipolarity," *Canadian Yearbook of International Law,* 1963, pp. 40 ff., as well as his "Changing International Law Method and Objectives in the Era of Soviet-Western Detente," *The American Journal of International Law,* vol. 59, 1965, pp. 1 ff. Cf. also G. I. Tunkin, "Theoretische Fragen des Voelkerrechts," *Modernes Voelkerrecht—Form oder Mittel der Aussenpolitik,* W. Wengler, ed. (Berlin, 1965). This distinguished scholar cited with approval: "*Die sozialistischen Laender (in the Erklaerung der Delegierten der kommunistischen Arbeiterparteien der sozialistischen Laender von 1957) gestalten ihre Beziehungen zu einander nach den Prinzipien der vollen Gleichberechtigung, der territorialen Integritaet, der staatlichen Unabhaengigkeit und Souveraenitaet und der Nichteinmischung in die inneren Angelegenheiten des anderen . . . ,*" pp. 266 ff.

37. On the Vietnam issue the literature has become very extensive. Cf. especially the Committee on Foreign Relations, J. William Fulbright, Chairman, *The Vietnam Hearings,* 1966; G. McT. Kahin and John W. Lewis, *The United States in Vietnam,* 1967; and H. E. Salisbury, *Behind the Lines—Hanoi,* 1967.

38. Cf. my discussion in *Introduction to Political Theory,* 1968, pp. 37 f.; also Eugene Kamena, "The Concept of a Political Revolution" in *Nomos,* vol. VIII: *Revolution* (1966), pp. 122 ff.; the conceptual problem is also treated by Johnson, *op. cit.* (note 22, above), esp. chs. 1 and 5, pp. 88 ff.

39. For this phenomenon, see my *Constitutional Government and Democracy,* 4th ed., 1968, ch. VIII.

40. Howard Fast's remarkable novel *Freedom Road,* 1944, depicts this tragedy. For the historical context, cf. Paul Buck, *The Road to Reunion, 1865–1900,* 1938, but he perhaps underplays the repression of the blacks.

41. For the theoretical context and its historical perspective see my

op. cit. (note 38, above), ch. 3. It is not to be wondered at that Lincoln's ideas are being put to a new use by the blacks and their sympathizers. Cf. Nelson, *op. cit.* (note 31, above), p. 145.

42. Even now, books like Nelson, *op. cit.* (note 31, above), maintain it. But, of course, Johnson, *op. cit.* (note 22, above), opposes it.

43. On founding, cf. my *op. cit.* (note 1, above), ch. 22; Arendt makes it central in her discussion of revolution, *op. cit.* (note 22, above), chs. 4 and 5.

44. Note the suggestive title of John D. Montgomery, *Forced to Be Free*, 1957. Cf. also John Gimbel, *The American Occupation of Germany: Politics and the Military, 1945–1949*, 1968, esp. ch. 13, pp. 226 ff. A good recent German reassessment has been given by Hans Peter Schwarz, *Vom Reich zur Bundesrepublik, 1945–1949*, 1966.

45. Rousseau, *Contrat Social* (1863), esp. Bk. I, ch. VII; my comments in *op. cit.* (note 38, above), ch. 12; and my paper "Law and Dictatorship" in *Annales de Philosophie Politique*, vol. V: *Rousseau et la Philosophie Politique* (Paris, 1965), pp. 77 ff. Compare now the comments in Judith N. Shklar, *Men and Citizens* (1969).

46. For the *Rechsstaat*, cf. my *op. cit.* (note 39, above) and translated into German as *Der Verfassungsstaat der Neuzeit* (1954), ch. 1; "Rebuilding the German Constitution," *American Political Science Review*, vol. XLIII, pp. 461 ff. and 704 ff.; and "Military Government as a Step toward Self-Rule," *Public Opinion Quarterly*, vol. 7, 1943, pp. 527 ff.

47. See my *Transcendent Justice*, 1964, esp. ch. 1.

48. Samuel P. Huntington, *Political Order in Changing Societies*, 1968.

49. Johnson, *op. cit.* (note 22, above), p. 119.

50. Feldman, *op. cit.* (note 30, above), p. 115.

4 Reflections on Political Violence in General

1. On legitimacy see my *Man and His Government*, 1963, ch. 13. See also Max Weber, *Wirtschaft und Gesellschaft*, 1921, 1925, pp. 17–19. His is a typical case of the conventional "definition." He inherited this definition from public law writings, e.g., Georg Jellinek, *Allgemeine Staatslehre*, 1900, pp. 160–161; 3rd ed., 1913, p. 183. For a recent instance cf. A. P. d'Entrèves, *La Dottrina del Stato*, 1962, p. 59 [English edition, p. 34]. Almond and other American political scientists have followed this tradition. Cf. Gabriel Almond and L. Bingham Powell, *Comparative Politics*, 1966, pp. 17 f.

2. Not only Sorel, but others have tried to draw a sharp distinction between "force" and violence, usually for ideological or propagandistic

reasons. Just recently Max Kampelmann in an otherwise significant article, "Dissent, Disobedience, and Defense in a Democracy," *World Affairs*, vol. 133, 1970, pp. 124 ff. wrote: ". . . it is fallacious to equate violence with force which is indeed essential to any ordered society. Violence is the illegal use of force . . . ," p. 126.

3. Georges Sorel, *Réflexions sur la Violence*, 3rd ed., 1912, with later appendices, p. 273. English edition, *Reflections on Violence*, with introduction by Edward Shils, London, N.D., p. 182. [They will hereafter be cited as Sorel (F) and Sorel (E).]

4. Sorel, *op. cit.*, ch. 6.

5. Sorel, *op. cit.*, (E) p. 186, and (F) p. 279.

6. Shils, Introduction to *op. cit.* (note 3, above), p. 25.

7. Sorel, *op. cit.*, (E) p. 279, and (F) p. 442.

8. *Ibid.*, (E) p. 285, and (F) p. 453.

9. Ida Wyss, *Virtù und Fortuna bei Boiardo und Ariost*, 1931; E. W. Mayer, *Machiavelli's Geschichtsauffassung und sein Begriff Virtù*, 1912; E. E. Cassirer, *Individuum und Kosmos in der Philosophie der Renaissance*, 1927.

10. Frantz Fanon, *Les Damnés de la Terre*, 1961 (English, *The Wretched of the Earth*, 1966).

11. James Baldwin, *Notes of a Native Son*, 1955, and *Another Country*, 1962. Malcom X, *The Autobiography*, 1964. Rap Brown, *Die Nigger Die*, 1965, and Herbert J. Storing, ed., *What Country Have I?*, with selections from these and other black writers, 1970, which affords an overview with a good selective bibliography. On this entire literature see the keen critical comments by another Negro writer, Albert Murray, *The Omni-Americans*, 1970. Cf. also John Hope Franklin's historical *From Slavery to Freedom*, 1947.

12. Frantz Fanon, *The Wretched of the Earth*, Grove Press edition, 1966, pp. 18 and 20.

13. Sorel, *op. cit.*, (E) pp. 181–182, and (F) p. 270.

14. *Ibid.*, (E) p. 182, and (F) p. 273.

15. Hugh Davis Graham and Ted Robert Gurr, eds., *The History of Violence in America: A Report of the National Commission on the Causes and Prevention of Violence*, 1969, esp. ch. 2, pp. 45 ff.

16. Richard Marsh Brown, in *op. cit.* (note 15, above), p. 154. The list is found on pp. 218 ff.

17. See Theodor Lindner, *Die Veme*, Muenster, 1888. Among earlier studies, which are quite numerous, mention might be made of Paul Wigand, *Das Femegericht Westphalens*, Hamm, 1825, and Theodor Bercke, *Geschichte der Westphaelischen Femgerichte*, Bremen, 1814–1815 (2 vols.). There had been a romantic tendency to glorify these courts

as manifestations of "Germanic" freedom, but Lindner comments: "Even in their native lands these courts did not contribute to the improvement of desperate conditions. Never was public order and security (safety) worse off than at the height of the Fehme Courts; the documents show clearly how these courts enabled rascals to trouble honest men. They did not clarify and improve the law, but increased the general confusion." (P. XXII.) "Their basic thought was to strengthen the law, and if they did not succeed they shared this fate with other attempts in those wild times." (P. XXXI.)

18. Brown, *op. cit.* (note 16, above), pp. 167–168.

19. William J. McConnell, *Frontier Law: A Story of Vigilante Days,* 1924; see also numerous references in Brown, *op. cit.* (note 16, above).

20. Brown, *op. cit.*, p. 177.

21. Brown, *op. cit.*, footnote 62.

22. Brown, *op. cit.*, p. 178.

23. In what follows we are following Brown, *op. cit.*, pp. 180 ff.

24. Carl J. Friedrich and Robert McCloskey, eds., *From the Declaration of Independence to the Constitution,* 1954; and Carl Becker, *The Declaration of Independence,* 1951, ch. 2, also esp. pp. 7 ff.

25. Carl J. Friedrich, *Constitutional Reason of State,* 1957; and Friedrich Meinecke, *Machiavellism,* 1957, a translation of *Die Idee der Staatsraison in der neueren Geschichte,* 1924, 1925.

26. Brown, *op. cit.* (note 16, above), cites Mott, *Regulators of Northern Indiana,* p. 17, which I was unable to get hold of.

27. Brown, *op. cit.*, pp. 183 ff.

28. Brown, *op. cit.*, pp. 196 and 201.

29. Willard A. Heaps, *Riots U.S.A., 1765–1965,* 1966.

30. Heaps, *op. cit.*, pp. 3–4.

31. Heaps, *op. cit.*, deals with the following: Stamp Act Riots; Doctors' Riot, 1788; Anti-Catholic Riots, 1844; Astor Place Riot, 1849; Draft Riots, 1863; Anti-Chinese Riot, 1871; Steel Lockout, 1892; Pullman Strike, 1894; Miners' Riot, 1899; Race Riot, 1917; Police Strike, Boston, 1919; The Bonus Army, 1932; Prison Riot, 1952; there are also chapters on contemporary tensions and riots.

32. Heaps, *op. cit.*, pp. 50 ff.

33. Cf. Carl Sandburg, *Abraham Lincoln, The War Years,* vol. II, 1936, p. 372: "There can be no army without men. Men can only be had voluntarily or involuntarily. We have ceased to obtain them voluntarily, and to obtain them involuntarily is the draft—the conscription." And at another point (p. 370) he said that either men must be drafted "or we must relinquish the original object of the contest, together with all the blood and treasure already expended in the effort to secure it." Cf. also

Lincoln's sage comments on his refusal to appoint a judge to make a searching judicial inquiry into these riots, p. 368.

34. Heaps, *op. cit.* (note 29, above), p. 52. Cf. also the entire ch. 6 on the Draft Riots.

35. Heaps, *op. cit.*, pp. 52–53.

36. Cf. the recent article by Edward Luttwak, "A Scenario for a Military Coup d'Etat in the United States," *Esquire*, July, 1970.

37. *Crime in the United States: Uniform Crime Reports, 1968*, released August 13, 1969, by J. Edgar Hoover for the F.B.I.

38. Gustave Le Bon, *The Crowd: A Study of the Popular Mind*, 1922, translated from the French *La psychologie des foules*, 1895.

39. Sorel, *op. cit.* (note 3, above), (E) p. 215, and (F) p. 329.

40. Chalmers Johnson, *Revolutionary Change*, 1966, ch. 6.

41. T. P. Thornton, "Terror as a Weapon of Political Agitation," in Harry Eckstein, ed., *Internal War: Problems and Approaches*, 1964, pp. 71 ff. esp. p. 73.

42. Carl J. Friedrich and Zbigniew Brzezinski, *Totalitarian Dictatorship and Autocracy*, rev. ed., 1965, chs. 13–15.

43. Brian Crozier, *The Rebels: A Study of Post-War Insurrections*, London, 1960. The problem of the rebel's outlook has been most incisively presented by Albert Camus, *The Rebel*—actually a rather unfortunate title for the French *L'Homme Révolté*, since the latter suggests the double entendre which is implied in the verb *to revolt* and *to be revolted* (disgusted).

44. Z. K. Brzezinski, *The Permanent Purge: Politics in Soviet Totalitarianism*, 1956. This is summarized in Friedrich and Brzezinski, *op. cit.* (note 42, above), ch. 15.

45. On the Cultural Revolution see Klaus Mehnert, *Peking and the New Left*, 1968; Mao is there reported as saying: "We must bring up millions of successors who will carry on the cause of proletarian revolution," p. 51. Cf. also Philip Bridgham, "Mao's Cultural Revolution: Origin and Development," *China Quarterly*, January-February, 1967, pp. 1–35. Also numerous articles giving contrasting views in *Problems of Communism*, 1967 and 1968, and in FEER.

46. Edward McWhinney, "Peaceful Coexistence and Soviet Western International Law," *American Journal of International Law*, vol. 56, pp. 951 ff.

47. Cf. the mocking remarks in Andrei Amalrik, *Will the Soviet Union Survive until 1984?*, New York Times, 1970, p. 28.

48. Thornton, *op. cit.* (note 41, above), p. 87.

49. The student revolt manifests this blind alley. Daniel and Gabriel Cohn-Bendit in their *Obsolete Communism: The Left Wing Alternative*,

1968 (first published in German under the title *Linksradikalismus -Gewaltkur gegen die Alterskrankheit des Kommunismus*, 1968—also in French), prescribe violence (a *Gewaltkur*) as the solution for the problems of the university after insisting that students now see "that their Rektor derives his power from the Prefect of Police." Unofficial violence by provoking official violence proved in fact no such thing, and to speak of police aggression in such a situation is to practice Hitler's doctrine of the big lie. Bryan Wilson, in *The Youth Culture and Universities*, 1970, has explored this problem for Britain, but without special attention to violence. He has emphasized, I believe rightly, the extent to which the mass media, by highlighting the sensational aspects of violence, contributed to its spread. "They have thereby helped to create a climate of greater tolerance for deviant behavior . . . and have presented deviant behavior as part of the youth culture. . . ." He also notes that they have "served as agencies of cultural diffusion, transmitting criminal ideas from one society to another . . . ," pp. 43–44.

5 The Ubiquity of Betrayal and Its Political Significance

1. Some of the points in this chapter were brought forward in my article in the *Political Quarterly*, "Political Pathology," January-March, 1966, pp. 76 ff. Some of the general literature there referred to is quite important here; see ch. 7 for further references (note 12 and 13 of article on p. 18).

2. Hans Magnus Enzensberger, *Politik und Verbrechen*, 1964, observes that "the traitors are the others."

3. *Ibid.*

4. Cf. esp. Jay Lifton, *Thought Reform and the Psychology of Totalism: A Study of Brainwashing in China*, 1962.

5. Cf. C. Vann Woodward, "Notes on Loyalty," *American Scholar*, 1964. Woodward explores once more the problem of the conflict of loyalties of the Southerner who is confronted with regional and national claims of identification.

6. See the writings cited in the next note.

7. James Baldwin, *Notes of a Native Son*, 1955; Eldridge Cleaver, *Soul on Ice*, 1968; Stokely Carmichael and Charles V. Hamilton, *Black Power: The Politics of Liberation in America*, 1967; *The Autobiography of Malcolm X*, 1964, e.g., p. 255, to mention only a few striking examples. See the next chapter for fuller development.

8. Albert Murray, *The Omni-Americans: New Perspectives on Black Experience and American Culture*, 1970, p. 6.

9. Claude Brown, *Manchild in the Promised Land,* 1965; cf. Murray's comment, *op. cit.*, p. 98.

10. Murray, *ibid.*

11. Rebecca West, *The Meaning of Treason,* 1947, pp. 366–367. In a later edition Miss West has presented comparative material from the United States. Cf. in this connection Ralph Toledano and Victor Lasky, *Seeds of Treason,* 1950; Adam Yarmolinsky, *Case Studies in Personnel Security*, 1955; and Morton Grodzins, *The Loyal and the Disloyal,* 1956.

12. Comparable situations were described by Louis de Jong, *The German Fifth Column in the Second World War,* 1956, and E. von Salomon, *Die Geächteten,* 1926. Cf. for the problem also Albert Camus, *L'Homme Révolté*, 1951.

13. Cf. my chapter "International Politics and Foreign Policy in Developed (Western) Systems," in R. Barry Farrell, ed., *Approaches to Comparative and International Politics*, 1966, esp. pp. 112 ff.

14. Alexander H. Leighton, *The Governing of Men,* 1945. Written on the basis of immediate practical experience, it is superior for our purpose to later reflected studies. Cf. also Grodzins, *op. cit.* (note 11, above). But cf. also the thorough recent reappraisal by Audrie Girdner and Anne Loftis, *The Great Betrayal: The Evacuation of the Japanese Americans during World-War II*, 1969.

15. This was done by Georg Jellinek in a famous essay, *Die Erklaerung der Menschen- und Buergerrechte*, 1895 (also in English). Jellinek's argument was, of course, contested in France. About his neglect of property cf. my *Man and His Government,* 1963, pp. 357 ff.

16. R. H. Bainton, *Christian Attitudes Toward Peace and War*, 1960; Central Committee for Conscientious Objection, *Handbook for Conscientious Objectors,* A. Tatum, ed., 10th ed., 1968. Abe Fortas, *Concerning Dissent and Civil Disobedience,* 1968; Milton R. Konvits, *Religious Liberty and Conscience: A Constitutional Inquiry*, 1968; Paul Ramsay, *War and the Christian Conscience*, 1961; Howard Zinn, *Disobedience and Democracy: Nine Fallacies on Law and Order*, 1968. It is clear even from the titles that these books are not primarily concerned with the treason aspect of objection, or its possible function. But their arguments lend credence to the hypothesis that that kind of treason often is functional and in any case is usually intended to be.

17. Baldwin, *op. cit.* (note 7, above), p. 26.

18. Murray, *op. cit.* (note 8, above), *passim.*

19. Cleaver, *op. cit.* (note 7, above), p. 132.

20. David Wise and Thomas B. Ross, *The Invisible Government*, 1964, chs. 14–17, while inclined toward overdramatization, give some descriptive accounts of these operations.

21. Albert Camus, *op. cit.* (note 12, above).

22. See my *Totalitarian Dictatorship and Autocracy* (with Z. K. Brzezinski) rev. ed., 1965, p. 121 f. where treason is placed within the context of a general expansion of criminal law; cf. Harold J. Berman, *Justice in the USSR*, 1950, for context, also later editions.

23. Friedrich Meinecke, *Machiavellism*, 1957—a rather misleading translation of the original title *Die Idee der Staatsraison in der neueren Geschichte*, 1921, 1925. Cf. also my *Constitutional Reason of State*, 1957, which explores the (by Meinecke neglected) constitutionalist angle of this problem.

6 Some Treason Cases Analyzed: Judas and After

1. Stanley Wolpert, *Nine Hours to Rama*, 1962, Bantam, 1963, p. 220.

2. The contrary is constantly demanded by people insisting upon commitment. They often do not realize that they are themselves traitors, as they betray the commitment to learning and truth, i.e., the *universitas* whose motto is *veritas*.

3. Eldridge Cleaver, *The Land Question*, as excerpted in Herbert J. Storing, ed., *What Country Have I? Political Writings by Black Americans*, 1970, pp. 184 ff.

4. Storing, *op. cit.*, pp. 189–190.

5. Storing, *op. cit.*, p. 185; *contra* Albert Murray, *The Omni-Americans*, 1970, who speaks on p. 6 of the "negative aspects" that are "constantly overemphasized" and of wishing to do "justice to U.S. Negroes, not only as American citizens, but also as fascinating human beings." Cf. also *Negro in Defense*, a wartime pamphlet of the Council for Democracy, published in 1942, and pleading for greater equality in the armed forces. It shows, of course, the stamp of wartime rhetoric, but contradicts the assertions of Cleaver, as cited.

6. Stokely Carmichael and Charles V. Hamilton, *Black Power: The Politics of Liberation in America*, 1967.

7. He was cited by a recent Royal Commission as saying: "I found two nations warring in the bosom of a single state." That was in 1839. A *Preliminary Report of the Royal Commission on Bilingualism and Biculturism*, Ottawa, 1965, p. 114.

8. Rebecca West, *The Meaning of Treason*, 1947, and even more in *The New Meaning of Treason*, 1964, has discussed this aspect.

9. Henri Michel, *Histoire de la Résistance*, 1950; Henri Michel and Z. Mirkine-Guetzevitch, *Les Idées politiques et sociales de la résistance*, 1954. H. E. Lichten (H. E. Riesser), *Collaboration*, Zurich, 1957. William L. Langer, *Our Vichy Gamble*, 1947.

10. Robert R. Bowie and Associates, *United States Foreign Policy: Ideology and Foreign Affairs,* 1959 (esp. contribution by Brzezinski). Cf. also my *Man and His Government,* 1963, ch. 4, and Carmichael and Hamilton, *op. cit.,* p. viii.

11. Friedrich and Brzezinski, *Totalitarian Dictatorship and Autocracy,* rev. ed., 1965, chs. 7 and 8.

12. Whittaker Chambers, *Witness,* 1952; cf. also the comment by Margret Boveri, *Der Verrat im Zwanzigsten Jahrhundert,* 4 vols. 1956–1957, English edition *Treason in the Twentieth Century,* 1961; I am citing the original edition in the notes that follow.

13. Boveri, *op. cit.,* vol. III, pp. 156 ff. agrees.

14. Speech of February 6, 1946, during the election being held in the Soviet Union.

15. In making such a statement, I may seem to get involved in the accusations and counter-accusations about Communism in the U.S. government. Roosevelt, in a forceful speech in 1944 at Boston ridiculed all such notions, and as these accusations were stated they deserved this ridicule; James McGregor Burns suggests this in his splendid new biography, *Roosevelt: Soldier of Freedom,* 1970, pp. 28–29. Cf. also Harold Ickes, *The Secret Diary,* vol. III, 1955, who deals with the accusations of the Dies Committee (on Un-American Activities) repeatedly. "As usual, I was listed as being sympathetic with Communism. I have not and never have been. . . ." (p. 356). In a conversation with Ickes, the author received a different impression.

16. Alger Hiss, *In the Court of Public Opinion,* 1957, completely neglects this aspect of the matter; one is puzzled whether to consider it deliberate and tactically motivated, or due to lack of self-understanding.

17. Boveri, *op. cit.* (note 12, above), pp. 156 ff. agrees.

18. Boveri, *op. cit.,* pp. 121–122.

19. Hiss, *op. cit.* (note 16, above).

20. *July 20, 1944,* published by Bundeszentrale fuer politische Bildung, in a number of editions; the one I used is of 1964. The quote is on p. 324.

21. *Ibid.,* p. 354. See also Annedore Leber, *Das Gewissen steht auf Lebensbilder aus dem deutschen Widerstand, 1933–1945,* Berlin, 1954. On p. 126 the same man reports to have written shortly before his death: "The most terrible thing is to know that it cannot succeed and that, in spite of that, it must be done for our country and for our children."

22. Hans Rothfels, *The German Opposition to Hitler,* 2d ed., 1948 (there are later German editions). Cf. also Walter Schmitthenner and Hans Buchheim, eds., *Der Deutsche Widerstand gegen Hitler,* 1966; and Dieter Ehlers, *Technik und Moral einer Verschwoerung—Der Aufstand am. 20 Juli, 1944,* Schriftenreihe, Heft 62, 1964.

23. Besides the work cited above in note 22, cf. the contribution of Hans Mommsen to Schmitthenner and Buchheim, *op. cit.*, pp. 73 ff., "Gesellschaftsbild und Verfassungsplaene des deutschen Widerstands." The Christian motivation was most impressively stated by Dietrich Bonhoeffer, whose *Letters and Papers from Prison*, London, 1953, have since been implemented by others of his writings not germane here.

24. Constantine Fitzgibbon, *20 July*, 1956; Gerhard Ritter, *Carl Goerdeler und die deutsche Widerstandsbewegung*, Stuttgart, 1954; A. W. Dulles, *Germany's Underground*, 1947; Saul Friedlaender, *Kurt Gerstein: The Ambiguity of the Good*, 1969, and many others.

25. Secretary of State Cordell Hull commented at the time that we hated the men who made the revolt as much as those against which it was directed—an unbelievable remark in present perspective.

26. Cf. the insightful discussion in Henry Dwight Sedgwick, *The Life of Marcus Aurelius*, 1922, esp. ch. 22 on "The Enforcement of the Law."

27. From an interview with the brother of Count Stauffenberg, in front of my seminar, on April 26, 1965. Cf. also Ernst Wolf, in Leber, *op. cit.* (note 21, above) and some of the writings cited.

28. Note the able and discriminating portrayal of his role in H. C. Deutsch, *The Conspiracy Against Hitler in the Twilight War*, 1968, where on p. 154 the inability of American officials to grasp his behavior is discussed; cf. also pp. 43 and 223 (on killing Hitler) and p. 159 (relation to Britain).

29. Deutsch, *op. cit.* (note 28), concluding chapter on pp. 353 ff.

7 The Heroic Traitor and His Function

1. Oleg Penkovskiy, *The Penkovskiy Papers*, 1965, with an introduction and commentary by Frank Gibney, pp. 27–28.

2. Rebecca West, *The New Meaning of Treason*, 1964 (this is an enlarged edition of the original *The Meaning of Treason*, 1945), p. 306. On page 369 she rightly comments that "a traitor can change the community into a desert haunted by fear."

3. This term has been explored in its various dimensions recently by Ada W. Finifter, "Dimensions of Political Alienation," *The American Political Science Review*, LXIV, 1970, pp. 389 ff. She gives some interesting statistics and bases some quantitative analysis upon it and concludes by saying: "The great popular unrest evident throughout the world today indicates that intensive exploration of the entire alienation domain constitutes a challenge of the highest priority for empirical political theory." She employs the term in the wider Hegelian connotation, as do we, rather than in Marx's specific sense of being alienated from one's work, and hence no longer identified with one's product. The

Hegelian notion owes some of its present-day popularity to Alexandre Kojève's work, especially his *Introduction à la lecture de Hegel,* 1947 (ed. Queneau). See also Heinrich Popitz, *Der entfremdete Mensch,* 1953.

4. West, *op. cit.* (note 2, above), p. 361.

5. West, *ibid.*

6. West, *op. cit.*, p. 363.

7. West, *ibid.*

8. West, *op. cit.*, p. 369.

9. Anne Morrow Lindbergh, *The Wave of the Future,* 1940; cf. my comment "We Build the Future," *Atlantic Monthly,* 1940–1941, pp. 33 ff.

10. Charles A. Beard, "Dizzy Minds and Foreign Quarrels," *Harper's Magazine,* 1940. Beard held these views long before the war and defended them to the author during the war.

11. Cited after West, *op. cit.* (note 2), p. 155.

12. *Ibid.*

13. The "end of ideology" has been discussed since Raymond Aron first suggested it in *L'opium des intellectuels,* 1955, and Daniel Bell took up the theory; cf. the discussion in Carl J. Friedrich and Z. K. Brzezinski, *Totalitarian Dictatorship and Autocracy,* rev. ed., 1965, ch. 7; and my discussion in *The Slavic Review,* vol. XXIV, pp. 591 ff; cf. also Penkovskiy, *op. cit.* (note 1, above). See also Allen Dulles, *The Craft of Intelligence,* 1963.

14. West, *op. cit.* (note 2, above), p. 266.

15. *New York Times,* July 3, 1970.

16. Margret Boveri, *Der Verrat im Zwanzigsten Jahrhundert,* 4 vols., 1956 ff. (English translation entitled *Treason in the Twentieth Century,* London, 1961.)

17. Boveri, *op. cit.*, vol. IV, pp. 314 ff.

18. *Ibid.*, pp. 326–327.

19. *Ibid.*

20. Carl J. Friedrich, *Europe: An Emergent Nation?,* 1969.

21. Boveri, *op. cit.* (note 16, above), vol. IV, pp. 275–276.

22. See *Times Literary Supplement,* June 28, 1957 (p. 390, column 4); the article deals with "loyalties."

23. Boveri, *op. cit.* (note 16, above), vol. IV, pp. 280–281.

24. Adam Yarmolinsky, *Case Studies in Personnel Security,* 1955. Cf. also the security case reported by Charles N. Miller in Herman Pritchett and Alan F. Westin, *The Third Branch of Government,* 1963.

25. Yarmolinsky, *ibid.*

26. Morton Grodzins, *The Loyal and the Disloyal,* 1966. Cf. also the references in note 14 of ch. 5.

27. Grodzins, *op. cit.*, p. 20.

28. Grodzins, *op. cit.*, p. 57. Bruce Jacobs contributed a fine analytical paper to my seminar on political pathology in 1969–1970 entitled, "Betrayal: An Examination of National Disloyalty among the Black Urban Poor"; it contains interesting quantitative analyses. Cf. also "The Meaning of Black Power: A Comparison of White and Black Interpretations of a Political Slogan," by Joel D. Aberbach and Jack L. Walker, *American Political Science Review*, LXIV, 1970, pp. 367 ff.

29. *The Middle of the Country*, edited by Bill Warren and subtitled *The Events of May 14th as Seen by Students and Faculty at Kent State University*, 1970, pp. 138 ff.

30. Cf. literature on Vietnam cited in ch. 3, note 37, above.

31. Ronald F. Bunn, *German Politics and the Spiegel Affair*, 1968; and David Schoenbaum, *The Spiegel Affair*, 1968.

8 Corruption in Historical Perspective

1. Arnold J. Heidenheimer, eds., *Political Corruption: Readings in Comparative Analysis*, 1970, p. 3.

2. Joseph J. Senturia, "Corruption, Political," *International Encyclopedia of the Social Sciences*, 1968; and Charles Aiken, "Corruption" in *Dictionary of the Social Sciences.*

3. On bureaucracy cf. Carl J. Friedrich and Taylor Cole, *Responsible Bureaucracy: A Study of the Swiss Civil Service*, 1933; Max Weber's classical treatment in *Wirtschaft und Gesellschaft*, 1922, 2d ed., 1925, and the comments in *Reader on Bureaucracy*, Robert K. Merton, ed., 1952 (includes a critique by myself); and my *Man and His Government*, 1963, ch. 18, which has extensive further references, as has my *Constitutional Government and Democracy*, 4th ed., 1968, ch. 2.

4. The statement is found not in one of Lord Acton's major writings but in a letter in which he criticizes another scholar for "the canon that we are to judge Pope and King unlike other men, with a favorable presumption that they did no wrong." The text of Acton's remark is given in context in John E. E. Dalberg Acton, *Essays on Freedom and Power*, G. Himmelreich, ed., 1948, p. 364.

5. Especially as developed by St. Augustine in *City of God*. Cf. my *Transcendent Justice*, 1964, pp. 11 ff.; and Herbert A. Deane, *The Political and Social Ideas of Saint Augustine*, 1956; as well as my *The Philosophy of Law in Historical Perspective*, 2d ed., 1965, ch. 5.

6. M. R. Werner, *Tammany Hall*, 1928; and V. O. Key, Jr., *Politics, Parties and Pressure Groups*, 4th ed., 1958, ch. 13, gives a scholarly analysis of a phenomenon which Bryce had emphasized in his *Modern Democracies* and *The American Commonwealth;* Werner's is a detailed

descriptive account of Tammany's workings at the time, soon to be superseded by the impact of La Guardia's welfare state operations and the New Deal's social security legislation.

7. Robert Penn Warren, *All the King's Men*, 1946, p. 134.

8. Walter L. Dorn, "The Prussian Bureaucracy in the Eighteenth Century," *Political Science Quarterly*, vol. 46, pp. 403 ff.; vol. 47, pp. 75 ff.; and vol. 49, pp. 259 ff., 1931–1932. Lewis B. Namier, *The Structure of Politics at the Accession of George III*, 1929; Norman Gash, *Politics in the Age of Peel*, 1953; Holden Furber, *Henry Dundas, First Viscount Melville, 1742–1811*, 1931.

9. Merle Fainsod, *How Russia Is Ruled*, rev. ed., 1963. For the comparable situation in Hitler's Germany cf. my *Totalitarian Dictatorship and Autocracy* (with Z. K. Brzezinski), rev. ed., 1965, pp. 241 ff., on the intermingling of government and business. A study is in preparation by Assessor Nebelung at Heidelberg which will soon appear, it is hoped. Soviet publications provide ample proof in their own articles against corrupt practices.

10. "Stenographische Niederschrift von einem Teil der Besprechung ueber die Judenfrage unter Vorsitz von Feldmarschall Goering im RLM am 12. November, 1938," to be found in *Der Prozess gegen die Hauptkriegsverbrecher vor dem internationalen Militaergerichtshof Nuernberg*, 1948, vol. XXVIII, p. 502 f.

11. Leon Trotsky, *Die Verratene Revolution* (*Revolution Betrayed*), 1937, p. 120; cf. also the works cited in note 9, above.

12. Cf. my *Introduction to Political Theory*, 1967, p. 138. The discussion on Caesar is found in Machiavelli's *Discourses*, bk. I, ch. 10.

13. C. D. Bowen, *Adventures of a Biographer*, 1946.

14. John Dickinson, *Death of a Republic: Politics and Political Thought at Rome, 59–44 B.C.*, G. L. Haskins, ed., 1963.

15. Montesquieu, *Considérations sur les causes de la Grandeur des Romains et de leur Décadence*, 1734; cf. also the bicentenary collection of papers on Montesquieu edited by Mirkine-Guetzevitch and Henri Puget, *La Pensée Politique et Constitutionelle*, Paris, 1948.

16. Rousseau, *Contrat Social;* see also the comments by Dita Shklar, *Men and Citizens—A Study of Rousseau's Theory*, 1969, esp. pp. 100, 103, and 110; Mario Einaudi's interesting *The Early Rousseau*, 1967, does not especially address itself to the problem, but cf. his pp. 114 ff.

17. Shklar, *op. cit.*, p. 111.

18. Friedrich, *op. cit.* (note 12, above), pp. 164 ff. dealing with equality.

19. Namier, *op. cit.* (note 8, above).

20. My *Constitutional Government and Democracy*, 4th ed., 1968, pp. 431–432; Namier, *op. cit.* (note 8, above), and more recently Samuel

E. Finer, "Patronage and Public Service: Jeffersonian Bureaucracy and the British Tradition," *Public Administration,* vol. 30, 1952, pp. 333 ff. and reprinted in Heidenheimer, *op. cit.* (note 1, above), pp. 106 ff. Cf. also Harvey C. Mansfield, Jr., *Statesmanship and Party Government: A Study of Burke and Bolingbroke,* 1965, esp. comments on pp. 66 ff. Concerning Bolingbroke, cf. Isaac Kramnick, *Lord Bolingbroke and His Circle: The Politics of Nostalgia in the Age of Walpole,* 1968.

21. On bureaucracy see the works cited above in note 3.

22. Rotteck-Welcker, the typical liberal progressive (cf. the study by Ursula Herdt [Albrecht] on Rotteck, Ph.D. thesis, Heidelberg), in his *Staatslexikon,* on p. 454.

23. Heidenheimer, *op. cit.* (note 1, above), in his Introduction, p. 13. There references are given to Montesquieu's *The Spirit of the Laws,* 1748, and Bentham's "The Rationale of Rewards," in his *Works,* vol. V, pp. 246–248.

24. For Burke see reference given in footnote 7, ch. 10. Cf. also in general E. and A. G. Porritt, *The Unreformed House of Commons,* 1901, ch. III; cf. also Karl Loewenstein's *Staatsrecht und Staatspraxis von Grossbritannien,* vol. I, 1965, pp. 95 ff. At one point, this author echoes Burke's argument when he writes: "Without the rotten and pocket borough the British parliament would not have been that incomparable gathering of the political and social elite which let England rise to the rank of the leading world power." Who knows? Like all arguments from history, it is inconclusive.

25. This instance incidentally shows how risky it is, and how misleading, to treat such conditions as stable, unalterable features of a "political culture." Cf. Samuel E. Finer's study, *op. cit.* (note 20, above).

26. On Prussia, Hans W. Rosenberg, *Bureaucracy, Aristocracy and Autocracy: The Prussian Experience, 1600–1815,* 1958, is valuable, in spite of its Marxist slant; cf. also Dorn's paper, cited above, in note 8; on France see W. A. Robson, *The Civil Service in Britain and France,* 1956, and Walter R. Sharp, *The French Civil Service: Bureaucracy in Transition,* 1931.

27. Friedrich and Brzezinski, *op. cit.* (note 9, above), chs. 16 and 18 and the literature cited there.

28. Harold J. Berman, *Justice in the USSR: An Interpretation of Soviet Law,* 1950, 2d ed., 1963, and John N. Hazard, *The Soviet System of Government,* 1964, who gives special attention to the legal aspect.

29. Ralph Braibanti, ed., *Asian Bureaucratic Systems Emergent from the British Imperial Tradition,* 1966, esp. entries under corruption, (Burma) pp. 414–415, 413, 383; 172–175 (India); 510–511 (Ceylon); 598–600 (Malaya).

30. Ralph Braibanti, "Reflections on Bureaucratic Corruption," in

Public Administration, vol. 40, 1962, pp. 357 ff. Cf. also P. S. Muhar, "Corruption in the Public Services in India," offprint of his presidential address to the Indian Political Science Association, December 26, 1964, pub. by Kurukshetra University.

31. M. McMullan, "A Theory of Corruption," *Sociological Review*, vol. 9, 1961, pp. 181 ff. (reprinted in Heidenheimer, *op. cit.* [note 1, above], pp. 317 ff.).

32. Joseph S. Nye, "Corruption and Political Development: A Cost-Benefit Analysis," *American Political Science Review*, vol. LXI, 1967, pp. 417 ff. (reprinted in Heidenheimer, *op. cit.* [note 1, above], pp. 564 ff.). Cf. also Samuel P. Huntington, "Modernization and Corruption," in his *Political Order in Changing Societies*, 1968, pp. 59 ff. (also reprinted in Heidenheimer, *op. cit.*, pp. 492 ff.).

33. McMullan, *op. cit.* (note 31, above), pp. 182–183. I am omitting from the list given by McMullan "injustice" as too general, "repressive measures" and "restrictions on governmental policy" as too unspecific.

34. These are modifications of McMullan, *ibid.*, pp. 183–184. Cf. also Nye, *op. cit.* (note 32, above). Nye goes far in delineating benefits of corruption, and weighing them against "costs," in estimating probabilities with due caution. He concludes that "at this point, however, not enough information is at hand to justify great confidence in the exact conclusions reached here." Cf. below, chapter 10.

35. McMullan, *ibid.*, p. 196.

36. Huntington, *op. cit.*, p. 59.

37. Matthew 21:12–13; Mark 11:15–18; Luke 19:45; Mark, significantly, adds that "the chief priests feared him and sought a way to destroy him."

38. Preserved Smith, *Erasmus: A Study of His Life, Ideals and Place in History*, 1923, 1962; P. S. Allen, *Erasmus: Lectures and Wayfaring Sketches*, 1934; Johan Huyzinga, *Erasmus and the Age of Reformation*, 1957.

39. Braibanti, *op. cit.* (note 30, above); McMullan, *op. cit.* (note 31, above); and Huntington, *op. cit.* (note 32, above)—all in Heidenheimer, *op. cit.* (note 1, above).

40. See references given above in note 6.

41. Muhar, *op. cit.* (note 30, above), pp. 30–31. The U.S. Congress has struggled with the problem of a code of ethics; see Robert S. Getz, *Congressional Ethics—The Conflict of Interest Issue*, 1966, esp. chs. I, VII, VIII–X.

42. Braibanti, *op. cit.* (note 30, above); p. 365 has reference esp. to Pakistan. Cf. also McMullan (on West Africa) and the other works cited above.

43. Noted by Huntington, *op. cit.* (note 32, above).

9 Cases of Corruption

1. Lord Denning's *Report* was reprinted in the *Times* of September 26, 1963. My seminar had the benefit of an analysis and discussion of the Profumo case with Professor W. A. Robson in 1965.

2. Catherine Drinker Bowen, *The Lion and the Throne,* 1956, an admirable biography of Bacon which seeks to understand Bacon's position, whereas Hastings Lyon and Herman Block, *Edward Coke, Oracle of the Law,* 1929, avoid the key issue.

3. An example is Charles Benoist, *Les Lois de la Politique Française,* 1928; Augustin Hamon, *Les Maîtres de la France,* in three volumes, 1936, 1937, 1938, offers from a Communist viewpoint a detailed panorama of the intertwining of government and business with the banks, with many names used as evidence. Any reader of *Action Française* and the writings of Charles Maurras, e.g., *Enquête sur la Monarchie,* 1900, is familiar with such broad accusations. They were frequently linked with anti-semitism in this literature. Cf. Ernst Nolte, *Der Faschismus in seiner Epoche: Action Francaise, Italienischer Faschismus, Nationalsozialismus,* 1963. Cf. also Leon Daudet and Jacques Bainville.

4. Hamon, *op. cit.* (note 3, above), *passim.*

5. A similar notion was developed for the United States by Charles A. Beard, *The Idea of National Interest,* 1934, esp. chs. II–VI, XII.

6. Hamon, *op. cit.* (note 3, above), has produced some evidence; cf. esp. vol. II, pp. 268 ff. Cf. also the entire section on the press in that volume. D. W. Brogan, *France Under the Republic, 1870–1939,* 1940 (English title, *The Development of Modern France*), and Alexander Werth, *France, 1940–1955,* 1956, are not very detailed on this topic. Some interesting sidelights in George Claude, *Souvenirs et Enseignement d'une expérience électorale,* 1931.

7. G. Casanova, *Memoirs.*

8. André Tardieu, *Révolution à Refaire,* 1936. The second volume deals with parliament. A brilliant sketch of this morass of corruption is given by William L. Shirer in *The Collapse of the Third Republic: An Inquiry into the Fall of France in 1940,* 1969, pp. 204 ff., where he states: "The Third Republic had been plagued from time to time with certain financial scandals in which a few cabinet ministers, past or even present, and members of Parliament had been shown to be in cahoots with shady or downright crooked promoters." And he adds that already at the turn of the century the Panama and other scandals had "aroused a certain amount of feeling against the corruptness of the republican parliamentary regime."

9. Lucius D. Clay, *Decision in Germany,* 1950, and the recent John

Gimbel, *The American Occupation of Germany: Politics and the Military, 1945–1949*, 1968, do not deal with corruption.

10. Cf. *Deutsche Zeitung*, especially February 2, 1961, for the pleading of the defense lawyer, Dr. Dahs; all German papers were, of course, full of the case at the time; cf. esp. *Die Welt, Frankfurter Allgemeine Zeitung, Stuttgarter Zeitung* (home town of Koennecke!).

11. In this connection it is interesting to recall in passing that one of the officials involved, a man named Brombach, was working for a parliamentary committee, and hence was a new type of official who cannot be said to be subject to the same duties of discretion and secrecy as the regular official. It was his job to secure information for his committee, and this makes the case instructive as illustrating how a significant political change may be causing the illusion of corruption.

12. *Statesman*, September 16, 1964, cited by P. S. Muhar, as cited in note 30, ch. 8 above, whom I follow.

13. *Statesman*, July 19, 1964.

14. Lloyd I. Rudolph and Susanne Hoeber Rudolph, "Cows, Corruption and Demonstrations," in *The Nation*, January 30, 1967, p. 139. Cf. also John B. Monteiro, "The Dimensions of Corruption in India," in that author's *Corruption: Control of Maladministration*, Bombay, 1966, pp. 39 ff. [and reprinted in Heidenheimer, *op. cit.* (above, note 10, ch. 8), pp. 220 ff.]. This article contains valuable quantitative data on the magnitude of corruption: in the year 1962, 20,461 complaints on corruption were filed, and 79 percent of these were dealt with (p. 220). Corruption, Monteiro says, "has spread far beyond the limits of general administration to the police and even the judiciary." One wonders whether it is not the reporting of corruption, rather than corruption itself, which has "spread." Monteiro cites an Indian judge as speaking of the police force (in Allahabad) as an "Augean stable" and adding that "There is no single lawless group in the whole country whose record of crimes comes anywhere near the record of that single organized unit, which is known as the Indian Police Force" (p. 225). In spite of the controversy these remarks occasioned, the author concludes that factual information "seems to warrant such an opinion."

15. Muhar, *loc. cit.*, p. 3.

16. *Report of the Committee on the Prevention of Corruption* (this committee was chaired by Professor Santhaham); cf. K. I. Santhaham, *Political Democracy and Economic Development*, 1967.

17. *Report* (as cited above, note 16), para. 3.14.

18. *Report* cit. 3.17.

19. *Report* cit. 3.18.

20. Muhar, *loc. cit.*, p. 6.

21. *Report* cit. 6.8; *ibid.*, p. 9.
22. Muhar, *loc. cit.*, p. 10.
23. *Report* cit. 2.10, 8.13, 6.6.4, 8.12.
24. Nathaniel H. Leff, "Economic Development Through Bureaucratic Corruption," *American Behavioral Scientist*, vol. 8, 1964, reprinted in Heidenheimer, *op. cit.* (note 11, ch. 8 above), pp. 510 ff. See the discussion in the next chapter. Cf. also the article by Abueva and Nye in Heidenheimer, pp. 534 ff. and 564 ff.
25. V. O. Key, Jr., *Politics, Parties, and Pressure Groups*, 4th ed., 1958, p. 152, footnote, where these statements are quoted from the *Congressional Record*, June 29, 1950, p. A5076.
26. Douglas Price, "Campaign Finance in Massachusetts in 1952" in *Public Policy*, vol. VI, 1955.
27. Joseph Borkin, *The Corrupt Judge*, 1962.
28. Borkin, *op. cit.*, p. 10.
29. Borkin, *op. cit.*
30. *Ibid.*, pp. 219 ff.
31. *Ibid.*, p. 210.
32. E. P. Herring, *Public Administration and the Public Interest*, 1936.
33. A very good thesis was prepared by Vincent Shally for my seminar on this subject entitled "Billie Sol Estes—A Case of Political Corruption." He built his analysis on the Reports in Congress, Hearings, Senate Committee on Government Operations, 87th Congress, "USDA and Billie Sol Estes—Cotton Allotments"; Hearings, Senate Committee on Government Operations, Senate Report No. 1607, 88th Congress, "Department of Agriculture Handling of Pooled Cotton Allotments of Billie Sol Estes"; Hearings, Senate Committee on Agriculture and Forestry, 86th Congress, "Investigation of Grain Storage Operations of CCC"; and House Committee on Government Operations, 89th Congress, House Report 196, "Operations of Billie Sol Estes." The matter was summarized in its complex business aspects in *Fortune*, July, 1962.
34. Julius Duscha, *Taxpayers Hayride: The Farm Problem from the New Deal to the Billie Sol Estes Case*, 1964, analyzes this aspect of the case.
35. Cf. Walter Goodman, *All Honorable Men: Corruption and Compromise in American Life*, 1963, *passim* and p. 8 f.

10 The Functionality of Corruption

1. Sir Ronald Syme, *The Roman Revolution*, 1939, 1960; Theodor Mommsen, *Roemisches Staatsrecht*, 1871–1888.

2. F. B. Marsh, "The Gangster in Roman Politics," *Classical Journal*, vol. XXVIII, 1932–1933. Cf. also his *A History of the Roman World, 146–30 B.C.* This and other works on corruption under the Republic were the basis of an excellent seminar paper by M. K. O'Sullivan, entitled "A Survey of the Nature and Uses of Corruption under the Roman Republic," 1965.

3. There are numerous references to corruption in Marsh, *op. cit.*, of course, as well as in Plutarch and Tacitus. The same is true of John Dickinson's fine posthumous study, edited by George Lee Haskins, *Death of a Republic: Politics and Political Thought at Rome, 59–44 B.C.*, 1963, esp. pp. 142 ff.

4. Leon Homo, *Roman Political Institutions,* 1929 (original French, 1927), esp. ch. IV.

5. R. O. Jolliffe, *Phases of Corruption in Roman Administration in the Last Half Century of the Roman Republic,* 1919, is central to our theme. Corruption is a recurrent theme in the standard histories of Rome, such as M. Cary's *History of Rome*, 1935 and later, and E. R. Boak, *A History of Rome to 565 A.D.*, 3d ed., 1946.

6. Lewis B. Namier, *The Structure of Politics at the Accession of George III*, 1929. Cf. also the discussion above in ch. 8.

7. Edmund Burke, in his speech to the House of Commons on May 7, 1782, on a motion by William Pitt the Younger for a reform of representation opposed the abolition of so-called rotten boroughs and argued that "you have an equal representation because you have men equally interested in the prosperity of the whole, who are involved in the general interest and the general sympathy; . . . they will stand clearer of local interests, passions, prejudices, and cabals than the others, and therefore preserve the balance of the parts, and with a more general view and a more steady hand than the rest." *Works,* vol. V, 1839, pp. 402 ff.

8. W. T. Arnold, *The Roman System of Provincial Administration,* Oxford, 1914, ch. III (for the Republic) and later ones for the Empire. Michael Rostovtsev in *The Social and Economic History of the Roman Empire,* 1926, gives at a number of points material on the corruption and bribery in the Roman Empire; in the later German edition (1929) these are found especially on pp. 220 ff. and 236 ff. At the latter point: "The officials grew rich by bribery and corruption" (after Diocletian).

9. S. N. Eisenstadt, in his imposing *The Political Systems of Empires,* 1963, does not give special attention to the problem of corruption in spite of its universality.

10. For the literature on bureaucracy see footnote 3 in ch. 8, above.

11. In the *Pendleton Act* of 1883, the *Hatch Act* of 1939 and its extension to state employees administering federal programs (*Little Hatch*

Act) 1940; see for comment V. O. Key, Jr., *op. cit.* (note 6, ch. 8, above), pp. 390 ff.

12. Heidenheimer, *op. cit.* (note 1, ch. 8, above), Introductory Essay, pp. 3 ff.

13. Jacob van Klaveren, "Corruption as an Historical Phenomenon," in Heidenheimer, *op. cit.*, pp. 67 ff. at p. 67. Cf. also (there cited) P. A. Means, *Ancient Civilizations of the Andes*, 1931, ch. VIII; it may be consulted though partly obsolete.

14. Karl Brandi, *Kaiser Karl V*, 2 vols., 1937, 1940 (Eng. ed., 1939).

15. On the theoretical issue cf. Walter Ullmann, *Medieval Papalism*, 1949, ch. 4. On the economic background Robert Latouche, *The Birth of Western Economy*, English translation, 1961. On the legal, Otto von Gierke, *Deutsches Genossenschaftsrecht*, vol. III, ch. 8.

16. Nathaniel H. Leff, "Economic Development Through Bureaucratic Corruption," in Heidenheimer, *op. cit.* (note 1, ch. 8, above), pp. 510 ff. at p. 514.

17. The expertise kind of elitism is candidly stated by Leff, *ibid.*, p. 518: "Moreover, the argument (for democracy) also exaggerates the extent to which economic growth depends upon a popular rallying-around rather than on many individual selfish activities." It is the automatism of old liberalism which would depend upon business leadership and initiative rather than planning.

18. John Nef, *Industry and Government in France and England: 1540–1640*, 1940. A somewhat different perspective is found in Robert T. Holt and John E. Turner, *The Basis of Economic Development: An Exploration in Comparative Political Analysis*, 1966.

19. India provides a striking instance; note the remarks by Jagota in his chapter in *Administration and Economic Development of India*, R. Braibanti and J. J. Spengler, eds., 1963, pp. 175 ff. Cf. also K. V. Rao, *Parliamentary Democracy of India*, 1961, and N. Srinivasan, *Democratic Government in India*, neither of whom, however, specifically addresses himself to this problem. John B. Monteiro, in his paper, "The Dimensions of Corruption in India" in Heidenheimer, *op. cit.* (note 1, ch. 8, above), pp. 220 ff. and Gunnar Myrdal in the same volume, "Corruption as a Hindrance to Modernization in South Asia" contribute significant reflections bearing on the issue.

20. This general reflection disposes of the arguments regarding taxation; for if it were true that the reasoning against it "attributes an unrealistically high propensity to spend for developmental purposes," as Leff argues, it would be mistakenly put. The right reason would be that taxes need to be collected for the purposes the majority favors, whatever they may be.

21. Gustav Schmoller, *Deutsches Staedteleben in der aelteren Zeit*, 1922, is approved of by van Klaveren as having "corrected the widely prevalent but erroneous idea" that "the free cities" were "democratic" communities, and having stressed that "these very cities were breeding places of oligarchic despotism and corruption." To be sure, they were at one point, namely in the days of their decline; but at an earlier day they were, if not "democratic"—whatever that may mean—then at any rate relatively free and open societies, and the precursors of later developments in the territorial states which the Enlightenment rightly praised and treated as paradigmatic. Cf. van Klaveren, *op. cit.* (note 13, above), p. 70.

22. Sherman Adams, *Firsthand Report*, 1961, as cited by Walter Goodman, *All Honorable Men: Corruption and Compromise in American Life*, 1963, p. 213.

23. Senator Wheeler as cited by Goodman, *op. cit.*, p. 176. Note also Goodman's comments and the remark (misleadingly restricted to Eisenhower) that "men from the industries to be regulated would make the best regulators." For this observation applies to practically all Presidents since the twenties for a good part of the time; such practice rests on the fetish of expertise.

24. Cf. the discussion of administrative justice in its application to American problems in my *Constitutional Government and Democracy*, 1968, pp. 117 ff.

25. This is the main point, it seems, of Edward C. Banfield's study *Political Influence*, 1961. Unfortunately, Banfield employs a number of key terms, notably *power, influence, authority*, in a sense so different from the one I prefer that it is difficult to quote him without creating confusion.

26. Banfield, *op. cit.*, p. 318.

27. Banfield, *op. cit.*, p. 323.

28. A striking illustration is provided by the so-called Cambridge Project, in the course of which such matters were to be analyzed by men like Karl Deutsch.

29. For a somewhat more detailed discussion see my "Foundations and the World of Science and Scholarship," *Polity*, vol. II, pp. 526 ff., where the discussion is focused on Warren Weaver, ed., *Philanthropic Foundations: Their History, Structure, Management and Record*, 1967, and the Agnelli Foundation's *Directory of European Foundations*, 1969.

30. The report of the Rockefeller Foundation on what it had done for India's agriculture: *India—A Partnership to Improve Food Production*, 1969; this report provides a striking illustration.

31. Weaver, *op. cit.* (note 29, above), pp. 152–153.
32. Weaver, *op. cit.*, p. 131.
33. Goodman, *op. cit.* (note 22, above), p. 230.

11 Nature and Function of Secrecy and Propaganda

1. See my *Constitutional Government and Democracy*, 4th ed., 1968, pp. 363 ff., where Bentham's views are placed in the context of his general outlook and the times; cf. also *ibid.*, pp. 55–57, for secrecy as a factor producing the trait of being discreet in a developed bureaucracy.

2. Georg Simmel in his general *Soziologie*, 2d ed., 1922, devoted an entire section, ch. V, to "the secret and the secret society," pp. 256 ff. The gist of this study is contained in an article for the *American Journal of Sociology*, vol. XI, pp. 441 ff., entitled "The Sociology of Secrecy and Secret Societies."

3. In my *The New Belief in the Common Man*, 1941, ch. III (rev. ed., *The New Image of the Common Man*, 1950; further revised and enlarged edition in German *Die Demokratie als Herrschafts-und Lebensform*, 1959—also in Spanish, *La Democracia como forma politica y de vida*) I sketched the problem of propaganda and mass communications; the adduced statements are found on pp. 86–87.

4. In my *The Age of the Baroque, 1610–1660*, 1952, pp. 21 ff. and Charles Howard McIlwain, *The Political Thought of James I*, 1918, esp. the introduction.

5. My *op. cit.* (note 1, above), pp. 363 ff. It was often a matter of keeping the proceedings secret from the king, not the public!

6. For Britain, the *Official Secrets Act*, 1911, as amended 1920 and 1939, is relevant. For the U.S. the *Espionage Act*, 1917, *The Alien Registration Act*, 1940, and the *Internal Security Act*, 1951.

7. The Profumo case is a striking instance; see for it above, ch. 9.

8. See L. G. Kraus, *Illegitimate Power*, 1964, where the argument is very forcefully stated and perhaps overstressed. For the Kentucky case see Harry M. Caudill, *Night Comes to the Cumberlands*, 1962, ch. X.

9. In the *Spiegel* affair, discussed above, ch. 7, a great many discussions suffered from this tendency to make freedom of the press an absolute value having priority over all others.

10. Robert Luce, *Legislative Procedure*, 1922, esp. 142 ff. More recent works on Congress have continued the discussion; cf. Clive Parry, "Legislatures and Secrecy," *Harvard Law Review*, vol. 67, 1954, pp. 737 ff.

11. My *Foreign Policy in the Making*, 1938, dealt with this issue.

12. Cf. Roscoe Pound, *The Organization of Courts*, 1940; and for

comparative purposes see R. C. K. Ensor, *Courts and Judges in France, Germany and England,* 1933.

13. An interesting article on this subject is "Dissenting Opinions in der Deutschen Verfassungsgerichtsbarkeit" by W. Heyde in *Jahrbuch des Oeffentlichen Rechts* (ed., Leibholz), 1970; it comments on a new norm of the Federal Republic of Germany, amending the law of the *Bundesverfassungsgerichts* (BVerf GG, March 12, 1951) by adding a paragraph to its paragraph 30: "*Ein Richter kann seine in der Beratung vertretene abweichende Meinung zu der Entscheidung oder zu deren Begruendung in einem Sondervotum niederlegen; das Sondervotum ist der Entscheidung anzuschliessen. . . .*" This author earlier published *Das Minderheitsvotum des ueberstimmten Richters,* Bielefeld, 1966.

14. William H. Prescott, *History of the Reign of Philip II of Spain,* Boston, 1858, vol. III, p. 415. Prescott there tells of a letter of Don Juan of Austria which with its numerous alterations by the royal hand can be seen in the archives at Simanca.

15. Woodrow Wilson, *Congressional Government,* 1885, pp. 81 ff. For Luce's criticism see his *op. cit.* (note 10, above), p. 152 f. These and related matters are discussed in my contribution to *Nomos,* vol. XII: *Privacy,* "Secrecy versus Privacy: The Democratic Dilemma," 1970. Still basic is the article by Samuel D. Warren and Louis D. Brandeis in the *Harvard Law Review,* 1890, dealing with the problems of the invasion of privacy not by the government but by private agencies, especially communication media.

16. See my *Totalitarian Dictatorship and Autocracy* (with Z. K. Brzezinski), rev. ed., 1965, pp. 295 ff.

17. U.S. Congress, Senate, Committee on the Judiciary, Subcommittee on Constitutional Rights, Summary Report of Hearings, 1958–1961, "Wiretapping and Eavesdropping," 1962. Cf. also Edward V. Long, *The Intruders: The Invasion of Privacy,* 1967.

18. For illustrations and the denial of the concept as a relevant one, cf. *Nomos,* vol. V: *The Public Interest,* 1962, esp. Glendon Schubert, "Is There a Public Interest Theory?," for the negative.

19. Edward A. Shils, *The Torment of Secrecy,* 1956, p. 238.

20. *Ibid.,* p. 235. Shils is not concerned with functionality as such, but contributes to its discussion by his vivid portrayal of the dialectic of secrecy and publicity in their polarity.

21. See below, ch. 13.

22. Wilson, *op. cit.* (note 15, above); also Luce, *op. cit.* (note 10, above).

23. It is worth noting that Wilson's argument is cast in moralistic terms: "pure" and "correct," rather than "effective" and "successful,"

are the terms used as measuring sticks for determining the issue.

24. Roland Young, *The American Congress,* 1959, p. 190.

25. Note the sharp criticism by Goodman of the handling of Goldfine by investigators, Walter Goodman, *All Honorable Men,* 1963, p. 207. "He [Goldfine] was an incident in a political skirmish, not guiltless by any means, certainly not as innocent as he professed, not merely a bystander or a tourist in Washington, yet demolished not on his own account but in passing."

26. See previous chapter and the references given there.

27. See the bibliography for ch. 23 of my work cited above in note 1, especially the writings of Harold D. Lasswell and his pupils.

28. Concerning the phenomenon of the vacuum, cf. work cited in note 14 above.

29. The term "publicistic" is suggested for attitudes and arguments which exaggerate the value of publicity.

30. Gottfried Dietze, *In Defense of Property,* 1963, has stressed the basic importance of these property notions at the time of the founding of the Republic.

31. The radical breach of enemy aliens' patents by the United States, through its Alien Property Custodian during World War I appears in retrospect a strange violation of the ideals the U.S. said it was fighting for.

32. Shils, *op. cit.,* ch. 2, pp. 36 ff. argues that privacy has declined in the United States, in contrast to Great Britain, and that is undoubtedly true. It is also true that this sense of privacy has something to do with Britain's aristocratic past. Georg Simmel, as cited below, relates private secrecy to aristocratic conditions.

33. Shils, *ibid.* But he is more concerned with another torment which results, he believes, from the traditional readiness for publicity characteristic of American society—a trait de Tocqueville had noted. Cf. Alexis de Tocqueville, *Democracy in America,* tr. J. P. Mayer and Max Lerner, pp. 580 ff; but de Tocqueville speaks of "private circles" rather than individuals here.

34. See my *Constitutional Reason of State,* 1957, pp. 116–117, where, in commenting on the several methods adopted in the U.S., Britain, France, and Germany, I observe that "basically, the problem remains unresolved." It is this: "When will any one of these methods actually result in undermining the faith in the constitutional order itself, to the extent that it disintegrates the will to maintain such a constitutional order?" That was precisely the charge of conservatives leveled at Senator McCarthy. Cf. *Investigations of Senators Joseph R. McCarthy and William Benton pursuant to S. Res. 187 and S. Res. 304,* Report of the Subcommittee on Privileges and Elections to the Committee on Rules and Ad-

ministration, Washington, 1952. This report dealt primarily with a case of alleged corruption.

35. See Elting E. Morison, *Admiral Sims and the Modern American Navy*, 1942, pp. 183 ff.; Tracy Barrett Kittredge, *Naval Lessons of the Great War*, 1921; Roger Burlingame, *General Billy Mitchell: Champion of Air Defense*, 1952, pp. 150 ff.; Emile Gavreau and Lester Cohen, *Billy Mitchell: Founder of Our Airforce and Prophet Without Honor*, 1942. Concerning the atomic submarine see "The Development of Nuclear Propulsion in the Navy" in the *Naval Institute Proceedings;* Clay Blair, Jr., *The Atomic Submarine and Admiral Rickover*, 1954; James Calvert, *Surface at the Pole*, 1960; and William R. Anderson with Clay Blair, Jr., *Nautilus 90 North*, 1959.

36. See ch. 7, note 31, and text.

37. Georg Simmel, *Soziologie*, 1922, pp. 274–275; Simmel's entire section on the *Geheimnis* is germane to our subject. Translations from it are my own, though it is available in English.

38. *Ibid.*, pp. 281 ff. discusses the secret societies, under the general assumption that "generally speaking, the secret society appears everywhere as a corollary of despotism and police restrictions" (p. 283), but while this is true, secret societies are also common in the United States, which most people would not describe as a despotism.

39. Dietrich Schindler, *Verfassungssrecht und Soziale Struktur Zuerich*, 1932, Part V, 2, pp. 135 ff.

40. Simmel, *op. cit.* (note 37, above), pp. 296 ff.

41. Simmel, *op. cit.*, p. 276.

42. Simmel, *op. cit.*, p. 277.

43. A vivid portrayal of this state of affairs is given by Merle Fainsod in his *Smolensk under Soviet Rule*, 1958, esp. chs. 7, 13, and 16. A more recent general assessment, but still preoccupied with Stalinist period, is found in Alex Inkeles and Raymond Bauer, *The Soviet Citizen: Daily Life in a Totalitarian Society*, 1959, esp. ch. 9, pp. 210 ff. The necessary corrective is sanely stated by Alfred G. Meyer, *The Soviet Political System: An Interpretation*, 1965, ch. 13, pp. 330 ff. Recent repressive action against writers protesting the occupation of Czechoslovakia are, if not a return to Stalinism, then at any rate a renewed tightening of the screw of terror. Cf. the recent reevaluation in Friedrich, Michael Curtis, and Benjamin Barber, *Totalitarianism in Perspective*, 1969, pp. 123 ff. Also A. Dallin and George W. Breslauer, *Political Terror in Communist Systems*, 1970.

12 Propaganda, Mass Communications, and Their Pathology

1. The most comprehensive treatise on propaganda in most of its ramifications is still Aristotle's *Rhetorics*. For a comprehensive bibliography, see Harold Lasswell, R. D. Casey, and B. L. Smith, *Propaganda and Promotional Activities*, 1935 and the edition of 1946; an updating of this valuable source is urgently needed. Aristotle's approach to the subject as rhetorics—he really wrote a *summa* of the extended teachings of the rhetorical sophists—has had a fascinating revival in Chaim Perelman's work, especially (with L. Olbrechts-Tytega) *La Nouvelle Rhétorique—Traite de l'Argumentation*, 1958—now also in English. The general literature on propaganda, the basic literature on communications, in the perspective of politics, such as Deutsch, de Sola Pool, Pye and others inspired by Norbert Wiener's *Cybernetics*, 2d. ed., 1961, are cited in my *Constitutional Government and Democracy*, 4th ed., 1968, ch. 23, pp. 686 ff. Basic, of course, for the political perspective are the well-known works by A. Lawrence Lowell, *Public Opinion and Popular Government*, 1913, and *Public Opinion in War and Peace*, 1923; Walter Lippmann, *Public Opinion*, 1922, and *The Phantom Public*, 1925, and John Dewey, *The Public and Its Problems*, 1927, to which Harold Lasswell's *Propaganda Technique in the World War*, 1927, is a worthy companion which marks the turning to newer techniques and questions as highlighted in his (with Dorothy Blumenstock) *World Revolutionary Propaganda*, 1939. Interesting also is Gorham Munson, *Twelve Decisive Battles of the Mind*, 1942, esp. chs. 3, 4, 9, and 12.

2. For the Institute of Propaganda Analysis, see their *Propaganda*, 1938, and my comments in *The New Belief in the Common Man*, 1942, ch. 3, pp. 96 ff. A similar view is offered by Charles Siepmann, *Radio, Television and Society*, 1950.

3. Zechariah Chafee, Jr., *Government and Mass Communications: A Report from the Commission on Freedom of the Press*, vol. I and II, 1947, *passim*.

4. The struggle over ORTF (Office Radio Télévision Française) has been the subject of extended press comment. A scholarly study under my direction is in preparation by Miss Gabriele Wölke at Heidelberg.

5. Cf. the works of Lippmann and Lowell, *op. cit.* (above, note 1).

6. Juergen Habermas, *Strukturwandel der Oeffentlichkeit*, 1962, argues more sophisticatedly that it has become different, pp. 200 ff.

7. V. O. Key, Jr., *The Responsible Electorate*, 1966; the argument is a statistical confirmation of the views set forth in my *op. cit.* (note 2, above).

8. This proposition is developed in my *op. cit.* (note 1, above), ch. 23; it also is central to Siepmann's analysis in *op. cit.* (note 2, above).

9. For this see chapter 11 of my (with Z. K. Brzezinski) *Totalitarian Dictatorship and Autocracy*, rev. ed., 1965, and the literature cited there, especially Nathan C. Leites, *A Study of Bolshevism*, 1953, where the notion of an operational code is developed. Cf. Munson, *op. cit.* (note 1, above) for the early phase.

10. Walter Millis has described the effect of the jingo press in the United States in bringing on the Spanish-American War; cf. his *The Martial Spirit*, 1931.

11. Cf. Harold Nicolson's *Peacemaking, 1919*, 1933; cf. also H. Bradford Westerfield, *Foreign Policy and Party Politics*, 1958, and similar works, including my *Foreign Policy in the Making*, 1938, and Alan Cranston, *The Killing of the Peace*, 1945, who is preoccupied with the U.S. failure to join the League of Nations.

12. V. O. Key, Jr., *op. cit.* (note 7, above), and the study by James W. Prothro and Charles M. Grigg, "Fundamental Principles of Democracy: Bases of Agreement and Disagreement," *Journal of Politics*, vol. XXII, 1960, pp. 276 ff., which statistically offered further confirmation.

13. I first suggested them in the work cited above in note 2, but they have not found wide acceptance; evidently neither the gander nor the geese found themselves flattered.

14. Edward L. Bernays, *Public Relations and the American Scene*, 1951, for many titles.

15. Charles E. Merriam, *The Making of Citizens*, 1931.

16. See my *Man and His Government*, 1963, pp. 620 ff.

17. This view was also expounded by Siepmann, *op. cit.* (note 2, above).

18. On this matter of manipulation, see Siepmann, *op. cit.*, p. 180 f. Cf. also Vance Packard, *The Hidden Persuaders* and the rather extravagant writings of McLuhan; an introduction to his views is provided by McLuhan's paper "Great Change-overs for You" in Harry J. Skornia and Jack William Kitson, *Problems and Controversies in Television and Radio: Basic Readings*, 1968, containing many valuable contributions.

19. Siepmann, *op. cit.* (note 2, above), pp. 181 ff.

20. My *op. cit.* (note 16, above), ch. 33; and my *op. cit.* (note 1, above), ch. 23; and my *op. cit.* (note 2, above) contain studies of propaganda from other perspectives, supplementing the analysis given here.

21. Siepmann, *op. cit.* (note 2, above), pp. 197 ff.

22. The election studies of recent years have brought this out; e.g., Bernd Vogel and Peter Haungs, *Wahlkampf und Waehlertradition*, 1965 (Heidelberg), esp. pp. 391 ff.; Erwin Scheuch and Rudolf Wildenmann,

Zur Soziologie der Wahl, 1965, esp. introductory chapter, p. 32 f.; Werner Kaltefleiter *et al.* "Im Wechselspiel der Koalitionen," in *Verfassung und Verfassungswirklichkeit,* 1970, esp. pp. 62 ff., 94 ff., and 131 ff. Cf. also Uwe Kitzinger, *German Electoral Politics,* 1959.

23. Bernard Rubin, *Political Television,* 1967.

24. Cf. Sidney Kraus, ed., *The Great Debates,* 1962, containing the texts. It also contains Earl Mazo's evaluation, "The Great Debates" and others. Cf. for quote, Rubin, *op. cit.,* p. 55.

25. Mazo, *op. cit.,* gives some of these estimates.

26. Theodore White, *The Making of the President,* 1960.

27. Reported by Rubin, *op. cit.* (note 23, above), pp. 192–193, and note 28 there. These expenditures appear disfunctional, since they enhance the candidates' dependence on contributors to their campaign funds; for European conditions and arrangements cf. Burton Paulu, *Radio and Television Broadcasting on the European Continent,* 1967, esp. ch. 5, pp. 151 ff.

28. Richard Rose and Arnold J. Heidenheimer, eds., "Comparative Political Finance: A Symposium" in the *Journal of Politics,* vol. 25, 1963, and the publications of the Citizens Research Foundation, concerned with political finance. The curious and complex problems of art. 315 of the *Federal Communications Act* are discussed in Rubin, *op. cit.* (note 23, above), pp. 139–140, and his note 37. The article provides for equal time, if a broadcaster provides free time for any candidate, to his competitors: the practical effect has been to "force" broadcasters to insist on payment for the time, which has greatly increased expenses to the candidates; in 1960 Congress suspended the rule for the presidential campaign, but failed to do so in 1964 and since.

29. There was widespread feeling that the reporting (including picturing) was slanted to heighten the impact of police brutality; yet the report by David Walker "*Rights in Conflict;* convention week in Chicago . . ." New York, 1968, avoids drawing conclusions from the facts presented.

30. Janet Harris' *Students in Revolt,* 1970, fails to make mention of it, but *The Middle Country,* 1970, edited by Bill Warren, contains striking illustrative material; for mass violence in the news media in America, cf. the *U.S. Riot Commission Report: Report of the National Advisory Commission on Civil Disorders,* pub. by the *New York Times* with a preface by Tom Wicker, who thinks "reading it is an ugly experience." In ch. 15 the media are discussed, pp. 362 ff. The Commission notes that "the Commission's content analysis (of press coverage) is the first study of its type of contemporary riot coverage, and it is extremely limited in scope." In light of this, we cannot speak with any assurance on these matters; the stress, however, is on the *lack* of coverage rather than its

slant. On ORTF see my *op. cit.* (note 1, above), pp. 523 ff., and literature cited there, as well as note 4, above. A recent report on the May upheaval of 1968, *The French Revolt: May 1968,* by Bernard E. Brown, 1970, stresses the difficulties of adapting to new technological conditions. "The political balance will shift, perhaps irrevocably, away from freedom towards power" (p. 22). The Commission did find, however, a "lack of cooperation between police officers and working reporters." They note the complaints of the press ("many experienced and capable journalists") and add that policemen (not qualified by laudatory adjectives) "charged that many reporters seemed to forget that the task of the police is to restore order" (p. 378 of the *Report*).

31. Janet Harris, *ibid.*, pp. 81 ff., gives an account, actually taken from Cohn-Bendit and hence student-oriented in its bias, on ORTF. See above, note 4.

32. The controversy concerning the fire and who laid it has continued. An excellent incisive assessment of the controversy with particular reference to the effects of the *Reichstagsbrand* was given by Hans Mommsen, "Der Reichstagsbrand und seine politischen Folgen," *Vierteljahrshefte fuer Zeitgeschichte,* vol. XII, 1964, pp. 351 ff., where the remarkable study by Fritz Tobias, *Der Reichstagsbrand, Legende und Wirklichkeit,* Rastatt, 1962, which disproved both the Communist and Nazi versions, is appropriately assessed.

33. Details may be found in the New York *Herald Tribune,* May 23, 1941, p. 1.

34. Peter Odegard has described the campaign of selling war bonds and its background in the new 1947 edition of his *American Politics: A Study of Political Dynamics,* with E. A. Helms.

35. Cf. the FCC reports cited in my *op. cit.* (note 1, above), note 33 in ch. 23; and my "The FCC Monopoly Report: A Critical Appraisal," in *Public Opinion Quarterly,* vol. 4, 1940, pp. 526 ff. The British press has been the subject of a number of reports of Royal Commissions, notably the *Ross Report,* cmd. 7700, 1947–1949; it has been superseded by more recent ones, notably the *Shawcross Report,* 1962. Interesting material on these questions is contained in *Rundfunkanstalten und Tageszeitungen -Eine Materialsammlung,* published by Arbeitsgemeinschaft der oeffentlichrechtlichen Rundfunkanstalten der Bundesrepublik Deutschland (ARD) May 1965, which is primarily concerned with the problem of competition between press and broadcasting, since the one is private and the other public, especially a proposal of the Springer concern to take over parts of television. Cf. for this problem in the U.S. Paul Lazersfeld's *Radio and the Printed Page,* 1940. The issue has also occupied the FCC as noted above and the controversy continues.

36. Chafee, *op. cit.* (note 3, above), *passim;* cf. Alfred McClung Lee, *The Daily Newspaper in America,* 1937, pp. 700 ff.

37. *Op. cit.* of Chafee, p. 717.

38. *Ibid.,* p. 718.

39. Voice of America is discussed with special emphasis on the policy problems in Robert E. Elder, *The Information Machine: The United States Information Agency and American Foreign Policy,* 1968, pp. 181 ff. Its historical background is broadly sketched by Wilson P. Dizard, *The Strategy of Truth: The Story of the U.S. Information Service,* 1961, pp. 69 ff. And its organizational framework is presented by John W. Henderson, *The United States Information Agency,* 1969, pp. 163 ff., ch. 6.

40. Cf. my *Europe: An Emergent Nation?,* 1970, esp. chs. 1, 2, and 10. There the opposing views are cited. On the general problem cf. Thomas Grandin, *The Political Use of Radio,* Geneva Studies, vol. X, no. 3 (no date, but probably 1939) for an early assessment, and Llewellyn White and Robert D. Leigh, *Peoples Speaking to Peoples, A Report from the Commission on the Press on International Communications,* 1946, for a more recent reassessment.

41. For the literature on Vietnam see ch. 3, note 37.

13 Intelligence and Espionage

1. For a well-balanced overall view, cf. Harry Howe Ransom, "Intelligence, Political and Military," in *IESS,* vol. 7, 1968; for an earlier sane assessment see Sherman Kent, *Strategic Intelligence,* 1949, where the quote is found on p. VII.

2. R. W. Rowan, *The Story of Secret Service,* 1937, who speaks of "thirty-three centuries of secret service."

3. See Michael Rostovtzeff, *The Social and Economic History of the Roman Empire,* 2d rev. ed., Oxford, 1957, *passim.*

4. *Op. cit.* (ch. 7, note 4, above).

5. G. Reitlinger, *The SS—Alibi of a Nation,* 1956; unfortunately, as the title indicates, the factual analysis is distorted by an unrelated political theme. Roger Manvell and Heinrich Fraenkel, in their *Heinrich Himmler,* 1965, and Hans Buchheim (ed. and contr.) *Anatomie des SS-Staates,* 1965, have avoided this danger.

6. See *Die Werke Friedrichs des Grossen,* vol. II (n.d., 1965?) pp. 409 ff. This extract is from "Generalprinzipien vom Kriege."

7. Cf. my *The Age of the Baroque,* 1952, pp. 199 ff. and elsewhere throughout.

8. E.g., the game of the balance of power; cf. Charles Dupuis,

L'Equilibre Européen, 1909, for a general review; see also Alfred Vagts, "The Balance of Power: The Growth of an Idea," in *World Politics*, vol. I, 1948, pp. 82–101; earlier my *Foreign Policy in the Making—The Search for a New Balance of Power*, 1938, esp. ch. 5.

9. Machiavelli, *Discourses*, book III, ch. XVIII; the argument is limited to war.

10. Regarding Ranke's discovery see Theodore H. von Laue, *Leopold Ranke—The Formative Years*, 1950.

11. This issue is involved in much of the controversy over the activities of Joseph McCarthy and McCarthyism; cf. the literature cited above, ch. 3, note 16.

12. Roberta Wohlstetter, *Pearl Harbor: Warning and Decision*, Stanford, 1962, pp. 394 ff. Beard, in his careful study of the Pearl Harbor attack, *President Roosevelt and the Coming of the War, 1941* . . . , New Haven, 1948, does not go into this aspect to any extent.

13. Robert F. Kennedy, *Thirteen Days—A Memoir*, 1969, esp. pp. 23 and 27–28.

14. Lucius D. Clay, *Decision in Germany*, 1950, esp. ch. 5; John Gimbel, *The American Occupation of Germany—Politics and the Military, 1945–1949*, 1968, esp. chs. 2, 5, 6, and 13. A recent and very able German reassessment is given by Hans-Peter Schwarz, *Vom Reich zur Bundesrepublik*, 1966, who is especially concerned with the problem of the text.

15. Tad Szulc, "CIA Is Accused by Bitter Rebels" *New York Times*, April 22, 1961. Cf. for a rather overdramatized journalistic account (with an axe to grind against the CIA) David Wise and Thomas B. Ross, *The Invisible Government*, 1964, of which it has been said that it (CIA) is neither invisible nor a government; for a more scholarly assessment cf. H. R. Ransom, *Can American Democracy Survive Cold War?*, 1963.

16. Machiavelli's advice against foreign advisers is given in ch. xxxi of book II of the *Discorsi sopra la prima deca di Tito Livio*, 1550.

17. See my *Totalitarian Dictatorship and Autocracy* (with Z. Brzezinski), rev. ed., 1965, ch 13 and the literature cited.

18. Oleg Penkovskiy, *The Penkovskiy Papers*, 1965, esp. the general introduction and ch. IX.

19. In the National Security Act, counter-intelligence is defined as "information on the intelligence activities of foreign intelligence agents. . . ." We are not going to enter here into the technical problems of this distinction, but it is clear that the FBI is involved in it for the purpose of uncovering "spies" and persons engaged in treason.

20. William J. Barnds, "Intelligence and Foreign Policy: Dilemmas of a Democracy," in *Foreign Affairs*, January, 1969, pp. 281 ff., p. 294;

a different view is taken by H. R. Ransom, *op. cit.* (note 15, above), ch. VII; it builds upon a more thorough analysis by the same author, *Central Intelligence and National Security*, 1959.

21. Barnds, *op. cit.* p. 283; my view contradicts the notion that the operational "cloak-and-dagger" activities should remain part of an intelligence agency, as Barnds holds.

22. *Op. cit.* p. 287; Barnds adds that "when this happens, he either becomes a time-server or else studies his subject only for its own sake rather than in the light of its importance to the United States."

22a. Barnds, *ibid.*

23. Immanuel Kant, "On Eternal Peace" in my *Inevitable Peace,* 1948, second edition, p. 265.

24. Rowan, *op. cit.* (note 2, above) and his article on "espionage" in *ESS,* has given a survey of this history. Though not scholarly in terms of the exacting standards of modern critical history, it is the best we have in English.

25. Rowan in *ESS*, p. 594.

26. Ransom, *op. cit.* (note 15, above), pp. 186 ff.

27. Penkovskiy, *op. cit.* (note 18, above) and my *op. cit.* (note 17, above).

28. Besides the treatment in Ransom, *op. cit.* (note 15, above) see Robert Kennedy, *op. cit.* (note 13, above).

INDEX

72 73 74 75 10 9 8 7 6 5 4 3 2 1